Theory and Evidence in Semantics

T0366958

Theory
and
Evidence
in
Semantics

edited by

Erhard Hinrichs

and

John Nerbonne

CSLI
PUBLICATIONS

Center for the Study of
Language and Information
Stanford University

Copyright © 2009
CSLI Publications
Center for the Study of Language and Information
Leland Stanford Junior University
Printed in the United States
13 12 11 10 09   1 2 3 4 5

Library of Congress Cataloging-in-Publication Data

Theory and evidence in semantics /
edited by Erhard Hinrichs and John Nerbonne.

p.   cm. – (CSLI lecture notes ; no. 189)

Includes bibliographical references and index.
ISBN-13: 978-1-57586-576-8 (pbk. : alk. paper)
ISBN-10:   1-57586-576-9 (pbk. : alk. paper)
ISBN-13: 978-1-57586-577-5 (cloth : alk. paper)
ISBN-10:   1-57586-577-7 (cloth : alk. paper)
1. Semantics. 2. Semantics, Comparative.
I. Hinrichs, Erhard W. II. Nerbonne, John A., 1951–

P325.T485 2009
401′.43–dc22   2008054121
CIP

∞ The acid-free paper used in this book meets the minimum requirements
of the American National Standard for Information Sciences—Permanence
of Paper for Printed Library Materials, ANSI Z39.48-1984.

CSLI was founded in 1983 by researchers from Stanford University, SRI
International, and Xerox PARC to further the research and development of
integrated theories of language, information, and computation. CSLI headquarters
and CSLI Publications are located on the campus of Stanford University.

CSLI Publications reports new developments in the study of language,
information, and computation. Please visit our web site at
http://cslipublications.stanford.edu/
for comments on this and other titles, as well as for changes
and corrections by the authors, editors, and publisher.

In honor of David Dowty on the occasion of his 60th birthday.

Contents

Contributors

CHRIS BARKER is Professor of Linguistics at New York University. His central interest is formal model-theoretic analysis for natural language semantics, particularly the internal structure of noun phrases, quantification, vagueness, crossover, and continuations.

ERHARD HINRICHS is Professor of General and Computational Linguistics at the Eberhard Karls Universität Tübingen. His research interests include model-theoretic semantics, constraint-based grammar formalisms, and data-driven approaches to computational linguistics.

JACK HOEKSEMA is Professor of Dutch Linguistics at the University of Groningen. He is interested in the use of corpora to study distributional properties of negative polarity items and other types of expressions, and in how these properties develop over time.

PAULINE JACOBSON is Professor of Cognitive and Linguistic Sciences at Brown University. Her research centers largely on the syntax/semantics interface, using model-theoretic semantics and categorial grammar. Particular interests include binding, quantifier scopes, extraction, anaphora, and especially the interaction between these phenomena.

MANFRED KRIFKA is Professor of General Linguistics at Humboldt-Universität zu Berlin and Zentrum für Allgemeine Sprachwissenschaft, Berlin. He has done work in semantics, e.g. on the interaction of aspect and nominal categories like the mass/count distinction, and on pragmatics, e.g. on the interpretation of focus.

PETER LASERSOHN is Associate Professor of Linguistics at the University of Illinois at Urbana-Champaign. His research interests include formal semantics, pragmatics, and the philosophy of language.

x / THEORY AND EVIDENCE IN SEMANTICS

JOHN NERBONNE is Professor of Information Science at the University of Groningen. He is a computational linguist who has worked on grammar, acquisition, and applications such as natural language interfaces and computer-assisted language learning. He currently focuses on computational methods for studying linguistic variation.

CRAIGE ROBERTS is Professor of Linguistics at The Ohio State University. She works on a variety of topics at the interface between formal semantics and formal pragmatics, including anaphora and definiteness, modality, presupposition and information structure.

GREGORY STUMP is Professor of English and Linguistics at the University of Kentucky. His research focuses on the properties of the morphological component within the larger architecture of grammatical theory; his work in this area draws upon evidence from a range of languages, very often from Sanskrit and Breton. In recent years, he has argued that the definition of a language's morphology makes essential reference to the notion of paradigms.

TIM VAN DE CRUYS is a Ph.D. candidate in computational linguistics at the University of Groningen. His research focuses on extracting lexical and grammatical information from large text reserves.

NEAL WHITMAN received his Ph.D. in Linguistics from The Ohio State University in 2002. His research focuses primarily on the syntax/semantics interface. Particular interests include passives and complex predicates; multiple- and coordinated-wh questions; and nonparallel coordinations. He also writes the linguistics blog Literal-Minded.

HOLGER WUNSCH is a Ph.D. student at Eberhard Karls Universität Tübingen, and a staff member of the Collaborative Research Center "Linguistic Data Structures". His research interests include the exploration of new computationally accessible linguistic knowledge sources for improving pronoun resolution in German.

Introducing Theory and Evidence in Semantics

ERHARD HINRICHS AND JOHN NERBONNE

1 The Occasion

This is a collection of papers from a one-day symposium, *Theory and Evidence in Semantics*, held on June 1, 2006 at the University of Groningen. The conference covered a good deal of ground semantically, and the present collection of papers reflects that range well, including papers on the syntax-semantics and morphology-semantics interfaces, computational forays experimenting with quantitative and application-driven approaches, and descriptive papers on problematic phenomena, including coordination, negative and collective predicates.

The broad range of topics addressed in this book will seem only appropriate if one recalls that the one-day symposium was held in honor of DAVID DOWTY, on the occasion of his sixtieth birthday. Dowty has been a far-ranging scholar in the field of linguistic semantics, and one of the most significant contributors to this field and to theoretical syntax. His well-received 1972 Texas dissertation on the temporal semantics of verbs (Dowty, 1972), supervised by Robert Wall and Emmon Bach, made some use of formal logic, but the succeeding years saw him whole-heartedly adopt the framework of logic and model-theory for his work in semantics, quickly making his mark in explorations of temporal reference and verbal aspect, culminating in the 1979 book *Word Meaning and Montague Grammar* (WMMG; Dowty 1979). Characteristically, the book was empirically ambitious, uniting analyses of inherent verbal aspect, the paradigms of tense and aspect variation, and vari-

Theory and Evidence in Semantics.
Erhard Hinrichs and John Nerbonne (eds.).
Copyright © 2009, CSLI Publications.

ous sorts of adverbial modification. Further, the WMMG analyses are spelled out in such complete semantic detail that attention to the syntax being interpreted follows naturally, earning the name 'grammar', and foreshadowing Dowty's later professional steps in which syntax figured prominently. But the book is likewise reflective, considering the cognitive implications of developing models of linguistic meaning in complex and powerful mathematical logics. In addition, the book was innovative in carrying the program of logic-based semantics from the domain of sentential semantics, in which it was beginning to enjoy success, to the domain of word (lexical) meaning, which researchers up till then regarded largely as the primitives on which the theory was to be built. Finally, WMMG was impressive for its attention to earlier scholarship in linguistic semantics, and for demonstrating how rewarding attention to more traditional work could be. If Dowty had written nothing else, the 1979 book would have assured him a place in scientific history.

Later, farther reaching, contributions confirm this assessment, even elaborating on some of WMMG's themes. The opportunity to extend logic-based semantic theories to lexical processes led to a number of specific empirical analyses of e.g. the relation between active and passive clauses (and active and passive verb forms), the functioning of quantificational adverbs, as well as to a number of influential theoretical conjectures concerning, *inter alia*, the nature of grammatical relations, the proper interaction of syntax and semantics, and the nature of *thematic roles* such as AGENT, THEME, etc., and the relation between deep, licensing grammatical relations and their concrete realizations.

Dowty has been very active professionally, touring, lecturing and appearing in summer schools frequently; serving as editor-in-chief of *Linguistics and Philosophy*, the leading journal in semantics, from 1988 until 1992, and also as associate editor of *Language*, the premier linguistics journal; and serving as chairman of the prominent Department of Linguistics of The Ohio State University for several years.

The foreword to a book in David Dowty's honor is a good place to note his professional contributions and, if we may, speculate on other aspects of Dowty's intellectual impact. For Dowty is known not only for creative and compelling linguistic analysis, but also for exacting empirical and scholarly standards. These standards have led him to frame his linguistic analyses in formalized grammars, grammars in principle capable of serving fairly directly in computational models. Dowty has always distrusted sloppiness and hand-waving, preferring pages of complicated, interacting definitions over the risk of equivocation, imprecision, and implicit appeal to intuition. This was, and still is, a minority stance in the larger field of grammatical analysis, where formalization and its required attention to detail in formulation is felt to distract research from the more profound questions. David Dowty's work is always concrete, detailed, and explicit. These standards have ensured respect for his work even among colleagues with whom he has disagreed.

2   The Papers

This section introduces the papers contributed to this volume. The discussion will relate the papers to different facets of David Dowty's research. For this reason, the order in which the papers will be introduced here differs from the book itself, where the authors appear in alphabetical order.

As we noted above, WMMG extended the program of logic-based semantics from the domain of sentential semantics, in which it was beginning to enjoy great success, to the domain of word (lexical) meanings. **Gregory Stump**'s contribution to this volume, "Cells and Paradigms in Inflectional Semantics", may be seen to continue that ambitious program.

Stump is the originator of WORD-AND-PARADIGM MORPHOLOGY, also known as REALIZATIONAL MORPHOLOGY. While morpheme-based approaches develop rules for combining morphemes into inflected forms, or for generating inflected forms from stems, word-based morphology states generalizations that hold between the forms of inflectional paradigms. The approach generally focuses on the way in which a cell "realizes" the distinctions on which the paradigm is based. The theory is laid out in Stump (2001).

In the present paper Stump takes up the degree to which semantic distinctions in paradigms may be seen to be orthogonal. He formulates the SEMANTIC FACTORIZATION HYPOTHESIS (SFH), which requires, in brief, that paradigmatic distinctions—say between present and past tense—be realized by a single semantic operator, which, additionally, must be used in the paradigms of all the words in which the paradigmatic distinction exists—following the example of tense used above, in all the verbs in which there is a present and past tense distinction. Stump further assumes that paradigms must be morphosyntactically motivated, meaning that either morphological or syntactic correlates are sufficient grounds for postulating paradigmatic distinctions, but that a semantic distinction, by itself, constitutes insufficient grounds for postulating a paradigmatic distinction.

The Niger-Congo Twi verbal inflection system includes one verbal tense distinction between the recent and the remote past that is not

consistently marked. The prefixes *à-* and *è-* are unexpectedly switched
in the negative section of the verbal paradigm. Since there is no syntactic motivation for the distinction (just as there is none in English),
and since paradigms must be morphosyntactically motivated, as noted
above, the switch is a *prima facie* counterexample to the SFH. Stump
examines several alternative avenues of analysis for this complicated
data, but finally concludes that the hypothesis is untenable.

Sanskrit distinguishes active and middle forms depending on whether
an action is conducted for the benefit of the agent or for the benefit of
someone else. But careful examination of this distinction across several
stem classes suggests that the morphological distinction is not semantically constant, again in contradiction to the SFH. Instead, the interpretation of the middle inflectional marker depends on whether the given
verb exhibits a distinction between active and middle. Stump notes
that both sorts of counterexamples fall within the group of phenomena
which Aronoff (1994) has called 'morphomes', phenomena whose only
coherent construal is within a morphological component of grammar.

Jack Hoeksema's contribution to this volume, "The *swarm* alternation revisited", re-examines the construction underlying sentences
such as (1), focusing on the use of the construction in Dutch, which
adds an impersonal variant to the alternation in English. Both languages allow an alternative in which *the bees* is the subject ('The bees
are swarming in the garden'):

(1)   a De tuin stikt van de bijen
      b The garden chokes of the bees
      c The garden is swarming with bees
      d Het stikt in de tuin van de bijen

Hoeksema reports on a collection of 1250 of these sentences that
he has gleaned from Dutch corpora, thereby adding further empirical
foundation to the discussion of a theoretically interesting phenomenon.
The data collection serves as the basis for comparison with the description given by David Dowty in " 'The garden swarms with bees'
and the fallacy of 'argument alternation' " (Dowty, 2000). Dowty dubs
his analysis the 'dynamic texture hypothesis' because the variant of
the construction in which the garden is subject describes a situation in
which there is a small and frequently repeated event that may be found
more or less throughout the location, giving it a "dynamic texture".

Hoeksema emphasizes that the predicates he finds are all predicates
of abundance, a point he strengthens via appeal to native-speaker intuition, noting that the constructions sound infelicitous in combination

with "downtoning" adverbials such as *a bit* or *somewhat*. This leads him
to hypothesize that we are dealing with a causative degree construction.
In sentences such as (1d), the object of *with*, *bees*, causes the subject
the garden to exhibit a high degree of a property, in this case presumably the property of appearing rather full. This construal explains
why subjects need not denote locations, as in 'John was bristling with
anger'. Interestingly, he likewise notes that the Dutch impersonal construction appears to be avoided when the otherwise personal subject is
not locative.

Hoeksema discusses the fact that the objects of the preposition *with*
in this construction are normally indefinite in English, a point which
follows naturally from Dowty's hypothesis, with its emphasis on the
frequently repeated events which make up the texture of the location.
Hoeksema's Dutch examples, on the other hand, are frequently "fake
definites" such as the one in the example above. (Note that there is no
suggestion in the Dutch version of the sentence that one is reporting on
a uniquely salient set of bees.) He does not add this to strengthen the
case for his alternative, only to admonish that subtle, perhaps stylistic
effects may rear their heads in corpus research of this type.

Craige Roberts' paper, *"know-how*: A Compositional Approach",
is concerned with the *know-how* construction in English, i.e. with verbs
that take infinitival question complements as in (2).

(2) Lingens doesn't know how to get out of the library.

Following Ryle (1949), Lewis (1979), and Abbott (2006), Roberts
claims that knowing-how and knowing-that should not be treated on a
par, as was recently proposed by Stanley and Williamson (2001), who
provide propositional accounts for both constructions. Rather, Roberts
agrees with Lewis that knowing-how, unlike knowing-that, crucially involves the property of self-ascription, i.e. attitudes *de se*. The paper
presents a compositional semantic analysis of the *know how to* construction that draws on contributions from a number of authors: an
account of *to* infinitival phrases due to Portner (1997), a semantics of
indirect questions developed by Groenendijk and Stokhof (1997), and a
semantics of infinitival questions as *hypothetical, unsaturated*, and *appropriate actions* in the sense of Dowty and Jacobson (1991). Roberts
argues in detail that these accounts can be "assembled" in such a way
that the stated requirements for the semantics of the *know how to*
construction are met. Again drawing on the insights of Dowty and Jacobson (1991), Roberts argues that verbs which govern *to* infinitival
phrases form a natural class of what she calls *epistemically reflective*

predicates and that infinitival questions are unsaturated in the sense that they do not contain a phonologically null PRO subject. This latter assumption distinguishes Roberts' account from the analysis of Stanley and Williamson. As linguistic evidence in support of their propositional account of the *know how to* construction, Stanley and Williamson crucially assume that infinitival questions contain a PRO subject. By contrast, Roberts adopts and refines a theory of control, first proposed by Jackendoff (1972) and Dowty (1985), which relies on the lexical semantics of the matrix verb, but crucially not on any syntactic element, to determine the controller of the subjectless non-finite complement. On the basis of examples such as (3), Roberts argues that control cannot be determined by the lexical semantics of the verb alone.

(3)   a John asked Mary to mow the lawn.

      b John asked Mary how to mow the lawn.

Roberts observes that *ask* subcategorizes either for an infinitival VP that denotes a goal, as in (3a), or for an infinitival question, as in (3b), with each choice of complement leading to distinct options for the entailed controller. In the case of (3a), the lexical semantics of the verb and the semantics of the infinitival VP together entail that the referent of the object NP is the one committed to perform the goal denoted by the infinitival VP. (3b), on the other hand, has either a generic interpretation or a subject control reading, but interestingly, no object control interpretation.

Roberts demonstrates that her compositional analysis is superior to Stanley and Williamson's analysis both in terms of descriptive adequacy and in terms of the principled and independent motivation of the various building blocks of the analyses involved.

The division of labor between semantics and pragmatics has been a long standing issue in linguistic theorizing. In his work on the nature of thematic roles (Dowty, 1991), on the *swarm* alternation (Dowty, 1991), and on the temporal interpretation of discourse (Dowty, 1986), David Dowty has addressed this question on a wide range of empirical facts. **Manfred Krifka**'s contribution, "Approximate Interpretations of Number Words: A Case for Strategic Communication", provides a pragmatic account for why "round numbers" in measure terms (such as 100) receive an approximate interpretation, whereas numbers such as 103 have a more precise interpretation.

The paper is a follow-up to previous work by the same author (Krifka, 2002) where the pragmatics of measure terms was investigated within the framework of bidirectional OT. The present paper places the overall issue within the context of strategic communication, which can formally be modeled by game theoretic means. This route has been taken by several researchers from the bidirectional OT community (such as Benz, Dekker, Jaeger, and van Rooij) and is well-motivated both conceptually and empirically.

The present paper expands on Krifka's previous analysis by comparing not just expressions of different complexity, but also scales of different granularity. This solves some of the empirical problems that the previous analysis was faced with. The theory that is put forward makes use of scales that differ insofar as they are more or less fine-grained, and proposes a principle that a number expression is interpreted on the most coarse-grained scale that it occurs on. This principle can be motivated in a game-theoretic setting of strategic communication that factors in the overall likelihood of the message. The emerging theory is refined in various ways. In particular, it is shown that complexity of representations, rather than the complexity of expressions, is of crucial importance. The paper concludes with the discussion of some surprising facts about the influence that the number system of a language has on which numbers are actually expressed in that language.

In a number of very influential papers, David Dowty has shown how the framework of categorial grammar can offer elegant solutions to a wide variety of linguistic phenomena, including bound anaphora (Dowty, 2007), non-constituent conjunction (Dowty, 1988), and the treatment of grammatical relations (Dowty, 1982). Among the papers contained in this volume, the contributions by Pauline Jacobson, Chris Barker, and Neil Whitman relate most closely to this aspect of the Dowty oeuvre.

Chris Barker's paper, "Reconstruction as delayed evaluation", addresses the interaction of binding and quantification in examples such as (4).

(4) [Which of his$_i$ relatives] does everyone$_i$ love _?

Such examples violate the empirical generalization derived from weak crossover facts as in (5).

(5) a. Everyone$_i$ loves his$_i$ mother. $\forall x.\textbf{loves}\,(\textbf{mother}\,x)\,x$
    b. *His$_i$ mother loves everyone$_i$. $\forall x.\textbf{loves}\,x\,(\textbf{mother}\,x)$

The contrast in (5) seems to suggest that a quantifier can bind a pronoun only if it linearly precedes it. In derivational theories of syntax, examples as in (4) have given rise to the idea that at some level of representation, (part of) the bracketed material is reconstructed in the gap position and then preceded by the binding quantifier.

The goal of Barker's paper is to show how a fully compositional account of scope and binding developed by Barker and Shan (2006) can naturally account for weak crossover and reconstruction effects without having to resort to movement or copying. The account assumes a categorial grammar with flexible type assignment and with two distinct modes of combination. Apart from the familiar forward and backward slash modes, Barker makes use of the two *continuation modes* which lead to additional categories: the functional category 'A$/\!\!/$B' (stands for: "A is missing a B, with B surrounding A") and 'B$\backslash\!\!\backslash$A' (stands for: "an A missing a B somewhere inside of A"). Informally speaking, the continuation mode allows a subexpression to combine with a context to form a larger expression, with the context either wrapping around ($/\!\!/$) the subexpression or with the subexpression occurring inside ($\backslash\!\!\backslash$) the context.[1] Each mode of combination comes with its own set of rule schemata for syntactic and semantic combination. The combination rules for continuation operators together with type-shifting operation of Lift and Lower yield a general mechanism for scope taking of, e.g., quantifiers. Two additional continuation-mode operators ▷ (with type-shifting operator Bind) and ? (with type-shifting operator Front) are introduced to account for pronominal binding and fronting of *wh*-phrases. Weak crossover and reconstruction, including functional answers for examples such as (4), can be derived in such a flexible type system if gaps, pronouns, and *wh*-words are treated as identity functions—an idea due to Jacobson (1999)—and as scope-taking elements—a proposal due to Dowty (2007).

Pauline Jacobson's paper, "Do Representations Matter or Do Meanings Matter: The Case of Antecedent Containment", raises one of the leading questions of semantic theorizing: the issue whether semantic interpretation crucially involves an intermediate level of semantic representations or whether semantic interpretation can be computed directly and without recourse to such an intermediary level representation. Jacobson considers cases of VP ellipsis that are referred to in the literature as *antecedent contained deletion* (ACD) and that have been frequently cited as key evidence in support of the view that semantic representations are crucial for semantic interpretation.

(6) Mary voted for every candidate that Bill will.

Jacobson contrasts two views of ACD and VP ellipsis: (i) the "stan-

---

[1]The concept of a *continuation* originates in computer science, where it is used, *inter alia*, to define control operators and to model the differences in call-by-name and call-by-value evaluation regimes (Plotkin, 1975).

dard view" that at least at the level of logical form (LF) there is actual linguistic material present in the ellipsis site of an elliptical VP such as *Bill will* in (6), and (ii) the alternative view that there is no material in the ellipsis site and that ellipsis is a case of anaphora, i.e. of reference to a property that is contextually salient in the discourse.

In particular, Jacobson discusses two related phenomena of antecedent containment that show parallel patterns of acceptability and that differ as to whether the modifier *also* is present or absent.

(7) a. Mary voted for every boy that BILL did ~~vote for~~.
     b. *Mary voted for every boy who corresponds with a girl that BILL did ~~vote for~~.
     c. *Mary voted for every girl who corresponds with a boy who lives next door to a boy that BILL did ~~vote for~~.

(8) a. Mary voted for every boy that BILL also voted for.
     b. *Mary voted for every boy who corresponds with a boy that BILL also voted for.
     c. *Mary voted for every boy who corresponds with a girl who lives next door to a boy that BILL also voted for.

Jacobson shows that, under the standard view, the analysis of examples such as (7) and (8) crucially involves the use of variables and representational constraints prohibiting the accidental reuse of variable names. In contrast to such a representational account, Jacobson shows that a directly compositional account can be cast in a variable-free semantics that does not make use of variables in the first place and thus can do without any representational constraints on the use of variables. The account is couched in the framework of Combinatory Categorial Grammar and builds on Jacobson's earlier work on variable-free semantics (Jacobson, 1999). The use of combinators makes it possible to compose meanings in such a way that they directly mirror syntactic composition.

In the present paper, Jacobson first develops such a variable-free, directly compositional account for (8a) and then shows how the contrasts in acceptability exhibited for (8) naturally fall out of such an account. In a second step, Jacobson shows how this analysis can be generalized to the patterns of acceptability for the ACD cases in (7).

Neil Whitman's piece "Right-Node Wrapping: Multimodal Categorial Grammar and the 'Friends in Low Places' Coordination" appears to describe a novel sort of construction, which he christens RIGHT-NODE WRAPPING. These coordinations have the form [*A* conjunction *B*] *C D* and are understood as if the element *C* were distributed over both sides

of the conjunction, while the element D is interpreted only with respect
to the second conjunct. Whitman offers the following example from the
Los Angeles Times, 16 Oct. 2003:

(9) The blast [upended] and [nearly sliced] a [...] Chevrolet in half

The bracketed phrases are the conjuncts A and B, a *Chevrolet* is the
distributed object C, while the underscored *in half* is understood solely
in combination with the likewise underscored second verb *sliced*, and
crucially not with the first conjunct *upended*. Whitman provides a long
list of examples from actual use, demonstrating the existence of the construction, in spite of the suspicion which Whitman himself confesses to
having felt when he first encountered it. Coordination has been studied
intensively in several grammatical frameworks, and especially within
categorial grammar, so that it is surprising to see a new sort of coordination discovered, even more so one which is readily instantiated in
newspaper prose (and elsewhere).

Whitman's work is a clear continuation of other work on coordination in categorial grammar, most specifically work on non-constituent
coordination, the earliest examples of which we are aware of being
Dowty (1988) and Steedman (1985, 1990). Dowty (1988) based his account of non-constituent coordination on functional composition and
type raising. In a sentence such as (10), the objects *Mary* and *Bill* are
first raised from the type NP to the type (VP/NP)\VP which then
compose leftwardly with the VP\VP-category adverbs *yesterday* and
today:

(10) John saw [Mary yesterday] and [Bill today]

This paves the way for straightforward cancellation with respect to the
VP/NP transitive verb *saw* and the subject.

Whitman formalizes his analysis within multi-modal categorial
grammar, using a Gentzen-style rule system with an accompanying
semantics. It turns out that it is sufficient to add a single rule of
"mixed associativity", which is assumed not to be universal, but rather
specific for English. The author contrasts this with an alternative analysis which makes uses of a unary constructor. Although both analyses
cover a good deal of the data, Whitman notes some overgeneration in
both analyses, as well as undergeneration of data with respect to the
first.

David Dowty's work has always been reflective about methodological issues, so it is only fitting that **Peter Lasersohn** picks up on the
nature of the compositionality requirement, a subject Dowty devoted
a lengthy paper to (Dowty, 2007). Lasersohn's piece, "Compositional

Interpretation in Which the Meanings of Complex Expressions are not Computable from the Meanings of their Parts", examines the nature of the compositionality requirement on semantic interpretation, the requirement that the meaning of a complex expression be a function of the meaning of its parts. Lasersohn notes that the requirement that meanings be compositional is occasionally defended as if it amounted to the requirement that meanings of complex constituents be computable on the basis of the meanings of their parts. This sounds psychologically plausible—after all, one might ask, how else could speakers and hearers be able to use complex expressions which they have never heard if they cannot compute them effectively? They must have some way of computing the meanings of the complex expressions based on the meanings of their constituents. But, as Lasersohn notes, there is actually ample reason to favor the weaker requirement that there merely be a homomorphism from syntax to semantics, the formulation inherited from Frege and Montague. In this form the compositionality requirement guarantees the substitutability of expressions of the same meaning, *salve veritate*. Computability goes beyond this.

Janssen (1997) had earlier proved that compositional semantic mappings are available for a very wide range of semantically interpreted systems, and Zadrozny (1994) had noted earlier that the judicious use of pointwise defined functions, which in fact are used widely in linguistic semantics, while preserving compositionality in the homomorphic sense, allowed extremely counterintuitive mappings. As an example, he showed how the numerals might be defined in a left-branching grammar and nonetheless be interpreted compositionally. So it has long been clear that compositionality, taken by itself, is a fairly tolerant requirement.

But Lasersohn works from the other side, noting that there are non-computable functions which nonetheless might serve as the basis for semantic interpretation, even suggesting that human speakers and hearers may communicate using them as a basis. The core technical idea is straightforward: we begin with the certainty that there are non-recursively enumerable sets. But then any function mapping one-to-one to this set will be non-computable, and mathematically, such one-to-one functions must exist. To the extent that we include non-recursively enumerable sets in our domain of discourse, and we are assured that one-to-one functions exist mapping into them, we are operating with non-computable predicates. The paper is valuable for showing how plausible it is that we indeed can do so. Lasersohn provides a simple example where we straightforwardly determine the truth value of a statement in a language talking about non-recursively enumerable sets.

This leads to a reflection about the nature of the compositionality requirement and to the argument that the familiar homomorphic requirement is on target, and to a rejection of the proposal that semantic operations be computable. Lasersohn notes *inter alia* that we are comfortable with the idea that we can determine the denotation of many complex expressions even without knowing the complete denotations of all their component constituents.

The papers by Hinrichs and Wunsch and by Nerbonne and Van de Cruys consider semantic phenomena from a computational linguistics perspective (Nerbonne, 1996). These authors use statistical methods to induce semantic regularities from large text corpora. **Erhard Hinrichs** and **Holger Wunsch**'s contribution, "Selectional Preferences for Anaphora Resolution", explores ways of extracting selectional restrictions from German text corpora for the task of computational anaphora resolution, i.e. the task of choosing the correct antecedent for a personal or reflexive pronoun in a discourse.

(11) The child munched on a cookie and smiled. It must have been {tasty/happy}.

Example (11) illustrates the importance of lexical semantics for this task. The pronoun *it* can potentially refer back to either *the child* or *a cookie*. The choice of antecedent depends crucially on the selectional restrictions of the predicate of the clause in which the pronoun appears: cookies can be tasty and children happy, but not vice versa.

While the importance of incorporating lexical semantics, particularly selectional restrictions, into anaphora resolution systems is generally recognized in computational linguistics, it is an open research question how this information can best be acquired by data-driven means.

Hinrichs and Wunsch apply latent semantic clustering (LSC), an unsupervised learning technique due to Rooth (1998), to two German newspaper corpora of radically different sizes: the manually annotated TüBa-D/Z treebank with 27,125 sentences and 473,747 lexical tokens and the automatically annotated TüPP-D/Z corpus with approx. 11.5 million sentences and 204,661,513 lexical tokens. The purpose of this comparison is to determine the quantity of data that is required to obtain meaningful results by means of unsupervised methods such as LSC.

Hinrichs and Wunsch show that the LSC method can yield reliable verb clusters only for the very large corpora TüPP-D/Z corpus. At the same time, automatic annotation of partial syntactic structure in combination with annotation of grammatical functions as in TüPP-D/Z suffices for LSC methods, as long as the annotation is sufficiently accurate and contains relevant information about clause structure.

John Nerbonne and **Tim Van de Cruys**'s contribution, "Quantitatively Detecting Semantic Relations: The Case of Aspectual Affinity", applies techniques from computational linguistics as well as from the statistics of dimension reduction to explore the degree to which aspect may be reflected in text. The investigation is inspired by the decades of work on temporal semantics by David Dowty and many more following him.

'Aspect' refers to the temporal make-up of predications, and in particular to whether predications implicitly refer to a completion or not. Those referring to a completion are known as TELIC and the others as ATELIC. Scholars of aspect have long noted that aspect is not marked explicitly in many languages, including Dutch and English. Thus *die* and *sing a song* are telic while *lie dying* and (intransitive) *sing* are not. The former imply completions in a way that the latter do not. The importance of the aspectual distinction is reflected in some aspects of grammar, e.g. the meaning of the progressive, as well as some inferences that depend on aspect, e.g., those involving completion.

But aspectual distinctions are not unambiguously marked on each verb, nor are verbs partitioned neatly into a small set of aspectual classes. If we wish to detect the implicit aspectual class of each verb, we must be prepared to sift through larger amounts of material, enough so that underlying dispositions are reflected in some concrete co-occurrence patterns. The "aspectual affinity" mentioned in Nerbonne and Van de Cruys's title refers to the different preferences of telic vs. atelic verbs for different classes of adverbials of duration. In brief, the telic predications take place *in, within a length of time*, while the atelic predications last *for a length of time*. This sort of affinity is also not unambiguous, however, for reasons which the semantic literature has carefully documented, and which the paper briefly reviews. The problems are reflected in the fact that one and the same predication may appear with a telic or an atelic adverbial of duration.

Nerbonne and Van de Cruys, working on Dutch, exploit a parsed corpus of 500 million words of newspaper text (approximately 27 years of daily newspapers) in order to seek the tell-tale affinities that should distinguish verbs that tend to be used to make telic as opposed to atelic publications. They build in this on the work of their colleagues in Groningen, Gertjan van Noord and Gosse Bouma, who have developed a dependency-based parser which assigns the correct dependencies in

a little more than 90% of the cases (Beek et al., 2002). But the full
corpus was parsed automatically and thus includes both the 90% that
was parsed correctly as well as the 10% that was not.

The authors extract all the instance of clauses which include adverbials of duration by essentially listing all the prepositions which head
such adverbials. They collect these into a large frequency table in which
each row represents the main verb and each column the adverbial sort.
The cells then represent the frequency with which the (column) adverbial occurred with the (row) head. They apply a two-dimensional
version of factor analysis (singular value decomposition) in order to
extract the most general affinities. While the authors are not satisfied
with the degree to which aspectual distinctions are reflect in the results,
they interestingly point out association strengths of some verbs with
durational adverbials that appear to reflect tendencies of use rather
than aspectual affinities.

References

Abbott, Barbara. 2006. Linguistic Solutions to Philosophical Problems. Paper given at the annual meeting of the Pacific APA, Portland, March,
2006.

Aronoff, Mark. 1994. *Morphology by itself: Stems and Inflectional Classes.*
Cambridge: MIT Press.

Barker, Chris and Chung-Chieh Shan. 2006. Types as Graphs: Continuations
in Type Logical Grammar. *Journal of Logic, Language and Information*
15(4):331–370.

Beek, Leonoor van der, Gosse Bouma, and Gertjan van Noord. 2002. Een
brede computationele grammatica voor het Nederlands. *Nederlandse
Taalkunde* 7(4):353–374.

Dowty, David. 1972. *Studies in the Logic of Verb Aspect and Time Reference
in English.* Ph.D. thesis, University of Texas at Austin.

Dowty, David. 1979. *Word Meaning and Montague Grammar.* Dordrecht:
Reidel.

Dowty, David. 1982. Grammatical Relations and Montague Grammar. In
P. Jacobson and G. K. Pullum, eds., *The Nature of Syntactic Representation*, pages 79–130. Dordrecht: Reidel.

Dowty, David. 1985. On Recent Analyses of the Semantics of Control. *Linguistics and Philosophy* 8(3):291–331.

Dowty, David. 1988. Type Raising, Functional Composition, and Non-
Constituent Conjunction. In R. Oehrle, E. Bach, and D. Wheeler, eds.,
Categorial Grammars and Natural Language Structures, pages 153–197.
Dordrecht: Reidel.

Dowty, David. 1991. Thematic Proto-Roles and Argument Selection. *Language* 67(3).

Dowty, David. 2000. 'The Garden Swarms with Bees' and the fallacy of 'Argument Alternation'. In Y. Ravin and C. Leacock, eds., *Polysemy. Theoretical and Computational Approaches*, pages 111–128. Oxford: Oxford University Press.

Dowty, David. 2007. Compositionality as an Empirical Problem. In C. Barker and P. Jacobson, eds., *Direct Compositionality*, pages 23–101. Oxford: Oxford University Press.

Dowty, David and Pauline Jacobson. 1991. Infinitival Questions. Unpublished manuscript for a talk delivered in colloquia at The University of California at Santa Cruz and Cornell University. The Ohio State University and Brown University.

Dowty, David R. 1986. The Effects of Aspectual Class on the Temporal Structure of Discourse: Semantics or Pragmatics? *Linguistics and Philosophy* 9(1):37–61.

Groenendijk, Jeroen and Martin Stokhof. 1997. Questions. In J. van Benthem and A. ter Meulen, eds., *Handbook of Logic and Language*, chap. 19, pages 1055–1124. Amsterdam: Elsevier Science/MIT Press.

Jackendoff, Ray. 1972. *Semantic Interpretation in Generative Grammar*. Cambridge, MA: MIT Press.

Jacobson, Pauline. 1999. Towards a Variable-Free Semantics. *Linguistics and Philosophy* 22:117–184.

Janssen, Theo. 1997. Compositionality. In J. van Benthem and A. ter Meulen, eds., *Handbook of Logic and Language*, pages 417–473. Cambridge: MIT Press.

Krifka, Manfred. 2002. Be brief and vague! And how bidirectional optimality theory allows for Verbosity and Precision. In D. Restle and D. Zaefferer, eds., *Sounds and Systems. Studies in Structure and Change. A Festschrift for Theo Vennemann*, pages 439–458. Berlin: Mouton de Gruyter.

Lewis, David K. 1979. Attitudes *de dicto* and *de se*. *The Philosophical Review* 88:513–543.

Nerbonne, John. 1996. Computational Semantics—Linguistics and Processing. In S. Lappin, ed., *Handbook of Contemporary Semantic Theory*, pages 459–482. London: Blackwell Publishers.

Plotkin, G. D. 1975. Call-by-Name, Call-by-Value and the λ-Calculus. *Theoretical Computer Science* 1:125–159.

Portner, Paul. 1997. The Semantics of Mood, Complementation, and Conversational Force. *Natural Language Semantics* 5(2):167–212.

Rooth, Mats. 1998. Two-dimensional Clusters in Grammatical Relations. In M. Rooth, S. Riezler, D. Prescher, S. Schulte im Walde, G. Carroll, and F. Beil, eds., *Inducing Lexicons with the EM Algorithm*, vol. 4.3 of AIMS, pages 7–24. Universität Stuttgart.

Ryle, Gilbert. 1949. *The Concept of Mind*. London: Hutchinson.

Stanley, Jason and Timothy Williamson. 2001. Knowing How. *The Journal of Philosophy* 98(5):411–444.

Steedman, Mark. 1985. Dependency and Coordination in the Grammar of English and Dutch. *Language* 61(3):523–568.

Steedman, Mark. 1990. Gapping as Constituent Coordination. *Linguistics and Philosophy* 13(2):207–263.

Stump, Gregory. 2001. *Inflectional Morphology: A Theory of Paradigm Structure*. Cambridge: Cambridge University Press.

Zadrozny, Wlodek. 1994. From Compositional to Systematic Semantics. *Linguistics and Philosophy* 17(4):329–342.

Acknowledgments

The editors of this volume had the honor and privilege of having David Dowty as the principal advisor of their Ph.D. theses. We would like to use this occasion to thank you, dear David, for your generous support, guidance and friendship over many years.

We are grateful to Dikran Karagueuzian of CSLI for agreeing to publish this volume in the CSLI Lecture Notes series and for his generous support throughout this project.

We are equally grateful to Monica Lău, our editorial assistant. Beyond the call of duty, she painstakingly went over all submitted manuscripts, carefully proof-read them, converted them to LaTeX when necessary, created the index and patiently corresponded with contributors over the course of many months to ensure as much as possible consistency of style across papers.

We would like to thank Bart Alewijnse, Yusuke Kubota, and Yannick Versley for their help with converting submitted manuscripts to LaTeX and to Cornelia Stoll for proof-reading.

Our special thanks go to the anonymous reviewers (you know who you are) for their detailed comments on the submitted manuscripts. Their care and acuity have improved the book immensely.

This publication would not have been possible without the financial support from the Department of Linguistics of the Eberhard Karls Universität Tübingen, from the Collaborative Research Center "Linguistic Data Structures" (SFB 441) at the University of Tübingen, from the Netherlands Organisation for Scientific Research (NWO), and from the Faculty of Letters at the University of Groningen.

1

Reconstruction as delayed evaluation[*]

Chris Barker

1.1 Quantificational binding in reconstruction examples

Not all logically coherent binding relationships are possible in English, of course. For instance, in weak crossover configurations, a quantifier generally cannot bind a pronoun without preceding it:

(1) a. Everyone$_i$ loves his$_i$ mother. $\forall x.\textbf{loves}\,(\textbf{mother}\,x)\,x$
    b. *His$_i$ mother loves everyone$_i$. $\forall x.\textbf{loves}\,x\,(\textbf{mother}\,x)$

In certain reconstruction configurations, however, a quantifier can bind a pronoun that linearly precedes it:

(2) [Which of his$_i$ relatives] does everyone$_i$ love _?

---

[*]Thanks to Pauline Jacobson, Oleg Kiselyov, Monica Lău, Chung-chieh Shan, Yoad Winter, and an anonymous referee. Special thanks to Pauline Jacobson for extensive and incisive discussion. The analysis presented in this paper is a modest extension of joint work with Chung-chieh Shan (see Shan and Barker 2006 and Barker and Shan 2006), and many of the insights developed here are due to conversations with Shan. However, I have drawn conclusions here that Shan may not necessarily endorse. Therefore I will speak of "our analysis", meaning Shan and Barker (2006), but I will express opinions about the interpretation of that analysis in the first person singular. Finally, I must acknowledge my debt to David Dowty. On one level, this paper explores the idea that pronouns are scope-taking elements, an unusual idea also proposed by Dowty in, e.g., Dowty (2007). But the true debt goes far, far deeper: for evidence, argumentation, explicitness, scholarship, intuition, depth, and lasting insight, David's work remains my inspiration, my model, my touchstone for recognizing genuine semantics.

Theory and Evidence in Semantics.
Erhard Hinrichs and John Nerbonne (eds.).
Copyright © 2009, CSLI Publications.

One popular idea is that (at least part of) the bracketed *wh*-phrase moves ('reconstructs') into the indicated gap position before binding relationships are established:

(3) [Which _] does everyone$_i$ love [_ of his$_i$ relatives]?

In the reconstructed configuration in (3), the quantificational NP *everyone* c-commands the pronoun in question, and the binding relationship looks perfectly ordinary. (There is a variation of this approach on which the gap contains a silent copy of the fronted *wh*-phrase, but we will not need to distinguish between movement versus copy reconstruction in this paper.)

On a descriptive level, my goal is to show how the system in Shan and Barker (2006), which accounts for weak crossover contrasts like (1), can handle reconstruction examples like (2) as well. I will argue that the resulting analysis has a number of empirical advantages over the direct-compositional account in Jacobson (1994, 2002a).

On an explanatory level, my goal is to search for a deeper understanding of what the phenomenon of reconstruction is. Following the lead of Sternefeld (1998, 2001), Shan and Barker (2006) and Barker and Shan (2006), I will explore the idea that reconstruction is a form of delayed semantic evaluation: roughly, that the evaluation of the fronted *wh*-phrase is delayed until the normal evaluation of the gap position. Sternefeld (1998, 2001) implements a delay mechanism by stipulating a formal distinction between variables and metavariables. In contrast to Sternefeld's analysis, on our account, delayed evaluation falls out automatically from the independently-motivated interaction of quantification and binding.

1.2   Four theories of reconstruction

I will briefly discuss four approaches to handling reconstruction facts. The first is classical syntactic reconstruction, on which a portion of the fronted material moves into gap position at LF, i.e., before semantic interpretation. There are many movement analyses that differ in important ways from one another (see, e.g., Heycock 1995 for a useful survey). What they all have in common that distinguishes them from the other three classes of analyses discussed here is that they make crucial use of a level of syntactic representation that is distinct from surface syntactic relationships.

The second class of analyses is a radically different approach on which the appearance of a binding relation is an illusion created by manipulating sets of functions. I will sometimes call this class of approaches 'apparent binding' accounts, or sometimes 'functionalist' accounts. Jacobson's (1994, 2002a) is the most highly developed instance of this approach, and I will discuss it in some detail.

The third is an approach called 'semantic reconstruction', on which there is no syntactic movement. Instead, reconstructed pronouns are interpreted as a special type of complex variable that Sternefeld calls a pseudo-variable, so that all of the maneuvering takes place in the semantics rather than in the syntax.

The fourth approach, of course, is our own.

1.2.1 So what's wrong with syntactic reconstruction?

The main objection to the classical analysis is simply "Why?": why must some material reconstruct? Certainly it would be perfectly semantically coherent to interpret a fronted *wh*-phrase in its syntactic position, with no binding or reconstruction effects. Why also postpone binding, since binding relationships are normally established before covert movement at LF? On our account, such questions do not arise. In fact, because reconstruction effects fall out automatically for us, it would require special stipulation to prevent them.

As a more methodological objection, syntactic reconstruction fails to be directly compositional in the sense of, e.g., Jacobson (2002b). In a directly compositional system, every syntactic constituent has a well-defined semantic interpretation. This is not the case for syntactic reconstruction. In particular, on the syntactic account, a fronted *wh*-phrase such as *which of his relatives* never receives a semantic value. On our account, every syntactic constituent has a meaning.

1.2.2 The apparent-binding strategy

Jacobson (1994, 2002b), Sharvit (1999), and Winter (2004) propose that certain cases of quantificational binding depends on analyzing some NPs as denoting functions (instead of individuals or generalized quantifiers). Sharvit attributes a similar strategy to unpublished work of von Stechow from 1990; Jacobson also traces the central idea back to the analysis of functional questions of Engdahl and of Gronendijk and Stokhof.

I will compare our account in some detail to the functionalist approach in Jacobson (1994, 2002a):

(4) a. [The woman that every man loves] is [his mother]. SPEC. COP.
    b. the [relative of his] [that every man loves]   NOM. MOD.

What these two constructions have in common is that a quantifier inside of a relative clause (here, *every man*) seems to bind a pronoun outside of the relative clause (*his*). Normally, relative clauses are scope islands,

4 / CHRIS BARKER

so these binding relationships require explanation.

Consider the nominal modifier case in (4b). On Jacobson's analysis, applying her **z** combinator to the denotation of *loves* yields an interpretation on which *that every man loves* denotes the set of functions f such that every man x loves fx (see Jacobson 2002a for technical details).

The ordinary denotation of a nominal does not have a type that allows it to combine with a set of functions, so Jacobson provides a combinator **m** such that $\mathbf{m}(\textit{relative of his}) = \lambda f \forall x.\textbf{relative}\, x\,(fx)$. Roughly, **m** takes a relation and returns the set of functions that are subsets of that relation. In this case, **m** returns the set of (partial) functions f such that for all x in the domain of f, fx is a relative of x. (Actually, in Jacobson's system, **m** must be a family of operators, one for each number of pronouns participating in the apparent binding relation.)

Finally, the relative clause will combine semantically with the nominal head by means of set intersection. In the case in hand, this intersection will include all functions f such that f maps each x to a relative of x, and for every man x, x loves fx. Assuming that the only salient such function is the function that maps each man onto his mother, then the definite description as a whole will denote the **mother-of** function.

One remarkable property of the functionalist analysis is that there is no binding relationship between the quantifier and the pronoun. Rather, there is only the appearance of binding, brought about by equating sets of functions.

Sharvit (1999), Jacobson (2002a), and Winter (2004) assume that the relative clause analysis can and should be generalized to at least some fronted *wh* cases. Sharvit (1999) in particular argues that there are strong parallels between the empirical behavior of functional relative clauses and *wh* reconstruction cases; for instance, both phenomena are sensitive to weak crossover violations (see section 1.6.4 below). However, none of these authors provide concrete details for the reconstruction cases:

(5) a. the [relative of his] [that every man loves _]

   b. Which [relative of his] [does every man love _]?

Presumably the semantics for *which* will result in a paraphrase such as 'tell me the function f such that for all x, fx is x's relative, and every man x loves fx'.

The apparent-binding strategy as developed by Jacobson is highly similar to ours in framework, philosophy, and a number of important assumptions. Both analyses are embodied in a combinatory categorial grammar obeying strict direct compositionality, and we rely heavily on the assumption that pronouns and other elements denote identity functions, an idea explored in detail in much of Jacobson's work.

On the empirical side, however, there are at least four significant differences between the apparent-binding approach and ours.

Radical context-dependency: plumbers and kittens. Consider the following example:

(6) The person that every plumber loves most is her mother.

Since $\mathbf{m}(person)$ returns the set of all functions whose range is included in the set of people, the prediction is that (6) will be true only if the mother function maps each plumber onto a person. So far so good. But the semantics of $\mathbf{m}$ also guarantees that (6) will be true only if every mother is a person. The reason is that a function f only gets into the set returned by the $\mathbf{m}$ operator if f maps every object x in its domain into the set of people, whether x is a plumber or not. But of course all sorts of creatures have mothers; after all, (6) can be true at the same time that the cat that every kitten loves most is *her* mother. The fact is, when evaluating (6), we need to limit our attention to how the functions involved behave when applied to plumbers, and kittens should be completely ignored. But this restriction is not guaranteed by the truth conditions of the functionalist analysis.

Perhaps the context restricts the mother function to the domain of plumbers (or kittens) on a per-use basis. One way to do this would be to assume that uses of pronouns routinely contribute domain restrictions, as Jacobson has proposed in other work relating to contrastive focus on pronouns. Then (6) will be appropriately used in a context in which *her* is a partial function defined only on female plumbers. The problem, as pointed out by Dimitriadis (2002), is that figuring out the domain restriction for a pronoun depends on distant semantic material in an arguably non-compositional way.

Spurious readings. The following examples are based on observations that Jacobson (personal communication) attributes to Heycock (personal communication):

(7) a. Which woman [that he loves] [does every man respect]?

b. Which woman [that he loves] [does John respect]?

On Jacobson's account, the (appearance of a) bound reading for (7a) arises by application of $\mathbf{m}$ to *that he loves*, where $\mathbf{m}(that\ he\ loves) = \lambda f \forall x.\mathbf{loves}(fx)x$ (see the discussion in Jacobson 2002a after her example (28)). This shift allows *that he loves* to denote a set of functions suitable for intersecting with the set of functions denoted by (the functional reading of) *does every man respect*. But the fact that *every man* is quantificational plays no role in constructing the functional reading: all that is required is application of **z** to *respect*. Consequently, *does John respect* will also have a functional interpretation, namely, $\lambda f.\mathbf{respects}(f\,\mathbf{j})\,\mathbf{j}$. The prediction is that (7b) should have an analysis such that *his mother* is a true answer only if every man loves his mother. But (7b) has no such reading.

Evidently, **m** should not be allowed to apply freely, but needs to be triggered by the presence of some overt quantifier elsewhere in the sentence. The main claim of the apparent-binding approach is that there is no formal link between the quantifier and the pronoun it seems to bind; but what examples like (7) show is that eliminating the formal link gives rise to spurious readings. Because our account does not rely on the **m** operator, these spurious readings do not arise.

Undergeneration: outbound binding. A third empirical problem involves cases in which the fronted *wh*-phrase contains a quantifier, rather than a pronoun.

(8) a. [Which of every applicant$_i$'s scores] did someone forget to record in his$_i$ file? (Engdahl)
  b. ...we summarize [what part of each model$_i$] is critical for producing its$_i$ fundamental behavior
  c. We're trying to find out [which aspect of each wine$_i$] has the strongest effect on its$_i$ quality.

I will call examples like (8), in which it is a quantifier that needs to be reconstructed, **outbound binding**. Outbound binding is unexpected on the apparent-binding account. The problem is that there is no obvious way to shift *of every applicant's scores* to a set of functions. The reason is that there is no gap or pronoun to get the functional interpretation started, as there was in the relative clause case, so **m** does not apply. I return to outbound binding in section 1.6.3 below.

How-many **questions.** Finally, the extension of the analysis in Jacobson (2002a) sketched above does not give an appropriate semantics for other types of questions:

(9) How many [relatives of his] [does every man love]?

Assume the men are John and Bill, who each love their parents, and no one else. Then **m**(*relatives of his*) will yield the following set of functions:

$$f_1(\mathbf{j}) = \mathbf{mom}(\mathbf{j}) \qquad f_1(\mathbf{b}) = \mathbf{mom}(\mathbf{b})$$
$$f_2(\mathbf{j}) = \mathbf{mom}(\mathbf{j}) \qquad f_2(\mathbf{b}) = \mathbf{dad}(\mathbf{b})$$

$$f_3(\mathbf{j}) = \mathbf{dad}(\mathbf{j}) \qquad f_3(\mathbf{b}) = \mathbf{mom}(\mathbf{b})$$
$$f_4(\mathbf{j}) = \mathbf{dad}(\mathbf{j}) \qquad f_4(\mathbf{b}) = \mathbf{dad}(\mathbf{b})$$

Since there are four functions, the simple-minded version of *how many* will incorrectly predict that *four* ought to be a true answer in the situation described. (The situation is more complex if we allow non-atomic entities in the range of the functions, but the answers still come out wrong.)

The problem is that we don't want a count of functions, we want a function from individuals to counts: for each individual x, the number of x's relatives that are loved by x.

Interestingly, there is an apparent-binding analysis that constructs exactly the right sort of function. Winter's (2004) approach is dual to Jacobson's: Jacobson starts with the functional meaning that her theory assigns to the relative clause and shifts the nominal head (via her **m**) so that it matches in type. Winter shifts instead the functional relative clause meaning (via his operator **RG**) into a function from individuals to sets (for instance, mapping each man onto the set of things he loves). As far as I can see, however, Winter's analysis shares (some version of) the other three empirical challenges with Jacobson's account.

These four empirical issues (the plumber problem, spurious readings, outbound binding, and *how-many* questions) motivate considering an alternative analysis of reconstruction. We provide such an account below, without needing an operator like **m** or **RG** (nor any operator specific to handling reconstruction). The result will be an analysis on which the apparent binding between the quantifier and the pronoun is genuine binding.

1.2.3 Semantic reconstruction

Several authors have suggested that reconstruction is primarily semantic in nature rather than syntactic. Versions of this idea are due to Cresti (1995, p. 85), Rullman (1995, p. 174), and Sternefeld (2001). There is a relevant discussion in Romero (1998, p. 82); von Stechow (1998) traces the idea back to a 1979 Bennet paper (no longer available from IULC), and relates it to the notion of dynamic binding as discussed, e.g., in Chierchia (1992). The basic idea is that syntactic displacement and its reconstruction is the same sort of syntactic reconstruction that characterizes beta-reduction in the lambda-calculus.

(10) a. Himself, everyone loves _.

 b. $(\lambda x \forall y.\mathbf{loves}\ y\ x)(\text{himself}_y)$

 c. $\forall y.\mathbf{loves}\ y\ \text{himself}_y$

This example, and (11) below, are adapted from Sternefeld. Though only marginally grammatical in English, translations of (10a) are better in other languages, including German.

Asserting a semantic equivalence between (10b) and (10c) captures the relationship between the surface position of the displaced constituent and its role in the semantic interpretation. Unfortunately, the reduction is not valid, since the variable y associated with *himself* comes to be bound by *everyone*. To see that this is not valid, note that (10b) is α-equivalent (and thus semantically equivalent) to $(\lambda x.\forall z.\textbf{loves } z\, x)(\text{himself}_y)$, which does not lead to the desired result.

Sternefeld shows how a more sophisticated approach can provide the desired effect without violating any of the rules of the lambda calculus.

(11) a. $\lambda g.(\lambda Y.\forall x.\textbf{loves } (Y g[x/1])\, x)\,\boxed{(\lambda g.g(1))}$

 b. $\lambda g.\forall x.\textbf{loves } (g[x/1](1))\, x$

Sternefeld assumes that sentences denote sets of assignment functions (as in many dynamic frameworks). If pronouns can denote functions from assignment functions to entities, as in the boxed expression $\lambda g.g(1)$, then the computation of (11b) from (11a) is perfectly valid according to the rules of the lambda calculus. Sternefeld calls denotations such as $\lambda g.g(1)$ 'pseudo variables', precisely because they are able to evade the normal rules of variable capture.

The way that pseudo-variables achieve delayed evaluation is by separating the process of evaluating a variable into two stages: in the first (outermost) stage, compute the appropriate assignment function. In the second, later (innermost) stage, apply the assignment function to the variable (index). Thus at the expense of adding a layer of indirection to the interpretation of (only some!) pronouns, we have a strategy for handling reconstruction semantically rather than syntactically.

The problem is that giving pseudo-variables free rein would provide a way for quantifiers to bind any pronoun that they take scope over. In other words, the difference between reconstruction situations in which binding is ok, and (for example) weak crossover situations in which binding is not ok, would become a matter of stipulation governing access to pseudo-variables. In addition, it is not clear how Sternefeld's analysis could be extended to cover outbound anaphora.

1.2.4   The continuation-based approach

Unlike the syntactic account, the system in Shan and Barker (2006) is directly compositional: it does not rely on movement, or copying, or any sort of LF. However, unlike Jacobson's functionalist account, we do not have any trouble ignoring kittens, nor do we generate the spurious readings due to overapplication of **m**. We do correctly generate outbound readings, and *how-many* questions do not pose any problem. In addition, on our direct compositional account, there is a bona fide binding relationship between the quantifier and the pronoun.

Like Sternefeld, we achieve delayed evaluation by assigning some uses of pronouns to categories with higher semantic types. Unlike Sternefeld, the availability of these more complex categories arises from type-shifting operators that are independently motivated in order to handle simple quantificational and binding, without any stipulation specific to reconstruction.

1.3 A general theory of scope and binding

This section presents the theory of scope and binding developed in Shan and Barker (2006). This theory was constructed without any consideration of either weak crossover or reconstruction examples. Nevertheless, we shall see that it automatically accounts for weak crossover contrasts like that in (1) as well as a range of reconstruction examples like that in (2).

The grammar is an ordinary combinatory categorial grammar in the style of Szabolcsi (e.g. 1992), Jacobson (e.g. 1999), Steedman (e.g. 2000), and others. As usual, for any categories A and B, the **default mode** of combination provides categories 'A/B' (an A missing a B to its right) and 'B\A' (an A missing a B to its left).

(12)   Syntax   Semantics

| A/B | **B** | $\Rightarrow$ A | f | x | $\Rightarrow fx$ |
| **B** | **B**\A | $\Rightarrow$ A | x | f | $\Rightarrow fx$ |

As usual, syntactic combination is a cancellation operation in which the bolded occurrences of the category B must match. The corresponding semantic operation is functional application, where the expression in the slashed category denotes a function f and the expression in the category B denotes an argument x.

In addition to the default mode, there is a second mode of combination. For any categories A and B, the **continuation mode** provides additional categories 'A⫽B' (an A missing a B where the B surrounds the A) and 'B⫽A' (an A missing a B somewhere inside of it).[1]

---

[1] Any category of the form B⫽A is a CONTINUATION; see Barker (2002) for motivation for the relevance of continuations in natural language semantics. Emmon Bach tells me that he used a double slash with a somewhat similar meaning, but he couldn't remember where, and I haven't been able to track down this use. Barker and Shan (2006) discuss the continuation mode within the framework of multi-modal Type Logical Grammar.

As a matter of notation, instead of using the ordinary ('linear') form of a category such as $C /\!\!/ (A \backslash B)$, I will usually display the category in the form of a *tower*, thus: $\dfrac{C \mid B}{A}$. At times below, however, I will revert to the linear notation according to the needs of the discussion at hand. In tandem on the semantics side, I define the stacked expression $\dfrac{g[\,]}{x}$ to be notation for the linear algebraic expression $\lambda\kappa.g(\kappa x)$.

One advantage of the tower notation is that it reveals how combination in the presence of continuations is a form of cancellation:

(13)   Syntax   Semantics

$$\frac{C \mid D}{A/B} \quad \frac{D \mid E}{B} \Rightarrow \frac{C \mid E}{A} \qquad \frac{g[\,]}{f} \quad \frac{h[\,]}{x} \Rightarrow \frac{g[h[\,]]}{f x}$$

$$\frac{C \mid D}{B} \quad \frac{D \mid E}{B \backslash A} \Rightarrow \frac{C \mid E}{A} \qquad \frac{g[\,]}{x} \quad \frac{h[\,]}{f} \Rightarrow \frac{g[h[\,]]}{f x}$$

Once again, bolded categories must match in order to cancel. In the corresponding semantic operation, '$g[\,]$' is an expression g containing a distinguished position somewhere within it, such that $g[x]$ is g with x inserted into that distinguished position.[2]

1.3.1   Quantification and scope

We will need two type-shifting operators to provide a general scope-taking mechanism: Lift and Lower.

Lift is an essential type-shifting operator familiar from Partee and Rooth (1983) and much subsequent work. (Indeed, Sternefeld's pseudo-variables are nothing more than Lifted variables.)

$$\text{Lift:} \quad \boxed{A{:}x \Rightarrow \frac{X \mid X}{A} : \frac{[\,]}{x}}$$

---

[2]Bracket notation is not commonly encountered in linguistics discussions, but is standard in theoretical computer science, especially in discussions of the lambda calculus (see, e.g., Barendregt, 1984). Crucially, unlike β-reduction, this substitution operation is variable-capturing. For instance, if $g[\,]$ is $\lambda x.\textbf{loves}\,\_\,\textbf{j}$, where $\_$ marks the distinguished position within $g[\,]$, then $g[x]$ is $\lambda x.\textbf{loves}\,x\,\textbf{j}$, in which x is bound by the lambda. I use bracket notation purely as a notational convenience; in particular, despite the discussion of semantic reconstruction above, the variable-capturing nature of the brackets plays no essential role in providing an interpretation for reconstruction examples. After all, these brackets are entirely dispensable: Shan and Barker (2006) present an equivalent grammar using the linear notation exclusively.

This rule says that if some expression is a member of category A and has semantic value x, then that expression is also a member of the category $\dfrac{\text{X} \mid \text{X}}{\text{A}}$ (in linear notation, $\text{X}/\!/(\text{A}\backslash\text{X})$) with semantic value $\dfrac{[\,]}{x}$ (in linear notation, $\lambda\kappa.\kappa x$).

Just as in Partee and Rooth, Lift allows expressions without any quantificational force of their own to participate in derivations with proper quantifiers. For instance, given lexical entries as follows:

(14) a. someone $\dfrac{\text{S} \mid \text{S}}{\text{NP}} : \dfrac{\exists x[\,]}{x}$

    b. everyone $\dfrac{\text{S} \mid \text{S}}{\text{NP}} : \dfrac{\forall y[\,]}{y}$

    c. loves $(\text{NP}\backslash\text{S})/\text{NP}:$ **loves**

In the presence of Lift, we have the following derivation:

$$\dfrac{\text{S}_3 \mid \text{S}_2}{\substack{\text{NP}_2 \\ \text{someone}}} \left(\dfrac{\text{S}_2 \mid \text{S}_1}{\substack{(\text{NP}_2\backslash\text{S}_0)/\text{NP}_1 \\ \text{loves}}} \quad \dfrac{\text{S}_1 \mid \text{S}_4}{\substack{\text{NP}_1 \\ \text{everyone}}} \right) = \dfrac{\text{S}_3 \mid \text{S}_4}{\substack{\text{S}_0 \\ \text{someone loves everyone}}}$$

Only for these first few derivations, I decorate category symbols with subscripts to help the reader figure out what cancels with what. Here, *loves* undergoes Lift with X = S. It combines first with *everyone*, at which point the NP_1's cancel and the S_1's cancel. When the verb phrase combines with the subject, the NP_2's and the S_2's cancel, producing the result on the right hand side of the equal sign.

The semantic calculation proceeds in parallel.

$$\dfrac{\exists x[\,]}{x} \left(\dfrac{[\,]}{\textbf{loves}} \quad \dfrac{\forall y[\,]}{y} \right) = \dfrac{\exists x(\forall y[\,])}{\textbf{loves}\ y\ x}$$

Since the final value contains an unresolved instance of [ ], we need an operator that is the dual of Lift in order to complete the derivation:

$$\text{Lower:} \quad \boxed{\dfrac{\text{X} \mid \textbf{S}}{\textbf{S}} : \dfrac{g[\,]}{x} \Rightarrow \text{X}{:}g[x]}$$

Unlike (13) above, Lower is a cancellation operation in which an S below the line cancels with the right top corner S (the two bolded S's in the diagram). In addition to its usefulness in various linguistic analyses (notably including Partee 1987), Lower is characteristic of continuation analyses (Plotkin 1975, Barker 2002, Shan and Barker 2006, etc.) as well as other types of dynamic systems (e.g., Chierchia 1995, as discussed in Barker 2002, p. 236).

Once we have Lower, the derivation of *Someone loves everyone* continues as follows:

$$\frac{S_3 \mid S_4}{S_0} : \frac{\exists x(\forall y[\ ])}{\textbf{loves } y\, x} \xrightarrow{\text{Lower}} S_3 : \exists x(\forall y(\textbf{loves } y\, x))$$

S_0 cancels with S_4, and the two-level denotation collapses to a single level.

1.3.2 Inverse scope and multiple continuation levels

In the derivation just above, the quantifiers take scope corresponding to their linear order. Arriving at the inverse scoping requires a second continuation layer.

At this point I must say a word about combining towers. In our system, any combination rule gives rise to another combination rule that operates under an extra continuation level. More precisely, any rule

$$A_1 \cdots A_n \Rightarrow B$$

gives rise to a rule

$$\frac{X_0 \mid X_1}{A_1} \cdots \frac{X_{n-1} \mid X_n}{A_n} \Rightarrow \frac{X_0 \mid X_n}{B}.$$

This is fairly intuitive in practice. For example, choosing $n = 2$, this is how the ordinary function application rules in (12) give rise to the continuation-aware function application rules in (13). Similarly, choosing $n = 1$, the ordinary Lift rule above gives rise to the following continuation-aware Lift rule:

$$\frac{X \mid X}{A} : \frac{f[\ ]}{x} \Rightarrow \frac{\dfrac{X \mid X}{Y \mid Y} \quad \dfrac{f[\ ]}{[\ ]}}{A \qquad x}$$

This derived Lift applies to the lexical entry for *everyone* given above in (14):

$$\frac{S_1 \mid S_1}{NP} : \frac{\forall y[\ ]}{y} \xrightarrow{\text{Lift}} \frac{\dfrac{S_1 \mid S_1}{S_2 \mid S_2} \quad \dfrac{\forall y[\ ]}{[\ ]}}{NP \qquad y}$$

We now have a derivation for inverse scope as follows:

$$\frac{\frac{\cdots}{\text{S} \mid \text{S}}}{\underset{\text{someone}}{\text{NP}}} \left(\frac{\frac{\cdots}{\cdots}}{\underset{\text{loves}}{(\text{NP}\backslash\text{S})/\text{NP}}} \quad \frac{\frac{\text{S} \mid \text{S}}{\text{S} \mid \text{S}}}{\underset{\text{everyone}}{\text{NP}}} \right) = \frac{\frac{\text{S} \mid \text{S}_2}{\text{S}_2 \mid \text{S}_1}}{\underset{\text{someone loves everyone}}{\text{S}_1}}$$

The derivation finishes by applying Lower twice: first to cancel the S_1's, and then to cancel the S_2's. The parallel semantic calculation shows how higher levels take scope over lower levels:

$$\frac{\frac{\cdots}{\exists x[\ ]}}{x} \left(\frac{\frac{\cdots}{\cdots}}{\text{\textbf{loves}}} \quad \frac{\forall y[\ ]}{\cdots} \right) = \frac{\frac{\forall y[\ ]}{\exists x[\ ]}}{\text{\textbf{loves } } y\, x} \overset{\text{Lower (twice)}}{\Longrightarrow} \forall y(\exists x(\textbf{loves } y\, x))$$

The generalization is that higher levels take scope over lower levels (by virtue of the interpretation of the tower notation), and within a single level, elements on the left take scope over elements on the right (by virtue of the details of combination given in (13)).

In addition to accounting for inverse scope, higher continuation levels will be crucial in the explanation of reconstruction.

Combination, Lift and Lower provide a general mechanism for scope-taking. We will need only two additional operators to account for reconstruction. The first governs binding, and the second characterizes fronted *wh*-constructions.

1.3.3   Binding

Let $\text{NP}\triangleright\text{S}$ be the category of clauses containing a bindable NP position somewhere within them. In general, inserting a pronoun into an expression that would otherwise be in some arbitrary category X creates an expression in category $\text{NP}\triangleright\text{X}$:

$$\text{his} \quad \frac{\text{NP}\triangleright\text{X} \mid \text{X}}{\text{NP}} : \frac{\lambda z[\ ]}{z}$$

Note that pronouns have a non-trivial effect at the first continuation level (i.e., above the horizontal line). That amounts to claiming that (unlike Jacobson's treatment) pronouns are quite literally scope-taking elements. Pronouns, then, are expressions that turn whatever contains them into something containing a bindable NP. Dowty (2007) also argues that pronouns are scope-takers, though his proposal is not compatible with our assumption that pronouns are also identity maps. Claiming that pronouns are identity maps is an assumption that we share with Jacobson, and that is crucial to our analysis in this paper.

So pronouns create expressions that can be bound into. The other half of establishing a binding relationship is accomplished via the following type-shifting operator:

$$\text{Bind:} \quad \boxed{\dfrac{\text{A} \mid \text{B}}{\text{NP}} : \dfrac{f[\,]}{x} \quad \Rightarrow \quad \dfrac{\text{A} \mid \text{NP}\triangleright\text{B}}{\text{NP}} : \dfrac{f([\,]x)}{x}}$$

This scheme says that any NP taking scope over an expression of category B can bind some NP within that B. The semantics copies the denotation of the NP (the x at the lower level) to serve as the value of the bound NP (the x at the higher level).

The binder and the bound pronoun find each other via cancellation:

$$\dfrac{\dfrac{\text{S} \mid \text{NP}\triangleright\text{S}}{\text{NP}}}{\underset{\text{everyone}}{}} \quad \dfrac{(\text{NP}\backslash\text{S})/\text{NP}}{\underset{\text{loves}}{}} \quad \left(\dfrac{\dfrac{\text{NP}\triangleright\text{S} \mid \text{S}}{\text{NP}}}{\underset{\text{his}}{}} \quad \dfrac{\text{NP}\backslash\text{NP}}{\underset{\text{mother}}{}} \right)$$

The idea is that the binding dependency created by the pronoun cancels with the binding value provided by the subject NP.[3]

$$\dfrac{\forall y([\,]y)}{y} \quad \textbf{loves} \quad \left(\dfrac{\lambda z[\,]}{z} \quad \textbf{mom} \right) = \dfrac{\forall y.(\lambda z[\,])\,y}{\textbf{loves}\,(\textbf{mom}\,z)\,y}$$

Lower
$$\Rightarrow \quad \forall y.(\lambda z.\textbf{loves}\,(\textbf{mom}\,z)\,y)\,y = \forall y.\textbf{loves}\,(\textbf{mom}\,y)\,y$$

In the semantics, the variable provided by the quantifier ends up binding the argument position of the relational noun *mother*, as desired.

1.3.4 Weak crossover

Remarkably, given this basic account of scope and binding, a wide range of weak crossover cases fall out for free.

$$\dfrac{\dfrac{\text{NP}\triangleright\text{S} \mid \text{S}}{\text{NP}}}{\underset{\text{his}}{}} \quad \dfrac{\text{NP}\backslash\text{NP}}{\underset{\text{mother}}{}} \quad \dfrac{(\text{NP}\backslash\text{S})/\text{NP}}{\underset{\text{loves}}{}} \quad \dfrac{\dfrac{\text{S} \mid \text{NP}\triangleright\text{S}}{\text{NP}}}{\underset{\text{everyone}}{}}$$

---

[3]Some technical details: *everyone* has undergone the Bind operator, *loves* undergoes Lift with X=NP▷S, the lexical category of the pronoun has been instantiated with X=S, and *mother* must undergo Lift with X=S.

In this derivation, cancellation proceeds without a hitch. The result, however, does not match the input schema of the Lower type-shifter (which requires S above the line, not NP$\triangleright$S). As a result, the expression cannot be collapsed into a final value. Intuitively, the reason is that the pronoun and the quantifier are facing away from each other, and neither is aware of the other: at the end of the derivation, the pronoun is still seeking a binder, and the quantifier is still waiting for something to bind.

Shan and Barker (2006) provide a more detailed discussion of the explanation for weak crossover, along with a wide range of examples.

1.4 Questions

In order to treat the reconstruction examples of interest such as (2), which have fronted *wh* phrases, it remains only to extend the grammar to handle *wh*-questions. The strategy will be to use a single lexical entry for both in-situ *wh*-questions and fronted *wh*-questions. Let an expression in category A?B be some expression in category B within which an element of category A has been questioned.

$$\text{who} \quad \frac{\text{NP?X} \mid \text{X}}{\text{NP}} : \frac{\textbf{who}(\lambda z[\,])}{z}$$

The structure of this lexical entry resembles that of a pronoun, except that in place of the syntactic connective $\triangleright$ there is ?. I can illustrate how this lexical entry works by pretending that English has in-situ *wh*-questions (somewhat marginally available as an echo question):

$$\frac{\overline{\text{NP}} \quad \frac{}{(\text{NP}\backslash\text{S})/\text{NP}} \quad \frac{\text{NP?S} \mid \text{S}}{\text{NP}}}{\text{John} \quad \text{loves} \quad \text{who}} \quad \begin{array}{l} \text{Lower} \\ \Rightarrow \quad \text{NP?S:} \; \textbf{who}(\lambda z.\textbf{loves} \; z \, \textbf{j}) \end{array}$$

Depending on your favorite semantics for questions (which I leave open; see also section 1.5 below), this could be glossed as 'Please identify a person z such that John loves z'.

Our fourth and final type-shifting operator allows *wh*-phrases to occur at the front of a sentence:

Front: $\boxed{(\text{X?Y})/\!\!/\text{Z}:f \Rightarrow (\text{X?Y})/\text{Z}:f}$

This operator takes an in-situ *wh*-phrase with category $(\text{X?Y})/\!\!/\text{Z}$, and modifies it in the tiniest way possible: by replacing $/\!/$ with $/$, with no change whatsoever in the semantics. For instance, we might have

$$(NP?S)/\!/(NP\backslash\!\backslash S) \quad \text{Front} \quad (NP?S)/(NP\backslash\!\backslash S)$$
$$\text{who} \qquad \Rightarrow \qquad \text{who}$$

This one syntactic change accounts for the difference between in-situ word order and fronted word order. Here's how: the continuation mode $/\!/$ allows an in-situ element such as a quantifier or a *wh*-word to combine with a larger phrase that encloses it, as we have seen above; the default mode $/$, of course, only allows an element to combine with a phrase that linearly follows it. The net result is that after shifting with the Front operator, a *wh*-phrase that originally (i.e., lexically) expected to be embedded in-situ within a larger expression now expects to find its semantic context packaged as a gap-containing phrase to its right.

Crucially, the Front operator does not affect the semantics of the *wh*-phrase at all. Because the expression with which the *wh*-phrase combines has the same syntactic category and the same semantic value regardless of whether the *wh*-phrase is in-situ or has been fronted (in the example below, for instance, the syntactic category the *wh*-phrase combines with is $NP\backslash\!\backslash S$ either way), the semantic value of the complete question does not differ when the *wh*-phrase is in-situ or fronted. As a consequence, if a pronoun could have been bound if the *wh*-phrase were in-situ, it can likewise be bound when the *wh*-phrase has been fronted.

Before we can complete our analysis of simple sentences with fronted *wh*-phrases, we need only provide an analysis of the *wh*-gap:

- $\quad X/\!/X : \lambda x.x$

This analysis says that silence (i.e., '$\_$') is the sort of expression that, when combined with an expression X containing it, forms an expression of category X. In other words, just like multiplying in arithmetic by $\dfrac{X}{X}$, combining an expression with a gap constitutes the identity function.

Since X can be any arbitrary category, there are many ways to instantiate a gap, and we will exploit this flexibility below. One of the simplest useful NP gaps instantiates X as $NP\backslash\!\backslash S$:

- $\quad (NP\backslash\!\backslash S)/\!/(NP\backslash\!\backslash S) = \dfrac{NP\backslash\!\backslash S \mid S}{NP}$

We have given the gap both in linear notation, to show that it is a legitimate instantiation of the general gap scheme, and the equivalent tower notation for use in the derivation of the expression *does John love* _:

$$\frac{\overline{\begin{array}{ccc} \text{S/S} & \text{NP} & \text{(NP\textbackslash S)/NP} \\ \text{does} & \text{John} & \text{love} \end{array}} \quad \begin{array}{c} \text{NP\textbackslash\textbackslash S} \mid \text{S} \\ \hline \text{NP} \\ \_ \end{array}}{} = \begin{array}{c} \text{NP\textbackslash\textbackslash S} \mid \text{S} \\ \hline \text{S} \\ \text{does John love} \_ \end{array}$$

$$\begin{array}{cc} \text{Lower} & \text{NP\textbackslash\textbackslash S} \\ \Rightarrow & \text{does John love} \_ \end{array}$$

This, of course, is just a question body, the gapped clause following the *wh*-word. The question body combines with *who* (which has undergone the Front operator):

$$\begin{array}{c} \text{(NP?S)/(NP\textbackslash\textbackslash S)} \\ \text{who} \end{array} \left(\begin{array}{c} \text{NP\textbackslash\textbackslash S} \\ \text{does John love} \_ \end{array} \right) = \begin{array}{c} \text{NP?S} \\ \text{who does John love} \_? \end{array}$$

The system guarantees that the semantics of the fronted question will be identical to the semantics of the in-situ version derived above, i.e., **who**($\lambda z.$**loves** $z\,$**j**).

The four type-shifters introduced above were motivated only by the most basic considerations of providing an analysis of scope, binding, and question formation: Lift, Lower, Bind, and Front. None of these operators were complicated in any way in anticipation of handling either weak crossover or reconstruction. Nevertheless, the system described above automatically accounts for a wide range of weak crossover examples, and, as we will see, reconstruction examples.

1.5   Functional questions

Since we claim (in common with Engdahl and many others) that reconstruction examples and functional questions arise through the same mechanisms, we must explain how functional questions work.

(15)   Q. Who does everyone love _?
        A1. the Queen
        A2. his mother

As is well known, the question in (15) has at least two sorts of answers. The first is closely parallel to the analysis given above, in which there is a single individual loved by everyone. A suitable answer for this interpretation would be (A1).

On the functional interpretation, there will be a potentially different loved person for each choice of lover. A suitable answer for this interpretation would be (A2): the person that each person x loves is x's mother. We will develop an account of this functional reading in some detail here, since many details of the analysis will be directly relevant for the analysis of reconstruction below.

1.5.1 Complex pronoun meanings as predicate modifiers

Before discussing functional questions, it will be helpful to discuss functional answers first. The classic answer to a functional question, of course, has the same category as a plain pronoun:

$$\frac{\dfrac{NP{\triangleright}S \mid S}{NP} \quad \dfrac{}{NP\backslash NP}}{\text{her} \qquad \text{mother}} = \frac{NP{\triangleright}S \mid S}{NP}$$
$$\text{her mother}$$

The claim is that *her* and *her mother* have the same category. We can call *her mother* a complex pronoun, in the same spirit that, e.g., *those men* counts as a complex demonstrative. That means that pronouns and complex pronouns should have equivalent syntactic distributions, and they should make interchangeable (but not semantically equivalent) contributions to the truth conditions of the larger expression. (See, e.g., Jacobson 1999 for motivation and discussion.)

Semantically, a pronoun adds a functional dependence to whatever expression contains it. If *John saw Mary* denotes a truth value, then *John saw her* denotes a function from individuals to truth values. As explained above, this is accomplished by instantiating the lexical category of *her* as $(NP{\triangleright}S)/\!/(NP\backslash\!\backslash S)$: a function from meanings of type $\langle e, t \rangle$ to meanings of type $\langle e, t \rangle$. But of course $\langle e, t \rangle$ is also the type of a nominal or other one-place predicate. Thus another valid perspective on the meaning of a pronoun is that it is a predicate modifier: it takes a predicate as argument and returns a modified predicate. Ignoring gender presuppositions, the specific function denoted by a pronoun is the identity function. But the complex expression *her mother* contributes content beyond the identity function. More specifically, given a predicate P as argument, the function denoted by *her mother* will return the composition of P with the **mother** function. For example, if *John saw her* denotes the function mapping each individual x to the proposition that John saw x, *John saw her mother* denotes the function from individuals x to the proposition that John saw x's mother.

1.5.2 Functional readings

Allowing gaps, *wh*-words, and pronouns to schematize over an infinite class of identity types provides considerable flexibility. Among the advantages of this flexibility is that it predicts not only functional readings, but, as we will see shortly, reconstruction examples.

In relying on functional gaps in this way, our account resembles the functionalist tradition of Engdahl (1986), Chierchia (1993), Jacobson (1999), and others. As Szabolcsi (1997) points out, one distinctive feature of this style of analysis is that the *wh*-phrase always takes wide scope over any (non-*wh*) quantificational element. But as she notes (p. 318), this does not limit the contribution of the quantifier to the semantics of the interrogative in certain important ways. In particular, it is possible to implement variations on Karttunen's or Groenendijk and Stokhof's semantics for a variety of question types. Therefore I leave the semantics of questions unanalyzed in this paper: since the choice of question semantics is independent of the phenomena we analyze here, the reader is free to supply their favorite conception of question meaning.[4]

Here is an instantiation of the schema for *who*, along with its corresponding gap, that will give rise to a simple functional reading of (15). Let 'pn' abbreviate the category of a simple pronoun, i.e., $(NP \triangleright S)/\!/(NP \backslash\!\backslash S)$.

who	$(pn?S) /\!/ (pn\backslash\!\backslash S)$
-	$(pn\backslash\!\backslash S) /\!/ (pn\backslash\!\backslash S)$

Unpacking this instantiation of the gap, we have

$$(pn\backslash\!\backslash S) /\!/ (pn\backslash\!\backslash S) = \frac{pn\backslash\!\backslash S \mid S}{pn} = \frac{\dfrac{pn\backslash\!\backslash S \mid S}{NP\triangleright S \mid S}}{NP}$$

The first step just converts from linear notation to tower notation, and the right hand side merely expands the abbreviation of the lower occurrence of 'pn'.

This instantiation of the gap enables the following analysis of the question body (i.e., *does everyone love _*). (This exact partial derivation will form part of the analysis of some of the reconstruction examples discussed below in the next section.)

---

[4]Szabolcsi, along with Beghelli (1997), goes on to criticize Chierchia's account in particular as failing to make sufficiently fine-grained empirical distinctions. We will have nothing to say on this occasion about most of the intricate facts presented there, including contrasting availability of functional and pair-list readings for *what* and *who* versus *which*, matrix versus embedded interrogatives, *every* versus *each*, etc.

$$
\begin{array}{c|c}
\text{pn}\backslash\backslash S & S \\
\hline
\text{NP}\triangleright S & S \\
\hline
\text{NP} \\
\text{everyone}
\end{array}
\qquad
\begin{array}{c}
\hline
(\text{NP}\backslash S)/\text{NP} \\
\text{love}
\end{array}
\qquad
\begin{array}{c|c}
\text{pn}\backslash\backslash S & S \\
\hline
\text{NP}\triangleright S & S \\
\hline
\text{NP} \\
\text{--}
\end{array}
\qquad
\begin{array}{c|c}
\text{pn}\backslash\backslash S & S \\
\hline
S & S \\
\hline
S \\
=
\end{array}
$$

In effect, the quantifier binds a virtual pronoun within the gap position.

$$
\begin{array}{c}
\hline
\forall y([\,]\,y) \\
\hline
y
\end{array}
\quad
\begin{array}{c}
\hline
\\
\textbf{love}
\end{array}
\quad
\begin{array}{c}
\lambda\mathcal{P}[\,] \\
\hline
\mathcal{P}(\lambda w[\,]) \\
\hline
w
\end{array}
\;=\;
\begin{array}{c}
\lambda\mathcal{P}[\,] \\
\hline
\forall y.\mathcal{P}(\lambda w[\,])\,y \\
\hline
\textbf{love}\; w\; y
\end{array}
$$

The semantic value of the gap looks complicated, but it is just an elaborate version of the identity function.[5]

We finish the derivation of this expression by applying the Lower operator twice:

$$
\begin{array}{c|c}
\text{pn}\backslash\backslash S & S \\
\hline
S & S \\
\hline
S
\end{array}
\text{Lower (twice)}
\qquad \Rightarrow \qquad
\text{pn}\backslash\backslash S : \lambda\mathcal{P}(\forall y.\mathcal{P}(\lambda w.\textbf{love}\; w\; y)\, y)
$$

Finally, the question-fronting operator applies to the instantiation of the lexical category of *who*:

$$
\text{Front}
$$
$$
(\text{pn?}S)/\!\!/(\text{pn}\backslash\backslash S) \quad \Rightarrow \quad (\text{pn?}S)/(\text{pn}\backslash\backslash S)
$$

which enables it to combine with the lowered question body just given to produce a question of category pn?S (i.e., a clause in which a pronoun has been questioned). The semantic value is simply the function denoted by *who* applied to the value of the question body:

$$
\textbf{who}(\lambda\mathcal{P}(\forall y.\mathcal{P}(\lambda w.\textbf{love}\; w\; y)\, y))
$$

---

[5]It is easier to see this if we convert from the tower notation into linear notation: $\lambda\gamma\lambda\mathcal{P}.\gamma(\lambda\kappa(\mathcal{P}(\lambda w.\kappa w)))$ To see that it is indeed an identity function, note that $\lambda w.\kappa w$ is η-equivalent to κ, $\lambda\kappa(\mathcal{P}\kappa)$ is η-equivalent to $\mathcal{P}$, and $\lambda\gamma\lambda\mathcal{P}.\gamma\mathcal{P}$ is easily recognizable as the identity function.

which can be paraphrased as 'for which pronoun meaning $\mathcal{P}$ is it true that everyone loves $\mathcal{P}$?' If the answer is the (complex) pronoun *his mother*, the prediction is that this will be a true answer only if inserting the answer into gap position expresses a true claim, i.e., only if it is true that everyone loves his mother.

Note that in any successful derivation of a fronted *wh*-phrase, the instantiation of the gap and of the *wh*-word must complement each other, in the sense that whatever the gap requires for completion (here, the pn part of pn\\S) must be exactly what the *wh*-phrase is questioning (here, the pn part of pn?S). In other words, the gap stands in the place the *wh*-phrase would have occupied if it were in-situ, and (metaphorically) transmits access to the gap position to the fronted *wh*-phrase.

1.6   Deriving reconstruction

We are now in a position to consider our core reconstruction case.

(16) Which relative of his does everyone love _?

We have already analyzed the question body, which receives the same functional analysis given above. Now we derive the fronted *wh*-phrase:

$$
\begin{array}{ccc}
\cfrac{(\mathrm{NP/N})?\mathrm{S} \mid \mathrm{S}}{\cfrac{\cdots}{\begin{array}{c}\mathrm{NP/N}\\ \text{which}\end{array}} \quad \cfrac{}{\begin{array}{c}\mathrm{N/NP}\\ \text{relative-of}\end{array}}} & \cfrac{\mathrm{NP}\triangleright\mathrm{S} \mid \mathrm{S}}{\cfrac{}{\begin{array}{c}\mathrm{NP}\\ \text{his}\end{array}}} & = \cfrac{(\mathrm{NP/N})?\mathrm{S} \mid \mathrm{S}}{\cfrac{\mathrm{NP}\triangleright\mathrm{S} \quad \mid \quad \mathrm{S}}{\begin{array}{c}\mathrm{NP}\\ \text{which rel of his}\end{array}}}
\end{array}
$$

The *wh*-word has undergone Lift. Because this *wh*-phrase will occur in fronted position, we now apply the Front operator. Using the 'pn' abbreviation, we have

$$
\begin{array}{ccc}
((\mathrm{NP/N})?\mathrm{S}) \;/\!\!/\; (\mathrm{pn}\backslash\backslash\mathrm{S}) & \text{Front} & ((\mathrm{NP/N})?\mathrm{S}) \;/\; (\mathrm{pn}\backslash\backslash\mathrm{S}) \\
\text{which relative of his} & \Rightarrow & \text{which relative of his}
\end{array}
$$

On the semantic side, we have

$$
\begin{array}{ccc}
\cfrac{\mathbf{which}(\lambda f[\,])}{f} & \cfrac{}{\mathbf{rel}} \quad \cfrac{}{\begin{array}{c}\lambda z[\,]\\ z\end{array}} & = \cfrac{\mathbf{which}(\lambda f[\,])}{\cfrac{\lambda z[\,]}{f(\mathbf{rel}\,z)}}
\end{array}
$$

The Front operator does not affect the semantics of the *wh*-phrase. In linear notation:

$$\lambda\gamma.\textbf{which}(\lambda f.\gamma(\lambda\kappa\lambda z.\kappa(f(\textbf{rel } z))))$$

Putting the pieces together:

$$\begin{array}{c} ((\text{NP/N})?\text{S}) \,/\, (\text{pn}\backslash\!\backslash\text{S}) \\ \text{which relative of his} \end{array} \left(\begin{array}{c} \text{pn}\backslash\!\backslash\text{S} \\ \text{does everyone love } \_\_ \end{array} \right):$$

$$\left(\lambda\gamma.\textbf{which}(\lambda f.\gamma(\lambda\kappa\lambda z.\kappa(f(\textbf{rel } z))))\right)\left(\lambda\mathcal{P}(\forall y.\mathcal{P}(\lambda w(\textbf{love } w\ y))\ y)\right)$$

$$= (\text{NP/N})?\text{S} : \textbf{which}(\lambda f\forall y.\textbf{love}(f(\textbf{rel } y))\ y)$$

A paraphrase of this denotation could be 'For which choice function f does every person y love $f(y$'s relatives)?' A suitable answer for this interpretation would be *the tallest*. This is a reconstruction interpretation on which the quantifier *everyone* binds the pronoun in the fronted *wh*-phrase. Moreover, unlike on the apparent-binding approach, this is genuine (not merely apparent) binding.

1.6.1   Reconstruction with functional answers

At this point, I have made good on my promise to show how a suitable theory of quantification and binding could automatically generate a reconstruction example involving displaced binding. However, the most natural reading of the question is one on which an appropriate answer might be *his mother*. Therefore we will go on to show how the same fundamental analysis automatically generates this interpretation as well. The details will be more complicated, but will involve no new techniques or assumptions.

The functional answer is a reading on which the answer depends not only on a specific set of relatives, but also on the identity of the person whose relatives we're considering. For example, on this doubly-dependent reading, the value could be different for Mary versus Bob even if they are siblings and have the same set of relatives.

Accommodating this reading involves exploiting the assumption that *wh*-words, like pronouns and gaps, can take on any identity type. The derivation of the fronted *wh*-phrase begins exactly as above, except that we start with $\dfrac{(\text{pn/N})?\text{S} \mid \text{S}}{\text{pn/N}}$ as the initial category for *which*, instead of $\dfrac{(\text{NP/N})?\text{S} \mid \text{S}}{\text{NP/N}}$. Thus:

$$\dfrac{(pn/N)?S \mid S}{\cdots} \quad \dfrac{}{\dfrac{N/NP}{\text{relative-of}}} \quad \dfrac{NP\triangleright S \mid S}{\dfrac{NP}{\text{his}}} \quad = \quad \dfrac{\dfrac{(pn/N)?S \mid S}{NP\triangleright S \mid S}}{\dfrac{}{pn}}$$

$$\dfrac{pn/N}{\text{which}}$$

Recalling that 'pn' abbreviates $\dfrac{NP\triangleright S \mid S}{NP}$, let 'ppn' abbreviate

$\dfrac{\dfrac{NP\triangleright S \mid S}{NP\triangleright S \mid S}}{NP}$. Then we have

$$\begin{array}{ccc} (pn/N)?S \mathbin{/\!\!/} (ppn\backslash\!\backslash S) & \text{Front} & (pn/N)?S \mathbin{/} (ppn\backslash\!\backslash S) \\ \text{which relative of his} & \Rightarrow & \text{which relative of his} \end{array}$$

Semantically, this gives us $\lambda\gamma.\mathbf{which}(\lambda\mathcal{F}.\gamma(\lambda\kappa\lambda x.\kappa(\mathcal{F}(\mathbf{rel}\,x))))$, where $\mathcal{F}$ is a variable over meanings in category pn/N (functions from nominal meanings to generalized pronoun meanings).

Since the analysis of the fronted *wh*-phrase is more complicated, the analysis of the question body must be correspondingly elaborated. Ignoring *does*, we have

$$\dfrac{\dfrac{S \mid NP\triangleright S}{S \mid NP\triangleright S}}{\dfrac{NP}{\text{everyone}}} \quad \dfrac{(NP\backslash S)/NP}{\text{love}} \quad \dfrac{\dfrac{ppn\backslash\!\backslash S \mid S}{NP\triangleright S \mid S}}{\dfrac{NP\triangleright S \mid S}{\dfrac{NP}{--}}}$$

In this case, the quantifier *everyone* binds twice (here is the type-shifting recipe for computing the category of *everyone*: Bind, then Lift, then Bind). It binds once for the reconstructed pronoun, and once for the virtual pronoun contributed by the *wh*-word. Once we combine and lower three times, the question body has category $ppn\backslash\!\backslash S$, which combines with the fronted *wh*-phrase.

The semantics of the question body:

$$\cfrac{\cfrac{\forall x.[\ ]x}{\cfrac{[\ ]x}{x}}}{} \quad \cfrac{}{\textbf{love}} \quad \cfrac{\cfrac{\lambda g[\ ]}{\cfrac{g(\lambda f[\ ])}{\cfrac{f(\lambda y[\ ])}{y}}}}{} = \cfrac{\cfrac{\lambda g[\ ]}{\cfrac{\forall x.g(\lambda f[\ ])\,x}{\cfrac{f(\lambda y[\ ])\,x}{\textbf{love}\,y\,x}}}}{}$$

Combining the fronted *wh*-phrase with the question body:

$$(\lambda\gamma.\textbf{which}(\lambda\mathcal{F}.\gamma(\lambda\kappa\lambda x.\kappa(\mathcal{F}(\textbf{rel}\,x)))))\Big(\lambda g\forall x.g(\lambda f.f(\lambda y.\textbf{love}\,y\,x)\,x)\,x\Big)$$
$$= \textbf{which}(\lambda\mathcal{F}\forall x.\mathcal{F}(\textbf{rel}\,x)(\lambda y.\textbf{love}\,y\,x)\,x)$$

This meaning is asking for a function $\mathcal{F}$ which, given some set of relatives, returns a pronoun function $\mathcal{P}$ such that x loves $\mathcal{P}$.

Degenerate answers and pair-list answers. A completely general answer will designate a potentially different loved relative for each individual: "Choosing among the set of John's relatives, John loves his mother; choosing among the set of Bill's relatives, Bill loves is his father; ...", and the analysis just given provides enough resolving power to accommodate fully general answers. But *his mother* is not such a fully general answer. How then does it come to be suitable as a reply to (2)?

If it happens that the correct pronoun function is constant for all of the relevant individuals, then the simpler functional answer *his mother* can be used, in which case the intended meaning is that for each individual x, the relative of x that x loves is x's mother. In other words, I am suggesting that answers often waste some of the resolving power available to them. In many situations, the only answers interesting enough to give are ones that are systematic in this fashion, what are often called "natural" functions in the literature.

Thus in this paper we are following the general strategy of Engdahl, Chierchia and others in assuming that functional readings are just a special case of fully general pair-list readings. This is more for the sake of expository simplicity than because of any deeply-set views; see Sharvit (1999) for arguments that this strategy may not be adequate.

1.6.2 *How-many* questions

Now I return briefly to *how many* questions. For the purposes of this paper, I will assume that *how many* is syntactically equivalent to *which*, predicting that they will have the same range of derivations. For instance, based on the analysis of the *which* question just given, we will have

(17) a. How many relatives of his does everyone love _?

    b. **how-many** $(\lambda \mathcal{F} \forall x. \mathcal{F}(\mathbf{rel}\ x)(\lambda y. \mathbf{love}\ y\ x)\ x)$

The complete answer will be a function $\mathcal{F}$ associating individuals x with numbers d in such a way that given the set of x's relatives, $\mathcal{F}$ returns a pronoun meaning such that x loves d-many of those relatives. The important point here is that the derivation provides exactly the information that the denotation of *how many* will need: an individual, a set, and a property that reveals which members of the set need to be counted.

1.6.3 Outbound binding

We have seen that a pronoun within a fronted constituent has a semantic effect as if it had been reconstructed into the gap position. It is perfectly possible for the fronted phrase to contain a quantificational NP instead of a pronoun, in which case the quantifier will take scope as if it had been reconstructed into the gap position. In particular, it is possible for such a quantifier to bind any pronoun that could have been bound from the gap position.

(18) Which relative of everyone$_i$ _ loves him$_i$ (the most)?

We instantiate the gap with X $= (S/\!/(NP\backslash\!\backslash(NP\triangleright S)))\backslash\!\backslash S$, and the rest of the derivation resembles the derivation for (16). The question body (_ *loves him*) will expect as its argument a quantificational NP that is ready to bind a pronoun (i.e., an argument of category $\dfrac{S \mid NP\triangleright S}{NP}$).

As long as *everyone* undergoes the Bind operator before combining with the rest of the fronted *wh*-phrase, this is exactly what the fronted *wh*-phrase delivers. The reduced semantic value of the complete derivation is **which**$(\lambda f \forall x.\mathbf{loves}\ x(f(\mathbf{rel}\ x))))$, in which the universal quantifier introduced by *everyone* clearly binds the variable introduced by the pronoun, as desired.

1.6.4 Interaction with crossover

The analysis correctly predicts that semantic reconstruction of fronted *wh*-phrases will obey weak crossover constraints on the interaction of the gap position with potential binders:

(19) a. Which woman that _ loves him$_i$ (do you think)
        every man$_i$ invited _?

    b. *Which woman that he$_i$ loves _ (do you think)
        _ invited every man$_i$?

See Shan and Barker (2006, pp. 123–4) for a derivation and discussion of a similar contrast involving *whose* instead of *which*.

1.7 Conclusion: reconstruction as delayed evaluation

The derivations above follow from unconstrained application of four general, independently motivated type-shifters (Lift, Lower, Bind, and Front), given suitably general lexical entries for *wh* words, pronouns, and gaps. The essential insight is the simple idea (championed by Jacobson) that pronouns, *wh*-words, and gaps all denote identity functions, combined with the idea that these items are scope-taking elements, as in recent work of Dowty. Because the identity function can be instantiated in various ways, gaps can in effect contain virtual pronouns. This makes it possible for a quantifier to bind into the gap, which in turn enables a (suitably instantiated) *wh*-phrase to accept a functional answer. When the fronted *wh*-phrase contains quantifiers or bindable pronouns, the fronting mechanism guarantees that these elements will behave semantically as if they had been interpreted in the gap position. Thus the system automatically provides reconstruction effects without movement or copying, without stipulating pseudo-variables, without stipulating a special functionalization operator such as Jacobson's **m**—indeed, without any special stipulation at all. The result is a directly compositional account that handles weak crossover and reconstruction, and on which the appearance of quantificational binding in reconstruction examples is in fact genuine binding brought about by delayed evaluation.

References

Barendregt, H. P. 1984. *The Lambda Calculus: Its Syntax and Semantics*, vol. 103 of *Studies in Logic and the Foundations of Mathematics*. Amsterdam: Elsevier.

Barker, Chris. 2002. Continuations and the nature of quantification. *Natural Language Semantics* 10(3):211–242.

Barker, Chris and Chung-Chieh Shan. 2006. Types as graphs: Continuations in Type Logical Grammar. *Journal of Logic, Language and Information* 15(4):331–370.

Beghelli, Filippo. 1997. The syntax of distributivity and pair-list readings. In A. Szabolcsi, ed., *Ways of Scope-Taking*, pages 349–408. Dordrecht: Kluwer.

Chierchia, Gennaro. 1992. Anaphora and Dynamic Binding. *Linguistics and Philosophy* 15(2):111–183.

Chierchia, Gennaro. 1993. Questions with quantifiers. *Natural Language Semantics* 1(2):181–234.

Chierchia, Gennaro. 1995. *Dynamics of Meaning*. Chicago: University of Chicago Press.

Cresti, Diana. 1995. Extraction and Reconstruction. *Natural Language Semantics* 3:79–122.

Dimitriadis, Alexis. 2002. Function Domains in Variable-Free Semantics. In *Proceedings of SALT 11*.

Dowty, David. 2007. Compositionality as an empirical problem. In C. Barker and P. Jacobson, eds., *Direct Compositionality*, pages 23–101. Oxford: Oxford University Press.

Engdahl, Elizabet. 1986. *Constituent Questions: The Syntax and Semantics of Questions with Special Reference to Swedish*. Reidel.

Heycock, Caroline. 1995. Asymmetries in reconstruction. *Linguistic Inquiry* 26:547–570.

Jacobson, Pauline. 1994. Binding connectivity in copular sentences. In *Proceedings of SALT 4*, pages 161–178.

Jacobson, Pauline. 1999. Towards a Variable-Free Semantics. *Linguistics and Philosophy* 22:117–184.

Jacobson, Pauline. 2002a. Direct compositionality and VFS: the case of binding into heads. In *Proceedings of SALT 12*, pages 144–163.

Jacobson, Pauline. 2002b. On the (dis)organization of the grammar. *Linguistics and Philosophy* 25:601–626.

Partee, Barbara. 1987. Noun Phrase Interpretation and Type-Shifting Principles. In J. Groenendijk, D. de Jong, and M. Stokhof, eds., *Studies in Discourse Representation Theory and the Theory of Generalized Quantifiers*, pages 115–143. Dordrecht: Foris Publications.

Partee, Barbara H. and Mats Rooth. 1983. Generalized conjunction and type ambiguity. In R. Bäuerle, C. Schwarze, and A. von Stechow, eds., *Meaning, Use and Interpretation of Language*, pages 361–383. Berlin: de Gruyter.

Plotkin, G. D. 1975. Call-by-Name, Call-by-Value and the λ-Calculus. *Theoretical Computer Science* 1:125–159.

Romero, Maribel. 1998. *Focus and reconstruction effects in wh-phrases*. Ph.D. thesis, University of Massachusetts Amherst.

Rullman, Hotze. 1995. *Maximality in the semantics of wh-constructions*. Ph.D. thesis, University of Massachusetts Amherst.

Shan, Chung-Chieh and Chris Barker. 2006. Explaining Crossover and Superiority as Left-to-Right Evaluation. *Linguistics and Philosophy* 29:91–134.

Sharvit, Yael. 1999. Functional Relative Clauses. *Linguistics and Philosophy* 22:447–478.

Steedman, Mark. 2000. *The Syntactic Process*. Cambridge: MIT Press.

Sternefeld, Wolfgang. 1998. The proper treatment of binding in pseudo cleft sentences. In G. Katz, S.-S. Kim, and H. Winhart, eds., *Reconstruction. Proceedings of the 1997 Tübingen Workshop*, Bericht Nr.127 des Sonderforschungsbereich 340, pages 39–58. Universität Stuttgart/Tübingen.

Sternefeld, Wolfgang. 2001. Semantic vs. syntactic reconstruction. In C. Rohrer, A. Rossdeutscher, and H. Kamp, eds., *Linguistic form and its computation*, pages 145–182. Stanford, CA: CSLI Publications.

Szabolcsi, Anna. 1992. Combinatory grammar and projection from the lexicon. In Sag and Szabolcsi, eds., *Lexical Matters*, vol. 24 of *CSLI Lecture Notes*, pages 241–269. Stanford: CSLI Publications.

Szabolcsi, Anna. 1997. Quantifiers in pair-list readings. In Szabolcsi, ed., *Ways of Scope-Taking*, pages 311–347. Dordrecht: Kluwer.

von Stechow, Arnim. 1998. Introduction. In G. Katz, S.-S. Kim, and H. Winhart, eds., *Reconstruction. Proceedings of the 1997 Tübingen Workshop*, Bericht Nr.127 des Sonderforschungsbereich 340. Universität Stuttgart/Tübingen.

Winter, Yoad. 2004. Functional quantification. *Research on Language and Computation* 2:331–363.

2

Selectional Preferences for Anaphora Resolution[*]

ERHARD HINRICHS AND HOLGER WUNSCH

2.1 Introduction

The goal of this paper is to investigate the possibility of incorporating lexical semantics, in particular selectional preferences of verbs, as an information source into the task of computational anaphora resolution, i.e. the task of choosing the correct antecedent for a personal or reflexive pronoun in a discourse.

(1) The child munched on a cookie and smiled. It must have been {tasty/happy}.

Example (1) illustrates the importance of lexical semantics for this task. The pronoun *it* can potentially refer back to either *the child* or *a cookie*. The choice of antecedent depends crucially on the selectional restrictions of the predicate of the clause that the pronoun appears in: cookies can be tasty and children happy, but not vice versa.

The importance of lexical semantics for this task has been widely recognized in the computational linguistics literature, dating back at least to Hobbs (1978). However, current implemented NLP systems for anaphora resolution are based mainly on morpho-syntactic and syntac-

[*]This article includes material previously published in Wunsch and Hinrichs (2006). We thank the Institute of Formal and Applied Linguistics of the Charles University Prague for permission to present an updated version of our work in the present volume. We would also like to thank two anonymous reviewers for their extensive comments and advice on a previous version of this paper.

Theory and Evidence in Semantics.
Erhard Hinrichs and John Nerbonne (eds.).
Copyright © 2009, CSLI Publications.

tic information.[1] The present paper aims to go beyond (morpho-)syntax
in anaphora resolution and investigates data-driven methods for obtaining selectional preferences from large text corpora. To this end,
the method of latent semantic clustering (LSC) (Rooth, 1998) will be
applied to two German text corpora of radically different size. The
purpose of this comparison is to determine the quantity of data that is
required to obtain meaningful results by means of unsupervised methods such as LSC. Even though the experimental part of this paper
focuses on German data, illustrative examples are mostly taken from
English for the following reasons: (i) many of the sentences cited are
classic examples taken from the previous literature whose significance
carries over to their German counterparts, (ii) English examples reduce
the amount of glossing required for German examples.

The paper is structured as follows: section 2.2 introduces the main research issues involved in the study of sentential and discourse
anaphora. Section 2.3 reviews the state of the art in computational
anaphora resolution and focuses on different syntax-based heuristics
for determining discourse salience. Section 2.4 shows that these heuristics are often in conflict with each other and therefore constitute soft,
defeasible constraints. By contrast, constraints based on selectional
preferences have to be considered hard constraints in the sense that
they constitute necessary, albeit not sufficient conditions for determining pronominal antecedents. Sections 2.5–2.10 are devoted to obtaining
selectional preferences from corpora. We will apply LSC to two annotated corpora of German newspaper texts and we will show that
adequate clustering results can be obtained only by very large automatically annotated corpora, but not by treebanks that have been
annotated semi-automatically by human annotators. The paper concludes with a comparison to related work and with an outlook to future
research.

2.2 Sentential and Discourse Anaphora

Anaphora resolution has been a central research issue in both theoretical and computational linguistics for more than three decades. In
theoretical linguistics, the focus of attention has been on the study
of intrasentential anaphora, in particular on donkey anaphora of pronouns and on the binding behavior of pronouns, reflexives and recip-
rocals. While computational linguists have incorporated the insights
on intrasentential anaphora gained in theoretical linguistics, the main

---

[1]A notable exception is Soon et al. (2001), who use WordNet class information
to capture coarse-grained semantic information about possible antecedents.

focus of their research has been on issues of intersentential anaphora. This focus on discourse anaphora is largely motivated by the types of applications in natural language processing that require resolution of anaphoric reference. One such application concerns information extraction systems, which have the goal of identifying those pieces of information in a large text repository that are relevant to a particular user query.

For a query as in (2a), the Wikipedia article on Alexander Graham Bell provides the relevant information.[2]

(2) a. From what university did Alexander Graham Bell graduate?

   b. **Alexander Graham Bell**, or A. Graham Bell, as he later prefered, was born in Edinburgh, on March 3, 1847. [...] **He** graduated from University College London.

The Wikipedia article starts with the first sentence in (2b). However, the subsequent sentence from the article that expresses the fact in question uses a pronoun instead of the proper name used in the query. Thus, the referent of the pronoun needs to be resolved to the appropriate antecedent in the Wikipedia article.

Machine translation, one of the classic applications of computational linguistics, also requires anaphora resolution if source and target language use different types of gender systems.

(3) a. Die Mutter gab **dem Mädchen [neuter]** *eine Tomate [fem]*. **Es [neuter]** mochte *sie [fem]* nicht.

   b. * The mother gave **the girl** *a tomato*. **It** did not like *her*.

   c. The mother gave **the girl** *a tomato*. **She** did not like *it*.

If one translates from German, a language with a grammatical gender system, to English, a language with a natural gender system, then a literal translation of the grammatical gender pronouns *es* and *sie* in German to their natural gender counterparts *it* and *she* results in the wrong translation shown in (2b). The correct translation in (2c) requires identification of the pronominal antecedents of the pronouns in the source language German and generation of the correct natural gender pronouns for these antecedents.

Computational linguists view the study of pronominal anaphoric reference as part of a larger task of coreference resolution in discourse. The latter involves reference resolution not only of pronouns, but also of other referring expressions such as definite descriptions such as *the Chancellor of Germany* and proper nouns *Angela Dorothea Merkel* in (4).

---

[2]`en.wikipedia.org/wiki/Alexander_Graham_Bell`

(4) *Angela Dorothea Merkel* (born in Hamburg, Germany, on July 17, 1954), as *Angela Dorothea Kasner*, is *the Chancellor of Germany*. Merkel, elected to the German Parliament from Mecklenburg-Western Pomerania, has been *the chairwoman of the Christian Democratic Union CDU* since April 9, 2000, and *Chairwoman of the CDU-CSU parliamentary party group* from 2002 to 2005. *She* leads a Grand coalition with its sister party, the Christian Social Union (CSU), and with the Social Democratic Party of Germany (SPD), formed after the 2005 federal election on November 22, 2005.

Discourse segments give rise to so-called *coreference chains* of referring expressions of various types, such as the coreference chain of expressions shown in italics in (4).

In this article we will limit ourselves to pronominal reference and will not discuss the larger topic of coreference resolution. This restriction seems justified in view of the fact that coreference resolution between definite noun phrases and their antecedents involves information that is rather different from anaphora resolution between a pronoun and its antecedent. In the case of non-pronominal coreference, resolution relies largely on extra-linguistic knowledge, e.g. that Angela Merkel is the current German chancellor, or substring comparisons, e.g. between the person's current name (Angela Dorothea Merkel) and her maiden name Angela Dorothea Kasner or between full name and last name only. Since pronouns are, apart from gender, number and case information, devoid of any descriptive contents, pronoun resolution has to rely on other factors.

2.3   The State of the Art in Computational Anaphora Resolution

While the anaphora resolution systems that have been suggested to date differ substantially in the algorithms they use, there is a striking convergence with respect to the features they consider. All of these features try to capture the notion of *discourse salience* of potential antecedents of pronouns. The main idea behind such salience-based accounts is the following: among potential antecedents for a pronoun, choose the one whose referent has the highest salience.

This section introduces some of the most widely used properties to capture the salience of discourse entities in the computational linguistics literature. Two classes of features in particular play a central role in the majority of resolution systems: features based on the syntactic properties of potential antecedents and features related to the relative distance of a pronoun and its potential antecedents.

Syntax-based features focus on specific syntactic constructions and on the relative salience ranking of discourse entities according to grammatical function.[3]

(5) a. **Existential Emphasis**:
There is **a pile of inflammable trash** *next to* **your car**. *You'll have to get rid of* **it**.

b. **Subject Emphasis**:
Autumn leaves *may cause a problem for* **the elderly**, *especially when* **they** *fall and become a wet and soggy mess on the ground*.

c. **Role Parallelism**:
Bill *contacted* **Joe**. **He** *called* **him**.

The existential-*there* construction in (5a) has the function of introducing a new discourse entity which becomes highly salient for the subsequent discourse. Accordingly, the pronoun *it* in (5a) has the indefinite NP in the previous sentence as its antecedent.[4] Another indicator for discourse salience is the grammatical function of a noun phrase that is used to refer to a discourse entity, with subjects ranking higher than objects. Such a salience ranking follows straightforwardly from David Dowty's seminal work on the relation between argument selections and what he calls *thematic proto-roles*. Dowty (1991) shows that subjects tend to be associated with agent-like properties, while direct objects are associated with properties that are typical of the patient of an event. The higher salience of discourse entities referred to by subjects is illustrated in (5b), where the correct antecedent for the pronoun *they* is the subject NP of the previous sentence. A second, related syntax-based feature applies to multiple pronouns in the same clause, as in (5c), where antecedent selection follows the principle of role-parallelism: the subject pronoun and object pronoun take as their antecedents the subject and object NPs of the previous clause, respectively.

In addition to structure-based features, linear order of the discourse and the distance between a pronoun and its antecedent need to be taken into account.

---

[3]The examples in this section are mostly taken from previous literature, in particular from: Hobbs (1978), Mitkov (2002), Jespersen (1954), and Lappin and Leass (1994)

[4]The example is taken from Hobbs (1978). Apart from the existential-*there* construction, cleft-sentences, e.g. *It was Sandy who I saw near the scene of the crime.*, and pseudo-clefts, e.g. *What Sandy gave to Robin was the new Harry Potter book.*, serve similar discourse functions.

(6) **Recency**: *Jack took* **the newspaper** *and then got hold of* **the magazine**. *He started reading* **it** *straight away.*

In (6) the pronoun *it* has two candidate antecedents, but it is the most recently mentioned NP that serves as the antecedent.

2.4 Beyond Syntax

In the previous section a number of heuristics for determining discourse salience have been reviewed. The current section considers possible interactions among these heuristics in order to determine their theoretical status in the context of the constraint-satisfaction problem of anaphora resolution. It turns out that basically any two heuristics are in competition with each other in the sense that they predict different preferred antecedents of a pronoun.

Consider the interaction between the heuristics of *subject emphasis* and *role parallelism* in examples (7).[5]

(7) *If* **the baby** *does not thrive on* **raw milk***, boil* **it***.*

For the pronoun *it* in (7), there are two potential antecedents: the noun phrase *the baby*, which is the subject of the sentence, and *raw milk*, which is a prepositional object of the main verb *thrive*. Since the pronoun is also in object position, the heuristics of role parallelism and of subject emphasis are both applicable for determining the pronoun's antecedent. The correct antecedent is chosen by the former heuristic. This seems to indicate that the heuristic of role parallelism should be ranked higher than subject emphasis. However, if we consider other examples, as in (8), then the opposite ranking seems to be required.

(8) *If* **the remote control** *does not open* **the garage door***, press* **it** *again.*

For (8) the correct antecedent is chosen if *subject emphasis* is given priority. Notice in particular that the examples (7) and (8) are in all relevant respects structurally identical and differ only in the their lexical material.

The same kind of competition can be observed in the interaction of the recency heuristics with the heuristic of object emphasis or of existential emphasis.

(9) *There is* **a problem** *with* **the disk** *you are using.* **It** *may be dirty or damaged.*

Recency would select *the disk* as the correct antecedent of the pronoun *it* while existential emphasis would wrongly select the head NP *a problem*.

---

[5]The example is due to Jespersen (1954).

However, a minimal pair to (9) is easily constructed, as in (10), where the opposite rank ordering of the two constraints is required.

(10) *There is* **a problem** *with* **the disk** *you are using.* **It** *must be solved.*

The same conflicting patterns also surface in the interaction between recency and object emphasis. The relevant minimal pair is shown in (11) and (12).

(11) *Vincent removed* **the diskette** *from* **the computer** *and then disconnected* **it**.

(12) *Vincent removed* **the diskette** *from* **the computer** *and then copied* **it**.

For (11) the correct antecedent is chosen if recency is the higher ranked constraint, while for (12) object emphasis has to outrank recency.

In sum, there seems to be no stable constraint ranking among salience heuristics that would yield the correct choice of antecedents for pronouns in discourse.

The reason for discussing the salience criteria and their potential interaction at some length is that they are heavily used in current systems for anaphora resolution, including the systems reported by Lappin and Leass (1994), Kennedy and Boguraev (1996), Mitkov (2002), and Preiss (2002), for English, as well as by Hinrichs et al. (2005) for German. There are a number of reasons for the popularity of these types of features. Any feature to be used by a computational anaphora resolution system must be accessible to the system for automatic processing. That means that the feature must be encoded explicitly in the data to be processed by the anaphora resolver. Features based on distance can be trivially extracted from the input data by the linear order inherent in language. Given today's parsers that operate at fairly high accuracy, it is moreover possible to enrich input data with the necessary information for the extraction of features that are based on syntax. Furthermore, throughout the last decade, there have been numerous efforts of annotating data in several languages with rich syntactic information. These manually annotated and corrected treebanks can provide the necessary gold data both for training resolution approaches based on machine learning techniques as well as for evaluating the performance of any automatic system.

In order to account for the defeasible nature of the salience constraints, all of the above systems use some notion of constraint weighting, with some constraints receiving higher weights than others. The

systems differ in the way these weights are obtained. Earlier systems
(e.g. Lappin and Leass 1994, Kennedy and Boguraev 1996, Mitkov
2002) use hand-crafted weights, while more recent systems (e.g. Preiss
2002 and Hinrichs et al. 2005) induce them directly from annotated
training data by machine learning methods. The best performance of
such systems reaches appr. 80% F-score, the harmonic mean between
recall and precision. The previous discussion offers one explanation as
to why these systems cannot reach higher performance: there is in principle no stable weighting scheme that would be able to model salience
of discourse referents in an empirically adequate fashion.

A closer look at examples (7)–(12) reveals the true explanation as
to why the salience principles fail to account for the facts. In each
case, only one of the two potential candidate antecedents should be
considered while the other candidate should be eliminated on semantic
grounds. Consider once more the near minimal pair for the interaction
of subject emphasis and role parallelism, which is repeated below as
(13) and (14).

(13) *If* **the baby** *does not thrive on* **raw milk**, *boil* **it**.

(14) *If* **the remote control** *does not open* **the garage door**, *press*
it *again*.

The selectional restrictions of the verbs *boil* and *press* are such that
only the *raw milk* and *the remote control* qualify as antecedents. Notice
also that once the other potential antecedents have been eliminated on
purely semantic grounds, the putative competition between the heuristics of subject emphasis and role parallelism vanishes since only one
antecedent remains as a candidate. The same explanation holds for the
other heuristics considered above.

Once we take lexical semantics into account, much of the problematic
rank ordering of salience constraints is no longer an issue. Thus, lexical
semantics in general and selectional preferences in particular can serve
as a prefilter to anaphora resolution in very much the same way as
morphological agreement is used.

(15) Wenn das Baby ([neuter]) kalte Milch ([feminine]) nicht mag,
dann koche sie ([feminine])

In the German counterpart of (13), the correct antecedent can be determined by morphological information alone. Only *kalte Milch* ('cold
milk') matches the pronoun in gender.

The comparison to the role of morphology in pronoun resolution is
particularly instructive because it clarifies the status of constraints on
anaphora resolution imposed by selectional restrictions. Selectional re-

strictions constitute hard, non-defeasible constraints just as agreement constraints do.

As mentioned above, one advantage of using features based on syntax or distance is that they can be extracted fairly easily from treebanks or parsed data. For semantic information, the situation to date is much more difficult. There are no manually annotated treebanks available (yet) that provide semantic analyses of sufficiently large scale as needed for automatic processing. Parsing systems that are capable of annotating semantics of both sufficient quantity and quality are not available either. It is therefore necessary to get access to semantic features by indirect means. In recent years, there have been a number of efforts of doing so, a selection of which will be reviewed in the next section.

2.4.1 Approaches for integrating semantics for coreference resolution

The need for incorporating semantic knowledge for the task of coreference resolution was observed already by Charniak (1972) and by Hobbs (1978). However, for quite some time it remained an open question how to obtain such knowledge on a broad scale and how to incorporate it into a running resolution system. With the advent of data-driven methods in computational linguistics, this situation has changed in recent years. There have been various attempts to use a variety of different knowledge sources to determine whether two potentially co-referent NPs are semantically compatible.

Soon et al. (2001) rely on the Princeton WordNet (Miller et al., 1988) hyponymy hierarchy to classify potential antecedents into broad semantic properties such as *person, time, location, object*, etc. However, due to the limited coverage of manually created resources, the utility of such an approach remains limited, as the authors themselves point out.

Apart from manually constructed lexical resources, semantic class information can also be obtained from large text repositories such as Wikipedia or from corpora such as the BBN Entity Type Corpus (Weischedel and Brunstein, 2005) or the ACE named entity corpora (LDC, 2005).

Ponzetto and Strube (2006) combine several semantic knowledge sources: the semantic similarity of two NPs based on WordNet and a measure of relatedness of NPs derived from Wikipedia's category taxonomy.[6] Additionally, they use Wikipedia to check whether there

---

[6] The Wikipedia measure of relatedness is a variant of path-length based WordNet measures of similarity.

exist interlinked[7] articles with titles equal to the head nouns of two candidate NPs.

Ng (2007) constructs a statistical semantic tagger that is trained on the BBN Entity Type Corpus and that discriminates among six broadly defined semantic classes. The class names PERSON, ORGANISATION, FACILITY, GEO-POLITICAL ENTITY (GPE), and LOCATION are taken from the ACE Phase 2 coreference corpus. A sixth category (OTHER) is assigned to those NPs that do fall under the other five categories.

It is important to note that testing the semantic compatibility of two potentially co-referent NPs applies primarily to definite descriptions and proper names. In fact, Ponzetto and Strube (2006), Ng (2007) and Soon et al. (2001) emphasize that their techniques were specifically developed for these types of NPs. The same is true for related approaches developed by Markert and Nissim (2005), by Ji et al. (2005), and by Mur and van der Plas (2006). However, they do not naturally generalize to pronominal reference since pronouns, apart from carrying grammatical gender information, are devoid of descriptive content. Therefore, semantic class information for a given pronoun cannot be determined directly. Instead, this information has to be obtained via the selectional restrictions imposed by the governing verb.

Apart from selectional restrictions, anaphoric reference resolution of pronouns can also benefit from *contextual role knowledge* in the sense of Bean and Riloff (2004). Bean and Riloff show how knowledge about prototypical actions and their participants, as in (16), can aid in correctly resolving the antecedent of a pronoun.

(16) a. Jose Maria Martinez, Roberto Lisandy, and Dino Rossy, who were staying at a Tecun Uman hotel, were kidnapped by armed men who took them to an unknown place.
   b. After **they** were released ...
   c. After **they** blindfolded the men ...

The release and blindfolding of victims are prototypical subactions of a kidnapping event. In continuation (16b), *they* refers to the kidnapped men while in continuation (16c) *they* refers to the agents of the kidnapping event. While tracking such contextual role knowledge is clearly worth-while, it is at best a technique that can be used in addition to selectional restriction information since information about the interdependence of events and their participants is always highly domain-specific.

---

[7]Ponzetto and Strube (2006) consider two articles interlinked if there exists either a direct link between the two articles, or an indirect one by means of a redirection or a disambiguation page.

The remainder of this paper explores how selectional preferences can be extracted from large linguistically annotated corpora by means of Latent Semantic Clustering (LSC), an unsupervised learning technique introduced by Rooth (1998). The following sections (2.5–2.10) represent an updated version of an earlier study (Wunsch and Hinrichs, 2006).

2.5 Linguistically Annotated Corpora

Treebank data have been utilized as data sources for a wide range of tasks in computational linguistics, including statistical parsing, anaphora resolution, induction of valence lexica, etc. More recently, researchers have experimented with extracting semantic information from syntactically annotated data. Here, treebank data have been used for the purposes of identifying selectional preferences of verbs and for the purposes of clustering verb classes (most notably using LSC).

The present paper follows this recent trend of extracting semantic information from syntactically annotated data. The goal of this work is to determine verb classes for German verbs by means of Latent Semantic Clustering. The ultimate goal of this research is task-oriented. We would like to investigate whether verb clusters obtained by the LSC method can be used as semantic knowledge for the purposes of anaphora resolution. In this sense, the current paper is a preparatory study and awaits a task-oriented evaluation in future work.

We will present experiments with two treebanks, TüBa-D/Z (Telljohann et al., 2003) and TüPP-D/Z (Müller, 2004b) that are both based on German newspaper text from the daily newspaper *die tageszeitung* (taz). The two resources differ significantly along the following dimensions:

1. **method of annotation:** The TüBa-D/Z treebank was manually annotated with the help of the tool *annotate* (Brants and Plaehn, 2000) and checked for consistency of annotation in a post-editing phase. The TüPP-D/Z was automatically annotated with the help of the KaRoPars parser described in Müller and Ule (2002) and not checked for errors of annotation in any way. However, as Müller (2004a) has shown, the quality of annotation produced by KaRoPars is quite competitive with the best results of other parsers of German for the categories that are annotated in TüPP-D/Z. The TüPP-D/Z experiments described in this paper corroborate this finding.

2. **granularity of annotation:** Both treebanks contain annotations about clause structure, topological fields, and grammatical functions of major constituents. However, at the clausal level,

the depth of annotation differs considerably. In TüPP-D/Z only chunks in the sense of Abney (1991) are annotated below the clause level, and attachments of chunks to other chunks is not provided. The TüBa-D/Z annotation, on the other hand, contains ordinary phrases (as opposed to chunks), and attachment among phrases is fully specified.

3. **size:** The version of the TüBa-D/Z treebank that was used in the experiments contains 27,125 sentences and 473,747 lexical tokens, while the TüPP-D/Z corpus is much larger in size: appr. 11.5 million sentences and 204,661,513 lexical tokens.

It turns out that the TüBa-D/Z data source is not sufficient in size for inducing good-quality clusters by the LSC method. Rather, the LSC experiments show that much larger resources such as TüPP-D/Z are needed to overcome the data sparseness issues that arise with smaller resources such as TüBa-D/Z. At the same time, automatic annotation of partial syntactic structure in combination with annotation of grammatical functions as in TüPP-D/Z suffices for LSC methods, as long as the annotation is sufficiently accurate and contains relevant information about clause structure.

2.6 The TüBa-D/Z treebank of German

Due to their fine grained syntactic annotation, the TüBa-D/Z treebank data are ideally suited as a basis for extracting the type of information relevant for LSC experiments, i.e. syntactic and semantic properties of verbs and their complements.

The TüBa-D/Z annotation scheme distinguishes four levels of syntactic constituency: the lexical level, the phrasal level, the level of topological fields, and the clausal level. The primary ordering principle of a clause is the inventory of topological fields, which characterize the word order regularities among different clause types of German and which are widely accepted among descriptive linguists of German (cf. e.g. Höhle 1986). The TüBa-D/Z annotation relies on a context-free backbone (i.e. proper trees without crossing branches) of phrase structure combined with edge labels that specify the grammatical function of the phrase in question.

Figure 1 shows an example tree from the TüBa-D/Z treebank for sentence (17). The sentence is divided into two clauses (SIMPX), and each clause is subdivided into topological fields. The main clause is made up of the following fields: VF (mnemonic for: *Vorfeld* – 'initial field') contains the sentence-initial, topicalized constituent. LK (for: *linke Satzklammer* – 'left sentence bracket') is occupied by the finite

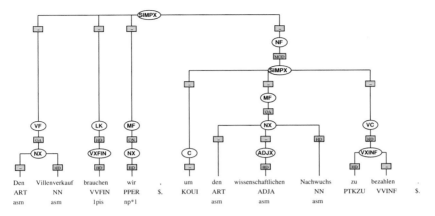

FIGURE 1   A sample tree from the TüBa/D-Z treebank.

verb. MF (for: *Mittelfeld* – 'middle field') contains adjuncts and complements of the main verb. NF (for: *Nachfeld* – 'final field') contains extraposed material. The subordinate clause is again divided into three topological fields: C (for: *Komplementierer* – 'complementizer'), MF, and VC (for: *Verbalkomplex* – 'verbal complex'). Edge labels are rendered in boxes and indicate grammatical functions. The sentence-initial NX (for: *noun phrase*) is marked as OA (for: *accusative complement*), the pronoun *wir* in the main clause and the NX in the embedded clause as ON (for: *nominative complement*).

(17) Den Villenverkauf   brauchen wir,   um den
      The sale of the villa need   we[subj], to   the
      wissenschaftlichen Nachwuchs zu bezahlen.
      young scientists   to pay.
      'We must sell the villa in order to pay young scientists.'

Topological field information and grammatical function information are crucial for the extraction of verbs and their complements. Topological fields provide the regions for grouping the right complements with the right verbs, and grammatical function labelling provides the necessary information for identifying the role of each complement.

2.7 The TüPP-D/Z treebank of German

TüPP-D/Z (Müller, 2004b) has been automatically annotated using the cascaded finite state parser KaRoPars. Four levels of syntactic constituency are annotated: the lexical level, the chunk level (in this respect, TüPP-D/Z differs from TüBa-D/Z), the level of topological

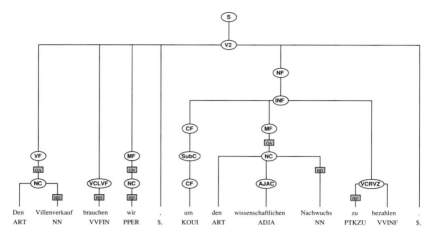

FIGURE 2 A sample from the automatically annotated TüPP-D/Z treebank.

fields, and the clausal level. Unlike TüBa-D/Z, which assumes a relatively deep syntactic structure, trees are quite flat in TüPP-D/Z. Due to limitations of the finite state parsing model, the attachment of chunks remains underspecified. Major constituents are annotated with grammatical functions. Figure 2 shows the example sentence (1) from section 2.6 in TüPP-D/Z annotation style. The automatic variant is fairly close to the manual annotation. The categories indicating left and right sentence brackets are merged with the categories of verb chunks.

Although the annotation of TüPP-D/Z provides less syntactic structure, the relevant information for the extraction of verb-object pairs, most importantly the annotation of topological fields and of noun chunks with grammatical functions, is present with sufficient accuracy.

2.8   Latent Semantic Clustering

The kinds of entities that can occur as complements (i.e. subjects and objects) of a verb are strongly determined by the verb's meaning. For the same reason, nouns preferably co-occur with certain classes of verbs. For example, nouns denoting types of *food* typically occur as objects of verbs like *cook* and *eat*, while verbs in the semantic field of *hear* may select objects like *music*, *opinion*, or *word*. It is extremely unlikely that *words* are *cooked*, and *cucumbers* are *heard*.

The selectional preferences of a verb are clear to a speaker or a hearer in the majority of all cases. For automatic methods however, it is much more difficult to get access to knowledge about a verb's selectional preferences (or verb semantics in general), since information about semantics is usually not available. Based on the observation that nouns that do belong to the preferred semantic field of a verb will occur with significantly higher frequency in a corpus together with that verb than nouns that do not, it is possible to infer a verb's selectional preferences by considering pairs or n-tuples of co-occurring verbs and objects. This requires that the amount of available data is sufficient to ensure that the frequencies obtained reach statistically significant levels. Combining verbs and nouns that co-occur with high frequency will result in groups that reflect classes of verbs with similar selectional preferences and the entities they prefer in their argument slots.

Latent Semantic Clustering (LSC) (Rooth, 1998) is a method for automatically extracting selectional preferences from large corpora. Originally, it was used for resolving attachment ambiguities in parsing. The algorithm accepts as its input tuples of verbs and their objects as they occur in a corpus. The tuples are then arranged in clusters in an iterative process. Both the number of clusters and the number of iterations must be pre-specified by the user. Apart from this, no further human intervention is required, which makes LSC an unsupervised approach.

Unlike other clustering methods that allow a tuple to become an element of only one cluster (so-called *hard-clustering methods*), LSC calculates for *each* cluster a probability of the occurrence of that tuple in that cluster. This means that in fact all tuples are members of all clusters, albeit with differently high probabilities (and mostly, very low probabilities). This is called *soft clustering*. Words that occur in a cluster with similar probabilities are to be interpreted as behaving similarly with respect to their preference of arguments (for verbs), or the verbs they usually co-occur with (for nouns). At the same time, this relatedness with respect to selectional preferences is also taken as a relatedness with respect to the semantic field of a verb or a noun. Soft-clustering methods are especially well suited to capture semantic properties: Words have multiple distinct readings, some more typical than others. Hard clustering methods that allow a word to occur only in one cluster put unnatural restrictions on the distribution of selectional preferences, while soft clusters provide much more fine-grained representations.

Compared to other approaches of acquiring selectional preferences such as techniques based on log-likelihood or mutual information, LSC has the advantage that due to clustering, it is able to discover verb/noun tuples that do not occur in the source corpus as such. This is an additional step of abstraction and smoothing helps to reduce problems of sparse data that other approaches frequently suffer from.

LSC employs three structures: Sets of verbs, sets of nouns, and sets of selectional types (i.e. semantic classes) (Rooth, 1998). It assumes probability distributions for all structures: The probability p^τ of a selectional type τ with respect to all other selectional types, the probability of any verb to be member of a selectional type (p_v^τ), and the probability of any noun to be member of a selectional type (p_n^τ). For any type, LSC constructs a probability distribution which gives the probability of a pair[8] of a verb and a noun being member of a selectional type:

$$p_{\tau,v,n} = p_\tau p_v^\tau p_n^\tau$$

The total probability of a verb-object pair is then the sum over all types:

$$p_{v,n} = \sum_\tau p_\tau p_v^\tau p_n^\tau$$

LSC iteratively estimates these probabilities by employing an expectation-maximization (EM) strategy.

2.9 Latent Semantic Clustering on TüBa-D/Z

The first set of experiments uses TüBa-D/Z as its data source. From the treebank, two sets of pairs were extracted. The first set of pairs comprises the lemmatized main verb and the lemmatized head of the subject noun phrase (grammatical function ON). The second set of pairs again consists of the main verb but this time the head of the accusative object (grammatical function OA) as the second element. For both sets, pair frequencies were calculated. The set of verbs and subjects contains 16,846 pairs, where the most frequent pair occurs 11 times (*sterben – Mensch* / 'die' – 'human being'). The set of verbs and accusative object contains 8,160 pairs. There, the most frequent pair occurs 35 times (*spielen – Rolle* / 'play' – 'role').

The results were used as the input to the *lsc* program (Schmid, 2006) which performed the actual soft clustering. *lsc* requires both the number of clusters and the number of iterations for the model estimation to be specified. A value of 40 was chosen for the number of clusters, a number which turned out to be optimal in previous work (Wagner, 2005, Schulte im Walde, 2003). 30 was chosen for the number of iterations. Altering this number did not noticeably change the clustering results.

Tables 1 and 2 show the top-ranked verb-subject and verb-object clusters as calculated by *lsc*. Each cluster consists of two features. Feature 0 contains the verbs and the corresponding probabilities that a verb has a selectional preference that is represented by the cluster.

---

[8]We assume pairs of verbs and nouns. For n-tuples, this generalizes in the obvious ways.

Cluster 31 (0.0401)			
Feature 0: verbs		**Feature 1: subjects**	
sein *be*	0.5007	Entscheidung *decision*	0.0217
lassen *let*	0.1974	Schröder	0.0182
fallen *fall*	0.1326	Krieg *war*	0.0105
feststellen *determine*	0.0179	Bombe *bomb*	0.0097
antworten *answer*	0.0166	Ergebnis *result*	0.0068
beenden *finish*	0.0156	Polizei *police*	0.0064
formulieren *formulate*	0.0129	Mann *man*	0.0061
festhalten *hold onto*	0.0108	Zeit *time*	0.0055
erfassen *capture*	0.0074	Demonstrant *demonstrator*	0.0055
lenken *steer*	0.0056	Rede *speech*	0.0055

TABLE 1 Top-ranked subject-verb clusters extracted from TüBa-D/Z.

This probability corresponds to p_v^τ described above. Feature 1 contains the nouns and corresponding values for p_n^τ. Note that for each feature, only the ten most probable words are shown. Due to the nature of the soft-clustering algorithm, all verbs and all nouns are in fact members of each cluster, but the ones not shown received very low probabilities.

It is obvious from manual inspection of the clusters that the LSC algorithm is not able to produce semantically coherent clusters with this input data. Consider the top-ranked verb-subject cluster in Table 1. The table shows the ten most prototypical (measured in terms of relative frequency) verbs (under feature 0) and nouns (under feature 1) for this cluster. Neither the verbs nor the nouns exhibit natural lexical fields. In particular the nouns are scattered among different ontological categories such as abstract entities (e.g. *decision* 'Entscheidung' and *Krieg* 'war'), humans (e.g. *Polizei* 'police' and *Mann* 'man') as well as inanimate objects (e.g. *Bombe* 'bomb'). Likewise, in Table 2 the verbs are almost equally divided between two disparate lexical fields:

Cluster 30 (0.0737)			
Feature 0: verbs		**Feature 1: objects**	
geben	0.9096	Alternative	0.0192
give		*alternative*	
starten	0.0236	Antwort	0.0148
start		*answer*	
ankündigen	0.0162	Mühe	0.0103
announce		*effort*	
unterrichten	0.0074	Auskunft	0.0103
teach		*information*	
plazieren	0.0046	Meinung	0.0089
place		*opinion*	
überreichen	0.0044	Position	0.0075
hand over		*position*	
aktivieren	0.0044	Absprache	0.0074
activate		*agreement*	
durchspielen	0.0032	Möglichkeit	0.0074
run through		*possibility*	
vernachlässigen	0.0030	Licht	0.0074
neglect		*light*	
leihen	0.0021	Krieg	0.0060
lend/borrow		*war*	

TABLE 2   Top-ranked verb-object clusters extracted from TüBa-D/Z.

change of possession verbs (e.g. *geben* 'give' and *leihen* 'lend') and verbs of mental action (e.g. *vernachlässigen* 'neglect' and *durchspielen* 'run through'). Moreover, the nominal objects that have been clustered for these verbs are only appropriate for the change of possession verbs, but do not represent realistic candidates for the verbs of mental action included in the verb cluster.

The two clusters are but two examples of the general picture that emerges from the LSC clusters obtained for the TüBa-D/Z data. Their lack of cohesion must be attributed to the relatively small size of the input data presented to the clusterer. With most of the pairs occurring only once, and the highest number of occurrences being below 40, the samples are nearly uniformly distributed. This means that the clustering algorithm cannot rely on much more information than random choice.

Cluster 19 (0.0456)			
Feature 0: verbs		**Feature 1: subjects**	
wollen	0.1998	Regierung	0.0258
want		*government*	
beschließen	0.0384	Senat	0.0207
decide		*senate*	
ablehnen	0.0325	SPD	0.0185
reject		*Social Democratic Party*	
aussprechen	0.0215	CDU	0.0102
articulate		*Christian Democratic Union*	
ankündigen	0.0205	Bundesregierung	0.0084
announce		*federal government*	
zustimmen	0.0188	USA	0.0082
agree			
einigen	0.0181	Parlament	0.0080
agree on		*parliament*	
fordern	0.0170	Präsident	0.0078
demand		*president*	
aufrufen	0.0165	Grünen	0.0076
call on		*green party*	
verabschieden	0.0159	Prozent	0.0058
pass (law)		*percent*	

TABLE 3 Top-ranked subject-verb clusters extracted from TüPP-D/Z.

2.10 Latent Semantic Clustering on TüPP-D/Z

The second set of experiments uses TüPP-D/Z as its data source. Sets of lemmatized verbs and subjects or accusative objects are extracted from the automatically parsed corpus and presented to the *lsc* clusterer in the same fashion as for the TüBa-D/Z experiments described in section 2.9. The size of the data sets extracted from TüPP-D/Z however exceeds the TüBa-D/Z data by several orders of magnitude. The set of verbs and subjects contains 4,309,330 pairs. The most frequent pair occurs 7,240 times (*Prozent – sein* / 'percent' – 'to be'). The set of verbs and accusative objects comprises 5,315,778 different pairs. The most frequent pair occurs 9,205 times (*spielen – Rolle* / 'play' – 'role').

Tables 3 and 4 show two clusters that were generated by *lsc* in this experiment and that are representative of the overall quality obtained.[9] Manual inspection of the results shows that the increased size of the

---

[9] Auxiliary verbs were removed from the clusters.

Cluster 16 (0.0372)			
Feature 0: verbs		**Feature 1: objects**	
sagen	0.0494	Menschen	0.0364
say		*people*	
verletzen	0.0298	Frau	0.0135
injure		*woman*	
töten	0.0246	Mann	0.0126
kill		*man*	
glauben	0.0173	Leute	0.0123
believe		*people*	
erschießen	0.0140	Kinder	0.0112
shoot		*children*	
fragen	0.0134	Frauen	0.0111
ask		*women*	
meinen	0.0102	Personen	0.0070
believe		*persons*	
ermorden	0.0095	Männer	0.0070
murder		*men*	
angreifen	0.0095	Soldaten	0.0054
attack		*soldiers*	
festnehmen	0.0079	Opfer	0.0047
arrest		*victim*	

TABLE 4 Top-ranked verb-object clusters extracted from TüPP-D/Z.

input data clearly improves the quality of the clusters. Especially the elements of the verb-object clusters yield intuitive selectional preferences. For example, the nouns in cluster 16 are all about people, and the verbs deal with actions that can be done to or with people. The verbs *verletzen* ('injure'), *töten* ('kill') , or *erschießen* ('shoot') belong to a more restricted domain of war, with corresponding nouns like *Soldaten* ('soldiers') or *Opfer* ('victim'). Likewise the subject-verb cluster in Table 3 also exhibits natural semantic classes of both verbs and nouns. The verbs are all members of the semantic field of communication verbs, with the subject nouns representing prototypical agents for this verb class.

2.11   Comparison with other work and conclusion

With the exception of Schulte im Walde (2003), Schulte im Walde (2004b), and Schulte im Walde (2006) we are not aware of any data-driven studies of German verb classifications. To the best of our knowledge, the present paper is the first study to employ LSC for soft-clustering of German verb classes. Schulte im Walde employs hard clustering algorithms for generating verb classes and limits herself to a detailed study of 168 German verbs. The main goal of her work is to see whether clustering techniques can yield empirically adequate results for the set of verbs that she considers. By comparison, the present work does not limit itself to a preselected number of verbs and uses soft clustering. Another interesting difference between Schulte im Walde's work and ours concerns the way in which she generalizes over the nominal complements obtained for a particular cluster. In Schulte im Walde (2004a), all nominal heads are projected to 15 most general concepts superimposed on the GermaNet hypernym hierarchy of nouns, the German version of WordNet (Hamp and Feldweg, 1997), so that selectional preferences of verbs can be expressed by very general ontological categories such as *situation, concrete object, abstract object*, etc.

An aspect that is currently missing from this research is an objective way of evaluating clusters. One possibility for evaluation of quality would be to map the elements of the clusters to their corresponding GermaNet concepts and then to search for hypernyms in the GermaNet hierarchy. If it is possible to find a restricted number of hypernyms that cover most, if not all, of the nouns in a cluster, this is an indication for the coherence of the cluster. An alternative way of measuring the quality of a cluster could be to consult lists of word associations as described in Dennis (2003) for English. Unfortunately, resources of this kind and of suitable size are not available for German. Yet another evaluation strategy could be to employ other techniques of corpus-based inference of semantic properties, such as Latent Semantic Analysis (Landauer and Dumais, 1997). However, the results of such a comparison would certainly have to be taken with a grain of salt since LSA is a much more general technique for measuring semantic relatedness.

We conclude with some brief remarks about two additional directions for future research. Wagner (2005) has shown for English how selectional preferences can be obtained by data abstraction on nominal argument positions of verb classes that are obtained by LSC. Wagner's approach differs from Schulte im Walde's in that the latter always generalizes to a set of very general ontological categories while Wagner tries to generalize up the hypernym hierarchy only as high as is supported by the data. This has the effect that ceteris paribus the selectional preferences that Wagner's approach produces are more specific than those obtained by other abstraction methods. This in turn leads to crisper selectional preferences. Another direction of future research concerns a task-based evaluation of the LSC clustering results. In the present paper we have limited ourselves to a purely manual inspection of the LSC clusters for the two treebanks we have considered. While this seems adequate for comparing the relative quality of clusters obtained by the two treebanks, it remains to be seen whether the clusters obtained from the TüPP-D/Z treebank are of sufficient quality to be used in NLP applications for which selectional preferences of verbs can play an important role. Automatic pronoun resolution seems to be a good candidate for such a task-based evaluation since it has often been argued that selectional preferences can provide an important source of knowledge for this task.

References

Abney, Steven. 1991. Parsing by chunks. In R. Berwick, S. Abney, and C. Tenny, eds., *Principle-based Parsing*. Boston: Kluwer Academic Publishers.

Bean, David and Ellen Riloff. 2004. Unsupervised Learning of Contextual Role Knowledge for Coreference Resolution. In D. M. Susan Dumais and S. Roukos, eds., *HLT-NAACL 2004: Main Proceedings*, pages 297–304. Boston, Massachusetts, USA: Association for Computational Linguistics.

Brants, Thorsten and Oliver Plaehn. 2000. Interactive Corpus Annotation. In *Proceedings of the Second International Conference on Language Resources and Evaluation (LREC-2000)*, pages 453–459. Athens, Greece.

Charniak, Eugene. 1972. *Toward a model of children's story comprehension.*. Ph.D. thesis, Massachusetts Institute of Technology Artifical Intelligence Laboratory.

Dennis, Simon. 2003. A Comparison of Statistical Models for the Extraction of Lexical Information from Text Corpora. In *Proceedings of the Twenty Fifth Conference of the Cognitive Science Society*, pages 330–335.

Dowty, David. 1991. Thematic proto-roles and argument selection. *Language* 67(3):547–619.

Hamp, Birgit and Helmut Feldweg. 1997. GermaNet – a Lexical-Semantic Net for German. In *Proceedings of ACL workshop Automatic Information Extraction and Building of Lexical Semantic Resources for NLP Applications)*. Madrid, Spain.

Hinrichs, Erhard W., Katja Filippova, and Holger Wunsch. 2005. A Data-driven Approach to Pronominal Anaphora Resolution in German. In G. Angelova, K. Bontcheva, R. Mitkov, N. Nicolov, and N. Nicolov, eds., *Proceedings of the 5th International Conference on Recent Advances in Natural Language Processing (RANLP 2005)*, pages 239–245. Borovets, Bulgaria.

Hobbs, Jerry R. 1978. Resolving pronoun references. *Lingua* 44:311–338.

Höhle, Tilman. 1986. Der Begriff "Mittelfeld", Anmerkungen über die Theorie der topologischen Felder. In *Akten des Siebten Internationalen Germanistenkongresses 1985*, pages 329–340. Göttingen, Germany.

Jespersen, Otto. 1954. *A Modern English Grammar on Historical Principles*. London: George Allen and Unwin.

Ji, Heng, David Westbrook, and Ralph Grishman. 2005. Using semantic relations to refine coreference decisions. In *HLT '05: Proceedings of the conference on Human Language Technology and Empirical Methods in Natural Language Processing*, pages 17–24. Morristown, NJ, USA: Association for Computational Linguistics.

Kennedy, Christopher and Branimir Boguraev. 1996. Anaphora for everyone: Pronominal anaphora resolution without a parser. In *The Proceedings of the 16th International Conference on Computational Linguistics*.

Landauer, Thomas K. and Susan T. Dumais. 1997. A Solution to Plato's Problem: The Latent Semantic Analysis Theory of Acquisition, Induction and Representation of Knowledge. *Psychological Review* 105:221–240.

Lappin, Shalom and Herbert J. Leass. 1994. An Algorithm for Pronominal Anaphora Resolution. *Computational Linguistics* 20(4):535–561.

LDC. 2005. *ACE Annotation Guidelines for Entity Detection and Tracking (EDT)*. Linguistic Data Consortium (LDC). Available at: http://www.ldc.upenn.edu/Projects/ACE/docs/English-Entities-Guidelines_v5.6.1.pdf.

Markert, Katja and Malvina Nissim. 2005. Comparing Knowledge Sources for Nominal Anaphora Resolution. *Computational Linguistics* pages 367–401.

Miller, George A., Christiane Fellbaum, Judy Kegl, and Katherine J. Miller. 1988. Wordnet: an electronic lexical reference system based on theories of lexical memory. *Revue quebecoise de linguistique* 17(2):181–213.

Mitkov, Ruslan. 2002. *Anaphora Resolution*. Longman Publishers.

Müller, Frank Henrik. 2004a. *A Finite State Approach to Shallow Parsing and Grammatical Functions Annotation of German*. Ph.D. thesis, University of Tübingen.

Müller, Frank Henrik. 2004b. Stylebook for the Tübingen Partially Parsed Corpus of Written German (TüPP-D/Z).

Müller, Frank Henrik and Tylman Ule. 2002. Annotating topological fields and chunks – and revising POS tags at the same time. In *Proceedings of the Nineteenth International Conference on Computational Linguistics (COLING 2002)*, pages 679–701. Taipei, Taiwan.

Mur, Jori and Lonneke van der Plas. 2006. Anaphora Resolution for Off-line Answer Extraction using Instances. In *Proceedings of the Workshop for Anaphora Resolution (WAR)*.

Ng, Vincent. 2007. Semantic Class Induction and Coreference Resolution. In *Proceedings of the 45th Annual Meeting of the Association of Computational Linguistics*, pages 536–543. Prague, Czech Republic.

Ponzetto, Simone Paolo and Michael Strube. 2006. Exploiting semantic role labeling, WordNet and Wikipedia for coreference resolution. In *Proceedings of the main conference on Human Language Technology Conference of* the North American Chapter of the Association of Computational Linguistics, pages 192–199. Morristown, NJ, USA: Association for Computational Linguistics.

Preiss, Judita. 2002. Anaphora resolution with memory based learning. In *Proceedings of the 5th UK Special Interest Group for Computational Linguistics (CLUK5)*, pages 1–8.

Rooth, Mats. 1998. Two-dimensional clusters in grammatical relations. In M. Rooth, S. Riezler, D. Prescher, S. Schulte im Walde, G. Carroll, and F. Beil, eds., *Inducing Lexicons with the EM Algorithm*, vol. 4.3 of AIMS, pages 7–24. Universität Stuttgart.

Schmid, Helmut. 2006. LSC. Institut für maschinelle Sprachverarbeitung, University of Stuttgart, http://www.ims.uni-stuttgart.de/projekte/gramotron/SOFTWARE/LSC.html.

Schulte im Walde, Sabine. 2003. *Experiments on the Automatic Induction of German Semantic Verb Classes*. Ph.D. thesis, Institut für Maschinelle Sprachverarbeitung, Universität Stuttgart. Published as AIMS Report 9(2).

Schulte im Walde, Sabine. 2004a. GermaNet Synsets as Selectional Preferences in Semantic Verb Clustering. *LDV-Forum – Zeitschrift für Computerlinguistik und Sprachtechnologie* 19(1/2):69–79. also published in Proceedings of the GermaNet Workshop, 2003.

Schulte im Walde, Sabine. 2004b. Induction of Semantic Classes for German Verbs. In S. Langer and D. Schnorbusch, eds., *Semantik im Lexikon*, vol. 479 of *Tübinger Beiträge zur Linguistik*, pages 59–86. Tübingen: Gunter Narr Verlag.

Schulte im Walde, Sabine. 2006. Experiments on the Automatic Induction of German Semantic Verb Classes. *Computational Linguistics* 32(2):159–194.

Soon, Wee Meng, Hwee Tou Ng, and Daniel Chung Yong Lim. 2001. A machine learning approach to coreference resolution of noun phrases. *Computational Linguistics* 27(4):521–544.

Telljohann, Heike, Erhard W. Hinrichs, and Sandra Kübler. 2003. Stylebook for the Tübingen Treebank of Written German (TüBa-D/Z). Tech. rep., Seminar für Sprachwissenschaft, Universität Tübingen.

Wagner, Andreas. 2005. *Learning Thematic Role Relations for Lexical Semantic Nets*. Ph.D. thesis, University of Tübingen.

Weischedel, Ralph M. and Ada Brunstein. 2005. *BBN pronoun coreference and entity type corpus*. Linguistic Data Consortium.

Wunsch, Holger and Erhard W. Hinrichs. 2006. Latent Semantic Clustering of German Verbs with Treebank Data. In J. Hajič and J. Nivre, eds., *Proceedings of the Fifth International Workshop on Treebanks and Linguistic Theories (TLT 2006)*, pages 151–162. Prague, Czech Republic.

3

The *swarm* alternation revisited[*]

JACK HOEKSEMA

3.1 Introduction

English has a special construction which allows names of locations to act as subjects of certain verbs and adjectives (see Salkoff 1983, Levin 1993, Dowty 2000, 2001, Rowlands 2002). While normally, these verbs have agentive or thematic subjects, as in (1a, 2a), in this special construction the agent or theme is expressed by a prepositional argument, while the subject is a locative expression (cf. 1b, 2b). David Dowty has called the construction in (1a), (2a) the A-Subject-construction, and the one in (1b), (2b) the L-Subject-construction (Dowty 2000, 2001).[1]

(1) a. Termites are swarming in my kitchen.
        [A-Subject construction]
     b. My kitchen is swarming with termites.
        [L-Subject construction]

[*]This paper was presented at the conference 'Theory and Evidence in Semantics', held on June 1, 2006, at the University of Groningen in honor of David Dowty. I am grateful to the audience, and especially to David Dowty, for their comments. It is my pleasure to acknowledge my indebtedness to David for his kind support and stimulating ideas which helped me along at crucial moments in my career in linguistics. I would also like to thank two anonymous reviewers for their comments and suggestions for improvement, and Gerlof Bouma and Erik-Jan Smits for some LaTeX first-aid. To Swarthmore College and its department of linguistics, I am much obliged for wonderful working conditions during the academic year 2005–2006.
[1]Somewhat confusingly, Dowty's L-Subject-construction is not the same as Salkoff's (1983) L-form. Salkoff's L-form corresponds to Dowty's A-Subject-construction, whereas Dowty's L-Subject-construction corresponds to Salkoff's T-form (for "transposed form").

Theory and Evidence in Semantics.
Erhard Hinrichs and John Nerbonne (eds.).
Copyright © 2009, CSLI Publications.

(2) a. Rumors are buzzing in Washington.
     b. Washington is buzzing with rumors.

The relation between (1a) and (1b), or (2a) and (2b), has been called the *swarm*-alternation, and sometimes been related to the *locative* alternation, cf. (3):[2]

(3) a. Fred sprayed DDT onto the doorposts.
     b. Fred sprayed the doorposts with DDT.

Counterparts to this English alternation have been noted in French (Boons et al., 1976), Czech (Fried, 2005), and Serbo-Croatian (Vasina, 1995, cited in Dowty, 2000). Some French examples (adopted from Boons et al., 1976) are given in (4) below:

(4) a. Les serpents venimeux pullulent dans ce   parc.
        The snakes   poisonous swarm   in   that park
        'Poisonous snakes are swarming/congregating in that park.'
     b. Ce   parc pullule de/en serpents venimeux.
        That park swarms of   snakes   poisonous
        'That park is swarming with poisonous snakes.'
     c. Des bravos enthousiastes éclatèrent dans la salle.
        The bravo's enthusiastic resounded in   the hall
        'Enthusiastic cheers resounded in the hall'
     d. La   salle éclata   de bravos enthousiastes.
        The hall resounded of cheers enthusiastic
        'The hall resounded with enthusiastic cheers.'

The alternation is not found in many other languages (Hindi (Narasimhan, 1998), Bangla (Khan, 1994)). Dutch (cf. Mulder, 1992) and German have a somewhat more complex pattern of alternations, involving three constructions, compare the sentences in (5)(Dutch), and (6)(German):

(5) a. [AGENTIVE SUBJECT]

        Mieren krioelen in de keuken.
        Ants   crawl   in the kitchen

        'Ants are crawling (in large numbers) in the kitchen.'

---

[2]For a good discussion of differences between the swarm alternation and the load/spray alternation, see Rowlands (2002). Throughout this paper, the term 'alternation' will be used as a conventional metaphor, without any assumption or implicit commitment as to its theoretical status: whether we should view the constructions involved as linked derivationally in some way, or whether they should be viewed as two separate and independent constructions. See Dowty (2001) for discussion of this point.

   b. [LOCATIVE SUBJECT]

     De   keuken krioelt van   de   mieren.
     The kitchen crawls with the ants

     'The kitchen is crawling with ants.'

   c. [IMPERSONAL]

     Het krioelt van de   mieren in de   keuken.
     It   crawls with the ants   in the kitchen

     'The kitchen is crawling with ants.'

(6) a. Ameisen wimmeln in der Küche. [German]
     Ants   swarm   in the kitchen
     'Ants are swarming in the kitchen.'

   b. Die Küche wimmelt von   Ameisen.
     the kitchen swarms   with ants
     'The kitchen is swarming with ants.'

   c. Es wimmelt von Ameisen in der Küche.
     it swarms with ants   in the kitchen
     'The kitchen is swarming with ants.'

A similar 3-way alternation has been noted for Czech (Fried, 2005, p. 481):

(7) a. V kuchyni voněla skořice.
     In kitchen smelled cinnamon[NOM]
     'Cinnamon smelled in the kitchen.'

   b. Kuchyň   voněla skořicí.
     Kitchen[NOM] smelled cinnamon[INSTR]
     'The kitchen smelled of cinnamon.'

   c. V kuchyni vonělo skořicí.
     In kitchen smelled cinnamon[INSTR]
     'In the kitchen, it smelled of cinnamon.'

The L-Subject-construction and the impersonal construction largely use the same predicates. There are some differences between the two constructions, however, in terms of predicate selection, to which I will return in section 3.4.

    My main concern in this paper will be to provide the reader with an overview of the *swarm*-alternation in Dutch, using corpus data from a sample of 1250 sentences, collected from the Internet and whatever books, journals or magazines I happened to read during the past 10 years or so. This overview will shed some new light on the status of the alternation, in particular David Dowty's dynamic texture hypothesis, but it is also interesting for its own sake, since there is virtually no literature on *swarm*-type constructions in Dutch. Before we look at Dutch, however, it will be useful to briefly turn to the situation in English.

3.2 Classification of predicates

Dowty (2001, p. 172), building on earlier work by Salkoff (1983), distinguishes 5 semantic classes of predicates that may be used in the L-Subject-construction, denoting:

1. Small local movements, typically occurring repetitively: crawl, drip, bubble, dance, dribble, erupt, flow, foam, froth, gush, heave, hop, jump, ripple, roil, rumble, run, shake, shiver, throb, vibrate, pulsate

2. Animal sounds and other simple sounds, often repetitive: hum, buzz, be abuzz, twitter, cackle, chirp, whistle, hiss, fizz, creak, boom, rustle, resonate, resound, echo

3. Kinds of light emission: beam, blaze, be ablaze, brighten, flame, glow, flicker, flare up, flash, glimmer, glisten, glitter, light up, shimmer

4. Smells and Tastes: reek, smell, be fragrant, be redolent, taste

5. Degree of occupancy/abundance: abound, brim, teem, be rich, be rife, be rampant

The 'simple' predicates all involve a type of action or process that is easy and quick to perceive. According to Dowty, it is easier to establish whether a fountain or a swamp is bubbling than whether a cow is grazing, and this difference is argued to explain the difference between (8a) and (8b):

(8) a. The swamp is bubbling with noxious gases.
    b. *The meadow is grazing with cows.

Dowty is careful to place this restriction at the level of individual predicates, and not at the level of the sentences in which they occur. Quite frequently, the object of *bubbling with* is some abstract noun, and it may in fact be a lot easier as well as faster in a real-world setting to observe that a cow is grazing than it is to find out whether someone is bubbling with anticipation or whether Utah is bubbling with cultural activities. Presumably once a verb or adjective is permitted in the L-Subject-construction, it may be used quite generally to describe arbitrary situations, regardless of how easy to perceive the situation is. Indeed, the proper place for the alternation, as envisaged by Dowty, is in the lexicon. The *swarm*-alternation has properties typical of lexical derivation, such as limited and variable productivity, as well as arbitrary lexical gaps. The variable productivity of the phenomenon is most obvious from cross-linguistic comparison: while Salkoff (1983) lists several hundred verbs and adjectives as appearing in the L-Subject-construction, Dutch only has several dozen, as far as I have been able to establish. This is not because Dutch lacks verbs in the relevant classes, but because the construction is simply less productive.

As an aside to this classification, let me add that etymology should not reign supreme here. A predicate like *crawling* might be viewed as a verb of motion or as a verb of abundance. When we say that a place is crawling with police, we are not just noting the fact that the policemen are moving, but also that their number is very large. Motion is still relevant, because we cannot use *crawl* for inanimate objects, as in (9a, b), unless they can move (as in 9c):

(9) a. *The jar is crawling with beans.
     b. *The cemetery is crawling with corpses.
         (OK in "Evil Dead" setting)
     c. The city center was crawling with cars.

On the other hand, the policemen, while in motion, need not move according to the precise meaning of *crawl,* on all fours. Other uses of *crawl* noted in the Oxford English Dictionary, such as 'moving slowly' or 'moving in a stealthy way', are also not entirely apt for the abundance reading.

More striking still than *crawl* is the case of *lousy*, which does not fit comfortably in any of the 5 categories if we just consider its basic meaning. However, usage in the L-Subject-construction suggests that it is a predicate of abundance:

(10) a. Saudi Arabia is lousy with princes.
      b. Philadelphia is lousy with murals.

Of the 5 classes identified by Dowty, the predicates of abundance are in my view the most central: if a predicate is used metaphorically, or without a clear relation to its etymology, it will be a predicate of abundance, not one of smell or light emission, or motion, or sound. They also appear to have the highest text frequency of all classes.

The 5 classes of predicates all serve to characterize a location in a holistic manner. One of the main differences between *Bees are swarming in the garden* and *The garden is swarming with bees*, is that the former sentence is about bees, and the latter about the garden. Another difference concerns the role of the location. In *Bees are swarming in the garden*, only a small part of the garden need be characterized by the presence of bees. On the other hand, to say that the garden is swarming with bees seems to imply that the entire garden is affected by the swarming bees. It seems reasonable to suppose that the abundance interpretation, which I claim to be associated with some predicates of motion, such as *crawl*, stems from this total affectedness requirement. If your entire garden is characterized by the crawling of ants or the swarming of bees, then that would entail that the amount of ants or bees is high.

Another property of the L-Subject-construction noticed by Dowty is that the objects of *with* tend to be indefinites, usually bare plurals or mass nouns. This suggests that individuation of the agents is suppressed or undesirable in this construction. The examples in (11), taken from Dowty (2000, p. 123), illustrate this point:

(11) a.   The room swarmed with mosquitoes.
      b.   The room swarmed with a hundred mosquitoes.
      c.   ??The room swarmed with seventy-three mosquitoes.
      d.   My philodendron is crawling with dozens of snails.
      e.   ??My philodendron is crawling with fifty-seven snails.

However, Dowty also noted some apparent exceptions to this generalization, such as

(12) The whole school buzzed with the rumor about the principal and the librarian.

While the object of *with* is a definite singular in this example, the sentence is nonetheless fine. Dowty argues that this is because we interpret the sentence to imply that there were many repetitions of the rumor. While the rumor itself may be unique as a type, there are as many tokens of it as there are retellings of the story. While examples like (12) are actually quite rare, there are also cases like (13), which are somewhat more common:

(13) a. The hills are alive with the sound of music.
      b. The school resounded with the laughter of happy pupils.
      c. The air reeked with the odor of burning flesh.

These were argued in Woisetschlaeger (1983) to be definites with the distributional characteristics of indefinites, as is clear from the fact that they appear without any problem in existential sentences. Note also that we can paraphrase all the examples rather precisely using just bare nominals:

(14) a. The hills are alive with musical sounds.
      b. The school resounded with happy-pupil laughter.
      c. The air reeked with burning-flesh odor.

From a small sample of 184 English examples, informally collected from books and newspapers I read during the preparation of this paper, I tabulated the types of noun phrases acting as objects of *with*, and these are presented in Table 1:

a(n) + singular	5	3%
numeral + plural	2	1%
def. NP	7	4%
the N of N	10	5%
something like N	1	0.5%
bare N	159	86%

TABLE 1 Objects of *with*

Note that pseudo-definites like *the sound of sleigh bells* or *the pitterpatter of little feet* are actually more common, in this construction, than regular definites like *the rumors about Brad and Angelina*.

The predominance of bare nouns in the L-subject construction is evidence for Dowty's *Dynamic Texture Hypothesis*. This hypothesis says, in brief, that locations are described by predicates which describe small and frequently repeated events in such a way that the predicates may apply equally well to each subpart of the location. These subregions are small and manifold, and create a "texture of movement" perception (to use Dowty's term). This is reminiscent, of course, of the effect of bare nominals on aspectual classes of verbal projections, a matter investigated at length in Dowty (1979). Whereas *build a house* is a telic predicate, *build houses* or *build furniture* is atelic. Each part of the process of building houses can be denoted by the same predicate *build houses*, whereas a proper subpart of building a house may not be termed *building a house*. E.g. if Jones was building houses between January and July, then he must have been building houses between March and May as well, even if he only built part of a house in that period. But if we know that Jones built a house between March and July, we may not conclude that he built a house between May and July, or between March and June. Bare plurals and mass nouns have the property of turning telic transitive verbs into atelic ones, because their denotations are closed under subparts. This is also why they fit in nicely with the dynamic texture hypothesis. In Dowty's words (2001, p. 177), "[t]his follows from the fact that an event occurs in every small subpart of the region, therefore each event has its own agent in that region. If the regions are so small as to create a texture-perception, then the minimal regions can't be clearly individuated or counted. There must be an agent in each of these regions, hence the total number of agents cannot be counted either."

3.3   Predicates in the Dutch *swarm*-construction

In Dutch, the 5 classes of predicates identified by Dowty can be found as well. On the basis of a sample of 1250 occurrences, from the year 1600 onwards, gathered mainly from the Internet[3] and personal reading, we can discern a gradual increase in productivity of the L-Subject-construction, even though our data are necessarily skewed toward the more recent periods. Especially rare predicates will therefore be underrepresented for the older periods. Noteworthy is the large number of verbs ending in *–eren/-elen*. Such verbs are traditionally referred to as frequentatives and intensives (cf. de Jager, 1875–1878).[4] The full list is given in the Appendix. The table given there gives an indication of the growth of the set of predicates in the period 1600–now, as well as of the types of predicates involved.

It is clear that the set of predicates involved in Dutch is roughly similar to that of English. Verbs and verbal idioms of sound and light emission, verbs of smell and motion are all attested, as well as verbs of abundance. Some do not appear to fit in so well, such as a group of predicates indicating life and death, illustrated by the examples in (15):

(15)   a. Het leeft hier van de konijnen.
           It   lives here of   the rabbits
           'This place is alive with rabbits.'

       b. Het sterft hier van de konijnen.
           It   dies   here of   the rabbits
           'This place is teeming with rabbits.'

       c. Het stikt   hier van de konijnen.
           it   chokes here of   the rabbits
           'This place is swarming with rabbits'

       d. De   weide was vergeven van de konijnen.
           The field   was poisoned of   the rabbits
           'The field is alive with rabbits.'

---

[3]Internet examples are mostly from the Digital Library of Dutch Literature (www.dbnl.org), where a huge collection of Dutch texts from all periods is brought together. For rare predicates, other sites were accessed as well, using the Google search engine.

[4]Verbs in –elen/-eren often have counterparts in English in –re/-le, e.g. tikkelen – tickle, flikkeren – flicker, smokkelen – smuggle. The nature of these English verbs was already noted by Samuel Johnson in his Grammar of the English Tongue (part of his famous 1755 Dictionary, cf. Kolb and Demaria (2005, p. 337)): "If there be an l, as in jingle, tingle, mingle, sprinkle, twinkle, there is implied a frequency, or iteration of small acts."

Although their etymology might not suggest it, the predicates in this set are verbs of abundance. The translations suggest that this group also exists in English, albeit on a smaller scale, with *alive* (cf. example 14a above). Similar cases with *choke* are also found, although the relation to real or metaphorical choking is more direct in English than in Dutch:

(16) a. The freeways were choking with traffic.
      b. Fido choked with passion when he smelled the bitch.

Many expressions that would seem to be predicates of light emission, such as *zwart zien* 'look black', can also be used as predicates of abundance:

(17) a. De kamer zag zwart van de rook.
         The room saw black of the smoke
         'The room was black with smoke.' (blackness caused by smoke)
      b. De stad zag zwart van de mensen.
         The town saw black with the people
         'The town was abounding with people.' (large number of people)

The differences may be subtle in individual examples, given that a place abounding with people may look dark because of the color of their attire, or because they block the light. It is clear, however, that sentences like (17b) normally refer primarily to the large number of the people.

3.4   Locative and other subjects

Dowty's L-Subject-construction is so-called because of the locative subject it displays. However, not in all cases the subject appears to be locative in nature. Consider e.g.:

(18) a. John's voice was dripping with sarcasm.
      b. John's beard was dripping with blood.

While it may be natural to say that John's beard is the location of a certain amount of blood, it does not make as much sense to say that John's voice can ever be the location of sarcasm. Of these two sentences, only (18b) has a counterpart with a locative PP:

(19) a. *Sarcasm was dripping from John's voice.
      b. Blood was dripping from John's beard.

Instead, I would prefer to say that John's voice was characterized, to a high degree, by sarcasm. Note that it is not sufficient to say that (18a) has an idiomatic or metaphorical interpretation. If we claim that John's voice is some metaphorical location in (18a), it is not entirely clear why (19a) does not support the same metaphor. Spatial metaphors, like the ones in (20), tend to be quite versatile:

(20) a. You will always have a place in his heart.
      b. He has a big heart: there will always be room for another honey.
      c. My heart is filled with joy.
      d. My heart was empty when she died.

Human subjects can be found in the L-Subject-construction, and not always in a strictly locative interpretation. Of course, a human body can be a location, but it is not entirely clear to me that this is the case with the examples in (21):

(21) a. When they were flush with cash, the city was flush with heroin.
      b. Dick was white with humiliation and fury.
      c. Thick with excitement, I ran around the office.
      d. Amy was oozing with pride.
      e. Orthodox families are flush with children.

Flush is a predicate of abundance. Being flush with cash means having a lot of it. Can we say that the owner of the cash is in some sense its location? Some metaphors seem to suggest this, for example, we say that someone who is flush with cash is loaded. Yet this seems tenable only up to a point. Compare:

(22) a. In John's house, the kitchen was crawling with ants.
      b. In John's house, Amy was oozing with pride.

While (22a) allows us to conclude that part of John's house was crawling with ants, (22b) does not seem to permit the inference that part of John's house is oozing with pride. Yet if all that Amy is doing in (22b) is providing a location for the pride, and if Amy is in John's house, then that inference should be valid, simply because of the transitivity of the localization relation: if X is localized in Y, and Y is localized in Z, then X is localized in Z as well.

The difference between true locatives and other subjects appears to be relevant in Dutch for the choice between personal and impersonal constructions. While there is a slight predominance of impersonal constructions in general (in my material, 52% of all sentences are impersonal, and 48% personal), the impersonal construction is avoided when the subject cannot be locative. Compare what happens with the verbs *stikken* 'choke' and *barsten* 'burst':

(23) a. De vijver stikt   van de kikkers.
             The pond chokes of   the frogs
             'The pond is crawling with frogs.'

      b. Het stikt   van de kikkers in de vijver.
             It   chokes of the frogs   in the pond
             'The pond is crawling with frogs.'

      c. Jan stikt   van de jaloezie.
             Jan chokes of   the jalousy
             'Jan is choking with jalousy.'

      d. *Het stikt   van de jaloezie in/bij   Jan.
             it   chokes with the jalousy in/with Jan
             'Jan is choking with jalousy.'

(24) a. Amerika barst van de illegalen.
             America bursts of   the illegals
             'America is rife with illegal aliens.'

      b. Het barst in Amerika van de illegalen.
             It   bursts in America of   the illegals
             'America is rife with illegal aliens.'

      c. Marie barst van verlangen.
             Marie bursts of   desire
             'Marie is bursting with desire.'

      d. *Het barst van verlangen in/bij   Marie.
             It   bursts of   desire   in/with Marie
             'Marie is bursting with desire.'

In Table 2 (see page 64), the distribution over personal and impersonal constructions is given, based on my corpus. Only the most common verbs are included in the table.

One of the more common idioms, *bol staan*, meaning 'be round, pumped up, bloated', is not all that often predicated of typical locations, but mostly of such things as newspapers, magazines and similar names for texts and containers of texts, although other subjects also occur. Compare:

(25) a. De kranten staan bol   van de geruchten over Berlusconi.
             The papers stand round of the rumors   about Berlusconi
             'The papers are replete with rumors about Berlusconi.'

      b. Het Nederlands elftal staat bol   van het talent.
             The Dutch   team stands round of   the talent
             'The Dutch team is overflowing with talent.'

For the 70 occurrences of this predicate, I found the distribution over semantic classes of subjects shown in Table 3 (on page 64).

Verb	Translation	Imp	Pers	% Imp
barsten	burst	42	51	44%
bol staan	be round	1	69	1%
bulken	abound	1	17	6%
gonzen	buzz	36	19	65%
grimmelen	swarm	12	14	46%
krioelen	crawl	116	72	62%
leven	live	5	1	83%
sterven	die	14	3	82%
stikken	choke	67	16	81%
vergeven	poisoned	5	38	12%
wemelen	teem	251	98	72%
weergalmen	resound	0	11	0%

TABLE 2 Impersonal versus Personal

Subject type	N	%
Texts	39	56%
Locations	11	16%
Groups	5	7%
People	3	5%
Events	5	7%
Periods	5	7%
Other	2	3%

TABLE 3 Subjects of BOL STAAN

Given that locative subjects are not completely ruled out with this predicate, we expect to find that the impersonal construction is possible, and this appears to be true. Sentences like (26), while not attested in my small sample, are grammatical and can be found on the Internet:

(26) Het staat   er   bol   van de geruchten.
     It   stands there round of   the rumors
     'It is rife with rumors.'

3.5   Fake definites

One of the most surprising properties of the Dutch data is the predominance of definite noun phrases in the PP-argument (noted in Mulder 1992). As Table 1 has shown, definite noun phrases in that position are quite uncommon in English, where bare plurals and mass nouns are by far the most common choice. In my Dutch examples above, I translated many definite noun phrases with English indefinites, simply by leaving out the article. Why did I do that? Because the definites in question are fakes: syntactically, they may look like definites, but they are interpreted as indefinites. This is intuitively clear for anyone who has attempted to translate modern Dutch into English, or vice versa. The usual discourse requirements of unique reference do not apply to these cases. The use of the definite article in this construction is not only unusual, given that German and English do not have it, it is also fairly new. The older stages of the language do not show this usage at all. Figure 1 shows the rise of fake definites from 0% of all noun phrases in the *van*-complement in the 18th century to 84% at the moment. Whether a definite is fake or not, is of course a judgment call. I decided to count as definite all occurrences of noun phrases that I would translate into English as indefinites.

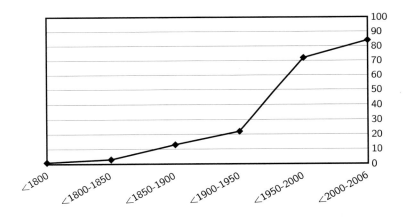

FIGURE 1 Increasing prevalence of fake definites

The use of fake definites is not easy to explain. There appears to be no reason whatsoever to use them, and every reason to avoid them. However, it should be pointed out that the use of expletive definites is not unheard of in Dutch. In a number of areas, Dutch uses the definite article without its usual definite interpretation, for instance in various measure constructions (cf. e.g. Corver and Zwarts, 2006):

(27) Hij heeft rond   de tachtig koeien.
      He has   around the eighty cows

'He has about eighty cows.'

(28) Hij is tegen   de tachtig.
     He is against the eighty
     'He is about/almost eighty years old.'

The definite article in these cases depends on the presence of the items *rond/ tegen*. Without these prepositions, the articles are prohibited on an indefinite reading:

(29) Hij heeft (*de) tachtig koeien.
     He has   the   eighty cows
     'He has 80 cows.'

(30) Hij is (*de) tachtig.
     He is the   eighty
     'He is 80.'

The choice of definite articles in the *swarm*-construction is still somewhat optional, and appears to be partly determined by syntactic complexity. For the most recent period, the data are distributed as indicated in Table 4. The percentage of spurious articles is highest among simple noun phrases consisting of just a noun, somewhat lower among A+ N combinations, and lowest among conjoined and post-modified nouns.[5] (The rare cases where no article was possible, e.g. because of the presence of a demonstrative determiner, were not included in the table.)

Class	+ article	- article	%-article
N	299	19	6%
A+N	69	18	21%
N+PP, N+Rel-Clause	40	11	22%
N conj N	23	11	32%

TABLE 4 Complexity Classes

The difference between simple nouns and complex noun phrases is highly significant. Collapsing the 3 types of complex noun phrases

[5] The relevance of modifiers was also noted in another connection in Salkoff (1983, pp. 292–3), where it was pointed out that indefinite singulars are sometimes possible in the T-type (Dowty's L-Subject-construction) when a modifier is present, whereas otherwise, this is not the case: His head reeled with hypotheses / ? an hypothesis / a curious idea / an hypothesis about God. It is conceivable that this observation is connected to the one in the main text about the absence of fake definite marking, although I do not yet see how.

listed in Table 4, and comparing them with the simple nouns yields a χ^2 of 33.7, p < 0.001.

The appearance of definite articles is interesting not only for their bearing on the issue of noun phrase complexity. They also provide a clue for another aspect of the analysis. Linguists like Salkoff and Dowty, working on the *swarm*-alternation, have generally assumed that examples like (31a,b) both exemplify the L-Subject-construction:

(31) a. The shore was jumping with people during Memorial weekend.

  b. Mary was jumping with anticipation when the package arrived.

Yet (31b) does not have a clearly locative subject, and Dowty's (2001) dynamic texture-hypothesis does not appear to apply to such cases. So the question is: Do these sentences really belong together, or do they represent different constructions? To answer this question, the Dutch data come in handy. Consider for example the sentences in (32):

(32) a. De kust barstte van de mensen afgelopen weekend.
    The shore burst of the people past   weekend
    'Last weekend, the shore was jumping with people.'

  b. Marie barstte van de zenuwen.
    Marie burst of the nerves
    'Marie was jumping with nerves.'

We see the tell-tale sign of expletive definites in both examples, suggesting that yes, they belong together, as instances of the same construction. We can also use the test in another way, to exclude certain semantically similar sentence types. Kutscher and Schultze-Berndt (2007) have suggested that the German examples in (33) are related to the English *swarm*-construction:

(33) a. Der Baum hängt voll Früchte.
    The tree   hangs full fruits
    'The tree is full of fruit.'

  b. Die Strassen lagen voll Schnee.
    The streets   lay   full snow
    'The streets were full of snow.'

  c. Beide Hunde saßen voll mit Metastasen.
    Both dogs   sat   full with metastases
    'Both dogs were full of metastases.'

These examples involve verbs of body posture with locative subjects. Indeed, the similarity is striking, with an interpretation that could easily support a translation into English using the L-Subject-construction, as in (34):

(34) a. The tree is heavy with fruit.
      b. The streets were thick with snow.
      c. Both dogs were riddled with metastases.

Dutch has an exact counterpart to the German construction:

(35) a. De boom hangt vol vruchten.
         The tree   hangs full fruits
         'The tree is full of fruit.'
      b. De straten lagen vol sneeuw.
         The streets lay   full snow
         'The streets were full of snow.'
      c. Beide honden zaten vol metastasen.
         Both dogs   sat   full metastases
         'Both dogs were full of metastases.'

The Dutch linguist Wobbe de Vries already noted the similarities between this and the *swarm*-construction back in 1910 (cf. de Vries, 1910).
He also noted an obvious difference: instead of the preposition *van*, the
adjective *vol* is employed. In 1910, quasi-definites could not be used to
provide further evidence for distinguishing the posture-verb construction from regular *swarm*-cases, because the use of quasi-definites was
just beginning to emerge. Today, however, it is striking just how bad
these examples become when we add definite articles to the examples
in (35):

(36) a. *De boom hangt vol de vruchten.
      b. *De straten lagen vol de sneeuw.
      c. *Beide honden zaten vol de metastasen.

This suggests that the Dutch/German construction with the verbs of
body posture, while semantically similar, must be viewed as nonetheless
distinct from the swarm-construction.

3.6 Conclusion

Finally, let me say what I consider to be the core meaning of the *swarm*-
construction. I do not think that David Dowty's dynamic texture-
hypothesis captures it completely, partly because of the possibility of
subjects that are not strictly locative, and partly because it does not
fully come to grips with the fact that the construction expresses a high

degree.[6] More precisely, I take the construction to be a causative degree construction. The object of *with* causes the subject to exhibit a high degree of some property by completely affecting it. Consider in this light the question-answer pairs in (37–39):

(37) Q: Were there many tourists?
     A: The streets were crawling with them.

(38) Q: Was John angry?
     A: He was foaming with fury.

(39) Q: Was the crowd loud?
     A: The walls were vibrating with their cheers.

Note that all answers are affirmative, and could be paraphrased as: "Yes, very."

The high-degree interpretation of the *swarm*-construction makes it compatible with adverbs like *just*, or *literally*, and less so with downtoners like *a bit* or *somewhat*:

(40) a. Smith was just bristling with anger.
     b. The place was just crawling with ants.
     c. The book is literally littered with typos.
     d. The yard was absolutely lousy with vermin.

(41) a. ??Smith was somewhat bristling with anger.
     b. ??The place was a bit crawling with ants.
     c. ??The book is a tad littered with typos.
     d. ??The yard was a mite lousy with vermin.

The oddness of the examples in (39) vis-à-vis the acceptability of those in (38) can be compared to the difference between predicates like *angry* and inherently high-degree predicates such as *livid* or *furious*:

(42) a. Jones was absolutely angry.[7]
     b. Jones was absolutely livid/furious.
     c. Jones was a bit angry.
     d. ??Jones was a bit livid/furious.

---

[6]During the presentation of this material at the conference 'Theory and Evidence in Semantics', David Dowty objected to this point by noting that nonlocative interpretations were typically idiomatic, e.g. John was boiling with anger or Mary was limp with laughter. This point is well-taken, but I would like to stress that Dowty's theory has nothing to say about these idiomatic cases, whereas they fit in perfectly with the analysis given here: they all express a high degree.

[7]The combination absolutely angry seems to be possible, to judge from numerous Google hits, but disprefered to absolutely furious or absolutely livid. This adverb appears to select for predicates that either express scalar endpoints such as empty, impossible, or high degree expressions such as furious, ludicrous etc.

The high-degree nature of the L-Subject-Construction might be related to the dynamic-texture hypothesis, but does not seem to follow from it. To see this point, consider once more the following example:

(43) The book was littered with typos.

The dynamic-texture hypothesis would state that the typos form an even pattern across the book, e.g. because there are ten on every page. The high-degree hypothesis, on the other hand, would simply say that the book had a very high number of typos, regardless of their distribution across the book. Intuitively, the latter characterization would appear to me to be more nearly correct.

Finally, given my hypothesis, it should come as no surprise that the *swarm*-construction has an intonation typical of emphatic sentence types, such as exclamatives. The verb has to be accentuated, except under very limited circumstances, in particular when contrastive focus is used to correct an earlier claim:

(44) a. The bar was just CRAWLING with cops.
  b. *The bar was crawling with COPS. [* in out of the blue context]
  c. The bar was crawling with COPS, not DRUNKS, you dummy!

Particularly striking is the possibility of emphatic lengthening. Emphatic lengthening is a phonetic process which is possible with some but not all degree expressions, such as English *so* or Dutch *zeer* 'very':

(45) a. You are SOOOOO right.
  b. The kitching was just CRAAAAAAWLING with ants.
  c. Het hotel was ZEEEER duur.   [Dutch]
     The hotel was very   expensive
     'The hotel was extremely expensive.'
  d. Het weeeeeemelde daar van de agenten.
     It crawled   there of the policemen
     'The place was crawling with cops.'

This option is entirely absent in the A-Subject-construction (or, for that matter, in any nonemphatic construction):

(46) a. *Ants are CRAAAAWLING in the kitchen.
  b. *Mieren weeeeeemelen in de keuken. [Dutch]
     Ants crawled   in the kitchen
     'Ants were crawling in the kitchen.'

References

Boons, Jean-Paul, Alain Guillet, and Christian Leclère. 1976. *La structure des phrases simples en français: Constructions intransitives*. Genève: Droz.

Corver, Norbert and Joost Zwarts. 2006. Prepositional Numerals. *Lingua* 116:811–835.

de Jager, Arie. 1875–1878. *Woordenboek der frequentatieven in het Nederlands*. Gouda: Van Goor. 2 vols.

de Vries, Wobbe. 1910. Opmerkingen over Nederlandsche syntaxis I. Usurpaties. *Tijdschrift voor Nederlandse Taal- en Letterkunde* 29:122–165.

Dowty, David. 1979. *Word Meaning and Montague Grammar*. Dordrecht: D. Reidel.

Dowty, David. 2000. 'The Garden Swarms with Bees' and the Fallacy of 'Argument Alternation'. In Y. Ravin and C. Leacock, eds., *Polysemy. Theoretical and Computational Approaches*, pages 111–128. Oxford: Oxford University Press.

Dowty, David. 2001. The Semantic Asymmetry of "Argument Alternations" (and Why it Matters). In G. van der Meer and A. G. ter Meulen, eds., *Making Sense: From Lexeme to Discourse*, Groninger Arbeiten zur germanistischen Linguistik 44, pages 171–186. Groningen: Centre for Language and Cognition.

Fried, Mirjam. 2005. A Frame-Based Approach to Case Alternations: The *Swarm*-class Verbs in Czech. *Cognitive linguistics* 16(3):475–512.

Khan, Zeeshan R. 1994. Bangla Verb Classes and Alternations. In D. A. Jones, R. C. Berwick, F. Cho, Z. Khan, K. Kohl, N. Nomura, A. Radhakrishnan, U. Sauerland, and B. Ulicny, eds., *Classes and Alternations in Bangla, German, English and Korean*, pages 36–50. MIT. A.I. Memo no. 1517, CBCL Memo no. 137.

Kolb, Gwin and Robert Jr. Demaria. 2005. *Samuel Johnson on the English Language*. New Haven: Yale University Press.

Kutscher, Silvia and Eva Schultze-Berndt. 2007. Why a folder lies in the basket although it is not lying: the semantics and use of German positional verbs with inanimate figures. *Linguistics* 54:983–1028.

Levin, Beth. 1993. *English Verb Classes and Alternations: A Preliminary Investigation*. Chicago: University of Chicago Press.

Mulder, René. 1992. *The Aspectual Nature of Syntactic Complementation*. Ph.D. thesis, University of Leiden.

Narasimhan, Bhuvana. 1998. Encoding complex events in Hindi and English. Unpublished MS, MIT.

Rowlands, Rachel. 2002. *Swarming with bees: property predication and the 'swarm' alternation*. Master's thesis, University of Canterbury, Canterbury, New Zealand.

Salkoff, Morris. 1983. Bees are Swarming in the Garden. A systematic study of productivity. *Language* 59(2):288–346.

Vasina, Svetlana. 1995. The Swarm-alternation and argument structure in Serbo-croatian. Unpublished Paper, Ohio State University.

Woisetschlaeger, Erich. 1983. On the question of definiteness in "an old man's book". *Linguistic Inquiry* 14:137–154.

Appendix

TABLE 5: List of all Dutch predicates

Dutch predicate	Translation	Count
aan elkaar hangen	hang together	7
abonderen	abound	1
barsten	burst	93
blaken	be hot	4
blauw staan	stand blue/be blue	3
blauw zien	look blue	5
bleek worden	turn pale	1
blinken	shine	3
bol staan	be round	70
bruisen	whirl	12
bulderen	roar	2
bulken	roar	18
daveren	roar	12
denderen	roar, thunder	2
doorweekt	soaked, drenched	1
dreunen	resound	10
drijven	float, drip	3
druipen	drip	9
duizelen	be dizzy, dazzle	2
dwarrelen	twirl	2
flonkeren	twinkle	5
fonkelen	twinkle	3
galmen	resound	3
geuren	smell, reek	1
glimmen	shine	7
glinsteren	shine, sparkle	5
godvergeven	god-poisoned	1
gonzen	buzz	55
grielen	crawl	1
griemelen	crawl	1
grijs zien	look grey	1
grimmelen	crawl	26
groen zien	look green	1
kabalen	be noisy	1

Continued on next page

Table 5 – continued from previous page

Dutch predicate	Translation	Count
kolken	whirl	1
krielen	crawl	53
krimmelen	crawl	1
krioelen	crawl	135
leven	be alive / live	6
loeien	bellow	1
miegelen	teem	13
op	used up	3
overkoken	boil over	1
overlopen	run over	3
overstromen	flow over	1
overvloeien	flow over	2
ritselen	rustle	11
rood zien	look red	6
schitteren	shine / sparkle	3
sidderen	shudder	1
smoren	smother / choke	2
spetteren	sputter	1
sterven	die	17
stijf staan	be stiff	13
stikken	choke	83
storm lopen	storm	1
stralen	radiate	1
suizen	sizzle	1
tinkeltwinkelen	twinkle	1
tintelen	tinge	7
trillen	trill	1
uit elkaar spatten	explode	1
uitpuilen	bulge	8
vergeven	poisoned	43
wedergalmen	resound	6
weergalmen	resound	5
wemelen	teem / crawl	349
wit zien	look white	5
zieden	boil	3
zinderen	be hot	10
zoemen	buzz	16

Continued on next page

Table 5 – continued from previous page

Dutch predicate	Translation	Count
zwart	black	7
zwart staan	be black	16
zwart zien	look black / abound	37
zwermen	swarm	4
Grand total		**1250**

TABLE 6: Dutch predicates, by period

Period	Predicate	Count
1550–1600	abonderen	1
	Total	1
1600–1650	dreunen	1
	grimmelen	6
	krielen	3
	krimmelen	1
	krioelen	1
	Total	12
1650–1700	barsten	1
	daveren	2
	grielen	1
	griemelen	1
	grimmelen	6
	krielen	5
	krioelen	3
	overvloeien	1
	zwermen	1
	Total	21
1700–1750	barsten	2
	blinken	1
	daveren	1
	dreunen	1
	grimmelen	7
	krielen	14
	wedergalmen	4
	Total	30

Continued on next page

Table 6 – continued from previous page

Period	Predicate	Count
1750–1800	daveren	1
	dreunen	2
	grimmelen	3
	krielen	13
	krioelen	1
	stikken	1
	wedergalmen	1
	weergalmen	1
	wemelen	1
	Total	24
1800–1850	daveren	1
	glinsteren	1
	grimmelen	2
	krielen	6
	krioelen	3
	overvloeien	1
	rood zien	1
	wedergalmen	1
	weergalmen	1
	wemelen	28
	Total	45
1850–1900	aan elkaar hangen	1
	blinken	2
	bulken	1
	daveren	2
	dreunen	1
	flonkeren	1
	fonkelen	1
	glinsteren	2
	grimmelen	2
	krielen	7
	krioelen	11
	miegelen	1
	rood zien	1
	weergalmen	1
	wemelen	47
	zwart	2

Continued on next page

Table 6 – continued from previous page

Period	Predicate	Count
	Total	83
1900–1950	aan elkaar hangen	2
	barsten	5
	blaken	1
	bleek worden	1
	bol staan	1
	daveren	3
	doorweekt	1
	dreunen	3
	flonkeren	1
	glimmen	1
	glinsteren	1
	gonzen	2
	krielen	5
	krioelen	32
	leven	2
	miegelen	2
	op	1
	rood zien	1
	stikken	3
	suizen	1
	tintelen	2
	weergalmen	1
	wemelen	59
	wit zien	2
	zieden	2
	zinderen	1
	zoemen	6
	zwart	3
	zwart staan	11
	zwart zien	4
	zwermen	1
	Total	161
1950–2000	aan elkaar hangen	2
	barsten	28
	blaken	1
	blauw staan	1

Continued on next page

Table 6 – continued from previous page

Period	Predicate	Count
	blauw zien	3
	bol staan	17
	bruisen	3
	bulderen	1
	bulken	1
	daveren	1
	denderen	1
	dreunen	1
	drijven	2
	druipen	1
	dwarrelen	1
	flonkeren	1
	fonkelen	1
	galmen	1
	geuren	1
	glimmen	2
	gonzen	18
	grijs zien	1
	kolken	1
	krioelen	57
	leven	2
	miegelen	2
	op	2
	overlopen	1
	overstromen	1
	ritselen	3
	rood zien	1
	schitteren	1
	sterven	8
	stijf staan	2
	stikken	23
	stralen	1
	tintelen	2
	trillen	1
	uitpuilen	2
	vergeven	10
	weergalmen	1

Continued on next page

Table 6 – continued from previous page

Period	Predicate	Count
	wemelen	104
	zieden	1
	zinderen	1
	zoemen	5
	zwart	1
	zwart staan	3
	zwart zien	8
	Total	333
2000–2007	aan elkaar hangen	2
	barsten	56
	bersten	1
	blaken	2
	blauw staan	2
	blauw zien	2
	bol staan	52
	bruisen	9
	bulderen	1
	bulken	16
	daveren	1
	denderen	1
	dreunen	1
	drijven	1
	druipen	8
	duizelen	2
	dwarrelen	1
	flonkeren	2
	fonkelen	1
	galmen	2
	glimmen	4
	glinsteren	1
	godvergeven	1
	gonzen	35
	groen zien	1
	kabalen	1
	krioelen	27
	leven	2
	loeien	1

Continued on next page

Table 6 – continued from previous page

Period	Predicate	Count
	miegelen	8
	overkoken	1
	overlopen	2
	ritselen	8
	rood zien	2
	schitteren	2
	sidderen	1
	smoren	2
	spetteren	1
	sterven	9
	stijf staan	11
	stikken	56
	storm lopen	1
	tinkeltwinkelen	1
	tintelen	3
	uit elkaar spatten	1
	uitpuilen	6
	vergeven	33
	wemelen	110
	wit zien	3
	zinderen	8
	zoemen	5
	zwart	1
	zwart staan	2
	zwart zien	25
	zwermen	2
	Total	540
	Grand Total	**1250**

4

Do Representations Matter or Do Meanings Matter: The Case of Antecedent Containment[*]

Pauline Jacobson

4.1 Introduction

This paper focuses on two related phenomena (both involving "antecedent containment") in an effort to address the question posed above. Of course the question as phrased here is a bit silly: no one doubts that meanings matter. But the central issue here is whether representations ever do. That is, are there principles and/or constraints in the grammar which are stated in terms of representational properties

---

[*]I chose this paper for the conference and the volume to honor David Dowty because it was from him that I learned to hope that in general the *meanings* and not the representations are what matters. Dowty's work continually strives to seriously illuminate the meanings of expressions, and to show how generalizations follow from these rather than from stipulative facts about representational properties. I do not expect David to necessarily agree with everything in the "worldview" presented below, but the spirit of this research is inspired by my contact with him and his work over many years. I think it is fair to say that I never would have learned semantics nor become a semanticist were it not for his work and its influence on the field (not to mention his friendship), and I fondly dedicate this paper to David.

An earlier version of some of this material is contained in Jacobson (2004). I would like to thank both Chris Barker and Irene Heim for a number of comments on that paper which have helped me significantly revise and sharpen the analysis, hopefully for the better. In addition, I have benefitted from extremely insightful comments from the referees for this volume; I regret that I have not had the time or space to properly address all of these comments, but hope to have at least addressed some of the more pressing ones.

of expressions (at any level)? Obviously no definitive answer to that can be given on the basis of one or two cases. My goal, therefore, is to take one case which has been thought to require crucial reference to representational properties—and which at first glance looks like a fairly convincing example of something which does—and to provide an account relying solely on the meanings of the relevant expressions— an account under which the facts fall out with no extra apparatus. To be sure, there remain pieces of the final analysis which are not completely nailed down and also open questions. For the most part, however, these are not artifacts of just this particular analysis; most of the open questions are ones which arise more generally, and must ultimately be answered in any theory. And, by looking at a closely related case which obviously relies purely on meanings and not representational properties, I hope to make a convincing case that this is the right strategy.

Let me first lay out the general worldview here. My point of departure is the hypothesis of "Direct Compositionality": the syntax "builds" (i.e., proves the well-formedness of) expressions while the semantics works in tandem to directly supply a model-theoretic interpretation of each expression as it is "built" in the syntax. If this is coupled with a reasonably constrained view of syntax, the prediction is that the grammar contains no principles referring to structured representations (such as trees); trees are nothing more than a convenient representation of the syntactic and semantic combinatorics and play no role in the statement of any grammatical processes. Obviously (all other things being equal) this is a much simpler conception of the grammar than one in which representations are computed and referred to, since it contains no apparatus as part of its basic architecture that is not needed under *any* theory. I will also assume (following Jacobson (1999)) a variable-free semantics—where the semantics makes no use of variable names nor assignment functions.[1]

I will be contrasting this with a different worldview: one in which the syntax computes representations which are then mapped into other representations (Logical Forms) which are then compositionally assigned a meaning. Under this view, representations play a crucial role in the grammar. For example, subtrees (generally local trees) are used in the statement of the compositional rules, since such rules are mappings

---

[1]Note that the adoption of a variable-free semantics is logically independent of the hypothesis of direct compositionality. In theory, one could have direct compositionality while making use of assignment functions (as in, e.g., Montague 1974), but this does give rise to some empirical difficulties. See Jacobson (1999) for discussion of the relationship between direct compositionality and variable-free semantics.

from trees to model theoretic objects. Since the grammar "keeps track" of the representations, such a grammar can also contain constraints on representations—and much work within this general program does in fact assume the existence of such constraints. This worldview has been assumed in a great deal of work since Chomsky (1976); the most recent thorough articulation of the semantic side is perhaps given in Heim and Kratzer (1998) (hereafter, HK), and so I will often refer to their particular version. I will, moreover, refer to this (and related) work as the "standard" view, realizing full well that it is standard only in certain places.

4.2   The two worldviews with respect to VP Ellipsis

Let us summarize (roughly) the "standard" view of VP Ellipsis (and Antecedent Contained Deletion, hereafter ACD). Of course there is no single "standard" view, but I think that the presentation here is a reasonable summary of the general gist of proposals within the standard view, and will serve for discussion. This view contains the following pieces. (i) There is actual linguistic material in the ellipsis site at some level of linguistic representation. In particular this material is at least present at LF and is interpreted compositionally just as if it were overt. (ii) There is an identity condition: this material is allowed to be silent or deleted in the actual pronounced sentence in view of it being identical to some other overt linguistic material (call that the "antecedent"). This has taken two forms. In some views the condition requires formal identity (see, e.g., Sag (1976) who required formal identity at LF) and in some the requirement is semantic identity (see, e.g., Merchant 2000). Given a condition on identity, the question arises as to what constitutes identity when there are unbound variables within both the antecedent and the elided VP. Notice that if we take seriously the idea that the semantic value of an expression is a function from assignment functions to something else, semantic identity will be met only if the variable names are the same (provided they are not bound within the expressions which need to be identical). Note that formal identity will lead to the same conclusion.[2] Here, however, strict formal identity would actually require the same variable names even if both are identically bound, whereas if both are bound within the domain relevant for "identity",

---

[2]Of course readers familiar with Sag (1976) will recall that he did not require identity of variable names, and had in fact a (rather complex) definition of "alphabetic variants" to allow distinct variable names in certain places. I will, however, not consider Sag's detailed proposal here; some of the pieces were motivated by supposed empirical generalizations which have since been shown to be incorrect (see, for example, Evans 1988).

semantic identity will no longer care about the variable names.

(iii) In addition, it has been assumed in much work since Rooth (1992b) that there is also a focus condition on ellipsis. Let VP_{ELL} stand for the elided VP and VP_{ANT} stand for the antecedent. Then Rooth's focus condition can be stated as follows: VP_{ELL} must be within some larger constituent C_{ELL} and VP_{ANT} must be contained within some larger constituent C_{ANT} such the meaning of C_{ANT} is or *implies (possibly in conjunction with other facts in the discourse context)* something which is a proper alternative to C_{ELL}. Put differently, using the focus semantics of Rooth (1985), $[[C_{ANT}]]$ must be a member of $[[C_{ELL}]]^{FOC}$ and must be distinct from the "regular" value of C_{ELL}. Notice that given this formulation, we require a linguistically overt antecedent not only for the identity condition but also for the focus condition, since this is stated in terms of the meaning of some C_{ANT} whose definition in turn requires a VP_{ANT}. We will be returning to this observation below.

(iv) Finally, the "standard" view assumes the usual wisdom on ACD. Consider the following:

(1) Mary voted for every candidate that Bill will.

The usual story is that the object DP (or, NP) *every candidate that Bill will* must be raised so as to leave a trace in the matrix VP, hence the matrix VP can serve as the antecedent (for present purposes we can think of traces as identical to variables). It is worth commenting on the identity condition with respect to the trace/variable. Consider (2), seen for now as an informal LF:

(2)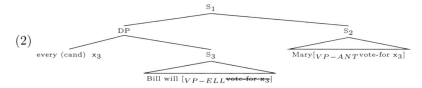

Here we have a case where the two VPs each contain variables unbound within that VP, but note that both a formal and a semantic identity condition are satisfied here since the variable names are the same. Things become a bit more interesting if we turn to a slightly more complex LF representation: one where the two expressions which are arguments of the quantifier *every* are actually of type <e,t> and are such that the unbound variable has been λ-abstracted over. Consider, for example (3), which is essentially the kind of LF adopted in HK:

(3)

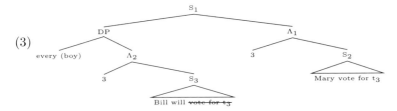

Notice that unless one adopts an additional stipulation (see below), such a representation should be allowed, and this too satisfies both a formal and a semantic identity condition. For the moment, then, we need not worry about the fact that the traces (variables) in the antecedent VP and in the elided VP are "bound" by different "operator" tokens (i.e., the integers whose semantic import is to perform λ-abstraction); they still can have the same index and hence correspond to the same variable. Thus restricting our gaze to the two VPs alone, again both formal and semantic identity are satisfied.

We turn now to an alternative view of VP ellipsis, one which is more in keeping with the general worldview here. Not all of the pieces that I lay out below come as a necessary package, but I will for convenience lay them out as a package. I will number each piece here as n', for n the corresponding piece in the above presentation of the "standard" view. (i') There is no material in the ellipsis site; ellipsis is really a matter of "anaphora" (see also Hardt (1993) and many others for this view). One concrete implementation of this idea is worked out in Jacobson (2003, 2007), and I sketch this out only informally here. To say that "ellipsis" is "anaphora" means, in terms of a variable free semantics, that a sentence like *John will (too)* is actually a function from <e,t> type meanings to propositions, and the listener picks out a contextually salient property from the discourse context. (This is exactly akin to the treatment of free pronouns in Jacobson 1999.) In syntactic terms, we will assume that the sentence contains the information that it has within it an "unbound proform", and thus its category (again following the details of Jacobson 1999) is S^{VP}, where the superscript here is just a record that there is a "VP proform" within the sentence. As to what that proform is, I assume that auxiliaries like *will* are listed in the lexicon as wanting VP complements; in Categorial Grammar terms, then, it is of category $VP/_R VP$ (it asks for a VP to its right to give a VP). I assume, however, that all auxiliaries (and *to*) map to a second syntactic category which is a "proform" and is thus VP^{VP}. The two have the same meaning and both are of type <<e,t>,<e,t>>; the difference is just that the proform does not actually expect a complement in the syntax. All that is actually crucial here is the claim that the final sentence contains the analogue of a "free pronoun" within it, and hence a contextually salient property is "picked up".

(ii') Given this view, there obviously is no identity condition (as is the case of other free pronouns). There is simply the illusion of an identity condition : the contextually salient meaning which is picked up can—and in fact likes to be—made contextually salient by being the meaning of some other linguistically overt expression, and so there will often be another expression whose meaning is identical to the meaning which is supplied. Of course immediately one must say something about the observation in Hankamer and Sag (1976) to the effect that it is quite difficult to supply a meaning in VP Ellipsis unless the relevant property is the meaning of an actual overt expression (i.e., "pragmatic control" is difficult). But subsequent literature is full of cases showing that pragmatic control does exist; see Webber (1978), Hardt (1993), Dalrymple et al. (1991) among many others.[3] To give two such cases, consider the following (I thank Stuart Shieber for (a) below).

(4) a. Context: We are hiking on a hot day and see a refreshing pool of water under a waterfall. I turn to you and say "I will if you will".

    b. Context: I see my friend Chris, about to ski down Inferno on cross-country skis, and say "He's not really going to, is he?"

(iii') will be the analogue of the focus condition which I will postpone discussion of until later. (iv') As to ACD, I assume that this is really an instance of "Transitive verb phrase (TVP) ellipsis" (see Cormack 1984, Evans 1988, Jacobson 1992). To elucidate, take first the account of "extraction gaps" in general within relative clauses in, e.g., Steedman (1987) and others within the Categorial Grammar tradition:

(5) Mary voted for every candidate that Bill will vote for.

In that account the two-place relation [[vote-for]] function composes with [[will]] (whose lexical meaning is of type $<<e,t>,<e,t>>$). I will revise this slightly and make use instead of the "Geach" rule (which is nothing more than a unary, or "Curry'd" version of function composition). This operation (call it **g**) takes a function f of type $<a,b>$ and maps it to a function h of type $<<c,a>,<c,b>>$ such that $h = \lambda X_{<c,a>}[\lambda c[f(X(c))]]$. This operation plays a crucial role in any

---

[3]Pointing out that there are cases of pragmatic control still leaves open the question as to why this is so much more difficult that for the case of ordinary personal pronouns. I will not address this here; for some rather preliminary discussion of this see Jacobson 2007.

case in the variable-free system of Jacobson (1999), since it is also what allows an expression of category A/B to combine instead with a B that has an unbound proform within it (passing up the information that there is an unbound proform here). I will treat extraction quite similarly (space precludes discussion of the syntax), but in a case like (5) where *vote for* is missing its object (and so is of type $<e,<e,t>>$) we can assume that *will* has undergone the **g** rule, to map into an expression of type $<<e,et>,<e,et>>$. Its new meaning is thus $\lambda R_{<e,<e,t>>}[\lambda x[[[\text{will}]] (R(x))]]$. When it then takes $[[\text{vote-for}]]$ as object, the result is exactly as if *will* had function-composed with *vote for*. (Thus note that $\mathbf{g}(h)(f) = h \, o \, f$.) (5) then is put together by combining this to type-lifted and Geach'ed *Bill* (just as if it had function composed with the type-lifted meaning). In the end *(that) Bill will vote for* is an $<e,t>$ type meaning as we would want (which presumably then intersects with $[[\text{candidate}]]$).

What about the corresponding ACD case like (3)? This is just like normal ellipsis; the auxiliary $\mathbf{g}(will)$ can shift into a proform over VPs with gaps—hence over 2-place relations. (Again, see Jacobson (1992) for full details.) This is what we get in the corresponding "ACD" case in (1). At the end of the day, the sentence contains an "unbound proform" over VPs with gaps and its meaning is a function from 2-place relations to propositions, and it picks up the highly contextually salient *vote-for* relation.

4.3 The puzzle

Consider the paradigm in (6), which is a variant of facts in Kennedy (1994, 2007) (note that these are not to be taken on a "stacking" reading; in (6b), the bad reading is one where the relative clause *that BILL ~~voted for~~* modifies *girl* (and not *boy*)):

(6)   a.   Mary voted for every boy that BILL did ~~vote for~~.
     b.   *Mary voted for every boy who corresponds with a girl that BILL did ~~vote for~~.
     c.   *Mary voted for every girl who corresponds with a boy who lives next door to a boy that BILL did ~~vote for~~.

(These can be improved with the right context, which is to be expected from the final analysis here.[4] For more thorough discussion,

---

[4]Sauerland (2004) points out that these are improved if the heads are the same; thus, for example, (4) is much better than (6b), and (4), which is much like one of Sauerland's actual examples, is perhaps even better:

(i)   ?Mary voted for every boy who corresponds with a boy that BILL did.
(ii) ?John visited every lake that was next to a lake that BILL did.

see Jacobson 2004.) The point of departure for my discussion is the analysis in Heim (1997), who suggests that the problem is that (6b) and (6c) fail to satisfy the focus condition (without additional context), but (6a) does satisfy the focus condition (no additional context needed). I will claim that this is exactly right, but that Heim's implementation—which requires reference to representational properties in order to determine when the focus condition is and isn't satisfied—is not. Rather, an (independently motivated) revision of the focus condition combined with a close look at the actual meanings will be enough to flesh out the intuition.

At first glance, Heim's solution would appear to be a purely semantic one—since the focus condition itself is stated in terms of meanings. But it turns out that representations are actually crucial here. To elucidate Heim's solution, consider an LF for the bad case in (6b) which is akin to what we have been calling the "informal" LF:

(7)

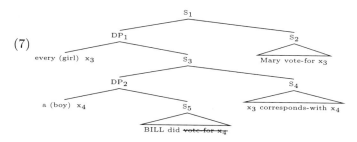

(The discussion here might seem somewhat confusing in that the *identity* condition is also not met here and so one might wonder why even

---

In Jacobson (2004) I argued out that the amelioration here is due precisely to the fact that these support the kinds of contexts which make such sentences good. Thus, with Heim (1997) I will suggest that the badness of (6b) and (6c) is due to an inability to satisfy Rooth's focus condition (Rooth, 1992b). This will be developed in more detail below; suffice it to say here that the reason that, for example, (4) is better than (6b) is that (4) allows us to imagine a background context where what is at issue is which of the boys different students voted for. In such a background context, we can be contrasting Mary's votees with Bill's votees. Indeed, with the right stress we can ameliorate cases like these even when the head nouns are not the same. Suppose that we are in a canoe club; each member has to canoe on at least one lake and at least one river in a certain region. I can report:

(iii) I canoed on the river that was next to the LAKE that BILL did.

Here the background question "at issue" is who canoed on which lakes/rivers, and so here ellipsis site is supported by an appropriate contrast. The remarks here are just informal; for fuller discussion see Jacobson (2004), and the full details of why these contexts provide appropriate amelioration should become clear after the analysis is developed in the subsequent sections of this paper.

bring up the focus condition. The reason is that ultimately Heim's analysis—like that of Sag (1976)—will actually have to allow the identity condition to ignore differences in variable names. We return to this below.) The key point here is that the only expression which could possibly be analyzed as C_{ELL} is S_4 (BILL did vote for x_4), and the alternatives to this are alternative propositions about who voted for x_4 . Thus the proposition that Mary voted for x_3 is not an alternative to this. (Note that, of course, these are actually assignment-function dependent propositions, but there are assignment functions such that $[[S_2]]$ is not a member of the focus value of S_5.) The insight, then, is that the Mary-votees and the Bill votees are in some sense not essentially connected (the way they are in the good case in (6a). Thus compare this to the good ACD case (6a). Continuing to use our "informal" representations, we see that we have the same variable and so there is no problem. (Of course we are for the moment calling these just "informal" representations, but as noted above we could still have the same variable in the more formal representation as shown in (3).

But there are key wrinkles that need to be addressed. The first, discussed in detail by Heim herself, is that we need a way to regulate the variable names such that we don't get accidental coindexation between two variables which are not really "the same". To show this for the "2-layered case" such as (6b) involves additional complications, and so it is easiest to exposit this point with reference to a "3-layered case" like (6c). Continuing with our informal LFs, the problem here is that nothing should block a representation like (8); yet here the focus (and the identity) condition is met, where C_{ANT} is S_2 and C_{ELL} is S_7:

(8)
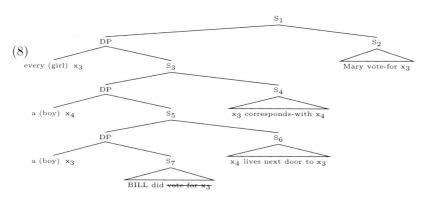

Heim thus proposes to rule out LFs of this sort with a condition against "accidental reuse" of variable names. This condition is given in (9):

(9) No Meaningless Coindexation: If an LF contains an occurrence of a variable v that is bound by a node α then all occurrences of v in this LF must be bound by the same node α.

Of course this does not mean anything without a definition of "bound". While Heim (1997) does not give such a definition, the discussion below is, I think, reasonably in keeping with the spirit of her proposal (and is similar, though not identical, to the discussion of this notion in HK). One could perhaps give a purely syntactic definition of this notion, but in keeping with the normal understanding of this notion we will define "bound" in terms of the semantic composition. To do that, we need to make explicit the interpretation of these LFs. It turns out that in fact what I am above calling the "informal" representation is closer to the LFs that Heim ultimately adopts, so let me spell this out using those representations. (The reason for using these, and not the HK-style representations as in (3) will become apparent shortly).

Suppose for the moment that we take the standard view of quantifiers that they take two <e,t> expressions as argument. Then assume that there is a semantic rule which takes as input LF structures like S_5 above, and does three things: (a) shifts the meaning of S_6 from an (assignment-function dependent) proposition to a set; (b) does the same for the meaning of S_7, and (c) take each set as argument of the quantifier (I ignore the head noun here). What do we mean by shifting the meaning of each sentence from propositions to sets? This is the "λ-abstraction" step. At the input, each sentence is an assignment-function dependent proposition. Take the set of assignment functions which differ only on the value that they assign to x_3 and call this set G_3. Then in general, the value of each of the sentences in question will be different for different members of G_3. Each is shifted, however, into an assignment-function dependent set, but in this case all members of G_3 will be mapped into the *same* set. This, of course, is what it means to "bind" or "close off" the variable x_3, and so this happens (given this particular semantics) at the level of the interpretation of S_5. Call the node which "binds" a variable x_i the lowest node whose interpretation is guaranteed to be constant on all members of G_i. Thus in this case the node which "binds" the occurrences of the x_3 within S_6 and S_7 is S_5. However, the full LF is ill-formed, because the occurrence of x_3 within S_2 is "bound" by S_1. Heim's condition is thus designed to rule this out.

Two points before continuing. As Heim notes, this view of "binding" within a domain means that it is crucial that we do *not* adopt representations along the lines of (3) shown above (the "HK style" representations). There, the λ-abstraction steps on both sentences do happen all at once when each sentence combines with the quantifier, but rather each sentence is separately and independently shifted from propositional to property meanings. Hence the two occurrences of x_3 are bound independently; one is bound by the node Λ_1 and the other by the node Λ_2, and so this too violates the "No Meaningless Coindexation" condition. But if LFs had to in general be of this form, (where the interpretation is such that each S separately shifts so that the variable is bound), and if (3) were ruled out, then VP Ellipsis would always be impossible! Not because the identity condition could not be met (since, as noted above, Heim's final solution will have to allow for different variable names), but because the focus condition could never be met. Hence she also adopts LFs which are closer to, e.g., (2) and (8). But a second point is that her interpretation of these is not as I have given here; she never shifts the meanings of the open Ss from a proposition. Rather, she takes these to always be propositions (thus, sets of assignment functions), and takes quantification to be over sets of assignment functions. That difference, however, is not really crucial to the discussion here since, as we see above, one can give an (albeit quite complex) procedure for interpreting LFs of this form without moving to the "Formulas hypothesis". (See Kennedy (2004) for related discussion)

In what sense is this solution representational? It is representational in two crucial ways. First, it crucially relies on LF representations as inputs to the semantics. Second, it relies on the No Meaningless Coindexation Constraint to regulate the representations. Actually the constraint itself as stated here is complex and should make us suspicious: for in order to know what "binds" a variable we need to actually consult the *interpretation* of the representations. Yet the work done by the constraint is to filter out certain representations (hence, it is a constraint on representation/meaning pairs). Of course one might attempt to recast it in purely representational terms (where "binding" is defined purely syntactically); such a constraint will still be on representations.

In addition to the complexity, there is one other suspicious aspect to this solution. Given the condition on no meaningless coindexation, it is necessary to allow the *identity condition* to ignore differences in variable names. This is necessary for all of the perfectly run-of-the-mill cases of sloppy identity, as in (the sloppy reading of) *John$_i$ loves his$_i$ mother, and BILL$_j$ does* ~~love his$_j$ mother~~ *too*. The two occurrences of *his* will have to correspond to different variables, as they are not bound by the same node. Note that the difference in variable names does not harm the focus condition because the domain meeting the focus condition is bigger (and is a domain in which they are already bound). The first conjunct is C_{ANT} and it is a member of the focus value of the second conjunct (which is C_{ELL}); the variables are not "open" in these. But the result that the grammar "ignores" the difference in variable names for the purposes of the identity condition is quite suspicious, since neither formal nor semantic identity is then met.

To be sure, Heim's analysis is not the last word here; different analyses and/or attempts to solve some of these problems are proposed in Fox (1999), Sauerland (2004) and Kennedy (2004) among others. Space precludes discussion of these, but in any case I am claiming that the basic insight in Heim's analysis is actually correct. I will, then, show below that it can be implemented without these difficulties, without representational constraints and, indeed, without the use of variables.

4.4 The lesson from antecedent contained *also*

The crux of my argument is that we find exactly parallel behavior in another case where it quickly becomes obvious that the solution has to lie entirely in the meanings of things, and that reliance on representational properties is doomed to failure. Thus we find an exactly parallel paradigm with respect to the behavior of *also* in an antecedent contained context:

(10) a. Mary voted for every boy that BILL also voted for.
  b. *Mary voted for every boy who corresponds with a boy that BILL also voted for.
  c. *Mary voted for every boy who corresponds with a girl who lives next door to a boy that BILL also voted for.

Two notes on these. First, I have indicated focal stress on BILL here. It is perhaps not required to be quite as prominent as in the case of ACD—and it is especially subtle since in fact *also* itself gets stress in these (which I have not indicated). Nonetheless, there does seem to be some stress on *Bill* in all of these, and so is notated throughout. Second, one can get things like (b) and (c) again with enough contextual support: that is where there is a background context such that the *also* is swallowing up some other background assumptions. But (10a) requires no special context, and this is what I mean by these contrasts here.

It is hard not to react to these contrasts by saying "Duh, it's the meanings, stupid!" and wondering why these even deserve comment. Obviously what is going on here has to do with their meanings: in (a) it somehow it follows that they are the same boys at issue, not so in (b) and (c). But to actually show how the semantics accounts for this is not so simple. Moreover, their parallel to ACD is striking, and we will see that once we have some handle on these, we are in a position to better understand the ACD contrasts. To really show the point, the strategy here will be to initially consider the contrasts in (10) under a rather "stupid" approach (not one that anyone would actually ever propose, but one that has an important analogue to the above representational approach to the ACD paradigm). Seeing what goes wrong and how to fix it will help illuminate what is going on in the ACD case.

For now, let us treat *also* as a sentential operator. Since we begin by fleshing out the analysis here in terms of the "standard" theory, we are free to assume that it raises to take an S in its scope, thus (11a) is mapped into the LF (11b):

(11) a. BILL also voted for Tom. $\longrightarrow$
      b. also [BILL voted for Tom]

Following Rooth (1985), we will assume that the value of an expression C is a pair $[[C]]$ (its "regular" value) and $[[C]]^{FOC}$, i.e. its focus value (a set of alternatives). We will further assume that *also* takes as arguments the full pair to return a regular value, and we will ignore the focus value of expressions of the form *also S*. Thus the interpretation of an expression *also S* is given in (12) (one could of course directly specify the meaning of *also* so that it takes the pair $<[[S]], [[S]]^{FOC}>$ as argument; I write (12) instead for expository ease:

(12) $[[also\ S]] = [[S]]$ if there is some other expression S' (in the discourse context) such that: (a) $[[S']]\ \varepsilon\ [[S]]^{FOC}$, (b) $[[S']] \neq [[S]]$, and (c) $[[S']]$ is true (at the relevant world and time). $[[also\ S]]$ is undefined otherwise.

Thus *also S* is defined only when the S has a focussed constituent within it (and hence a non-singleton focus value), and where there is some other sentence in the discourse context which is true and is a proper alternative to $[[S]]$.

Enter a sophisticated skeptic, who is immediately thinking the following: "Do we really want to require that there be a *linguistically overt S* whose meaning is the proper alternative? After all, this is a presupposition. Shouldn't we just require that the context contain a true proposition which is a member of the focus value of $[[S]]$ (and is distinct from $[[S]]$), and not worry about whether this proposition has been overtly expressed?" Of course the skeptic is exactly right. But recall that the project here is to go down the wrong path, so let us for now silence our skeptic, and continue to assume that the alternative has to have been expressed.

Consider, then, the following LF representation for (10a):

(13)

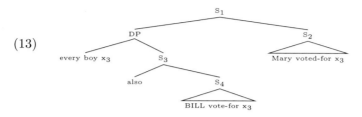

Our condition for interpreting S_3 is met and so $[[S_3]]$ (and the rest) is defined. This is because $[[S_2]]$ is a member of the focus value of S_4. Of course I am glossing over something fairly serious here: it is not enough for $[[S_3]]$ to be a member of the focus value of S_4; it must also be true. Whether or not it is depends on the assignment (in particular, the value assigned to x_3) so more needs to be said, but since we will be arguing that this is not really the right tack to take in the end I will gloss over this problem here.

The reason for insisting on the alternative proposition being the value of some *overt* expression is to try to pursue an explanation of the ungrammaticality of (10b) in a way that parallels Heim's explanation for the corresponding ACD case (6b). Thus let us consider the following LF for (10b):

(14)

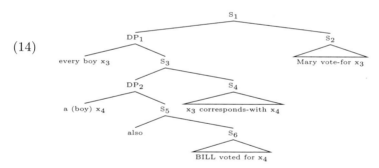

We are looking for some proper alternative to $[[S_6]]$. But here the truth of S_2 cannot possibly be relevant for *also*, since $[[S_2]]$ is not a member of the focus value of S_6. This is true, in short, because the are "about" different votees. Thus this is exactly parallel to Heim's story about the badness of ACD with (6b).

It should be obvious that to make the story work, we will need here too to adopt the convention on No Meaningless Coindexation. Again trying to show this for the two-layered case in (10b) introduces a few additional points into the discussion (see Jacobson (2004) for details), but the reader can convince themselves that this would be needed to rule out *also* in the case of (10c); the story here is again parallel to (6c). (The interested reader can fill in the details.)

But let us now listen to our enlightened skeptic, who points out that it is obviously misguided to look just at the representation of a little piece like S_2 in each case. This is because we need not just the existence of an expression with a certain meaning—but the expressed proposition *needs to be true*. (This is the difficulty which we suppressed earlier). This is the key difference between the case of *also* and the case of ACD: the latter just required something to be "salient"—not "true"—and so it becomes tempting to look at a small bit like S_2 since its truth is irrelevant.

But an analysis which fails to look globally at the *truth* of the relevant alternatives will clearly be doomed. After all, consider the contrasts in (15) which show that just looking at S_2 (which will be the same representation in all cases) cannot possibly be right:

(15) a. Mary voted for every boy that BILL also voted for.
     b. Mary voted for some boy that BILL also voted for.
     c. *Mary voted for no boy that BILL also voted for.

Moreover, we know independently that it would be odd to require the alternative proposition to have to be overtly expressed, since this is a presupposition. And indeed, it has been known for decades that the alternative need not be overt; consider the following (updated) classic case:

(16) John called Mary a friend of Cheney's. BILL also insulted her.

Of course we could now revise (12) to say that the relevant overt expression S′ must either have as its meaning an alternative to the focus value of *also*'s sister or must *imply (possibly pragmatically)* such an alternative. (See Rooth's focus condition, to which we will return.) But in fact the presupposition (not surprisingly) need not come from anything which is linguistically overt. Suppose I see my friend Chris about to try to ski down Inferno on cross-country skis, I can—with no other sentences having been introduced in the discourse—turn to you and say: You know—BODE also tried that.

In light of this, we should revise (12) as follows:

(17) [[also S]] = [[S]] if there is a proposition p in the discourse context such that: (a)) p ε [[S]]^{FOC}, (b) p $\neq$ [[S]], and (c) p is true (at the relevant world and time).
    [[also S]] is undefined otherwise.

The only question, then, is whether this will all work out when *also* is within a relative clause as in (10a), and where *also* is contained within something which will constitute the alternative.

The answer is yes. And in fact we could just as easily show this using the "standard" kinds of LFs shown here: the point is that we won't need to worry about constraints on alphabetic variants because everything will be a property of the meanings. (This in fact will be spelled out in Jacobson in preparation.) But rather than show this using the standard account, I will spell it out under a direct compositional and variable-free account. The reason is not because the standard account cannot succeed, but because I wish to ultimately show that this entire domain (including the ACD case) provides no evidence *against* a direct compositional view (and also no evidence for variable names which, note, were quite crucial in Heim's analysis).

Before continuing, I will make one expository simplification—which is to continue to treat *also* as a sentential modifier and pretend that it is actually "raised" as in the treatment above. This of course is a cheat: *also* in the sentences at issue shows up as a VP modifier and "raising" it at LF is obviously not possible if there is no LF. But this "cheat" is harmless: one can simply take the lexical meaning of *also* to be the "Geach'ed" version of what it would mean if it were a sentential operator (the meaning of the latter is spelled out below in (18).) But since this adds more λs to the formulas making them that much harder to read, I will make this expository simplification and pretend that it is in pre-sentential position.

To show how to account for the paradigm in (10), we need two background pieces both of which, I believe, can be motivated independently. First, consider an expression with a "gap" in it such as *(who) BILL likes*, or an expression with a pronoun unbound within it, such as *BILL likes him* (which, given the apparatus in Jacobson (1999) is of category S^{NP}). In Jacobson (1999) I claimed that for both, the regular semantic value is of type <e,t>. But what is its focus value? There are actually two possibilities. One is that it is a set of alternative functions of type <e,t>. The second is that it is a function from individuals to a set of alternative propositions. The analysis here rests crucially on the assumption that (b) is correct. At the moment I have to leave it as a promissory note that the combinatorics can be worked out so as to get this effect. Hopefully, though, the reader will agree with my intuition that this is what we would expect and is the "natural" way to think about things. Notice that one can think of this result as taking a cue from what *does* work out nicely with variables: the name of an unbound variable remains constant in both the regular semantic value and in all of the alternatives to some expression; in a sense the variable name (or assignment function) has widest scope over everything. The idea that the focus value is a function from individuals to alternatives in cases of expressions with unbound pronouns (or gaps) within them is a way to capture that same intuition.

The second background assumption relies on generalizing the **g** rule, a move with independent motivation which will be discussed in Jacobson (in preparation) but which in any case seems quite natural. The **g** rule as stated earlier maps a function of type $<a,b>$ into one of type $<<c,a>,<c,b>>$. But it is easy enough to generalize this to n-place functions. Illustrating with just the 2-place case, a function f of type $<a,<b,d>>$ would be mapped into a function h of type $<<c,a>,<<c,b>,<c,d>>>$ where $h = \lambda X_{<c,a>}[\lambda Y_{<c,b>}[\lambda C_c[f(X(c)) (Y(c))]]]$. (It is interesting to note that one can derive the polymorphic *and* of Partee and Rooth (1983) by simply thinking of the base case as being of type $<t,<t,t>>$ and noting that all of the other cases are simply the application of generalized **g** to this.)

This is all we need. Note that above we gave a direct semantic rule interpreting expressions of the form *also S*, but let us now just give a meaning instead for *also*. As noted earlier, [[also]] is taking a pair as argument: the "regular" meaning and the focus value. In other words, it takes a pair $<p.S>$ as argument, where S is a set of propositions. Let us Curry this, so that [[also]] is as follows (I again ignore the focus value of the result):

(18) $\lambda p[\lambda S[p$ iff $\exists p'$ such that p' is true and $p' \neq p$ and $p \varepsilon S]]$

(where the combinatorics are set up such that the sister of *also* will be such that its regular value will be the first argument of this and its focus value will be the second). Then the generalized **g** rule will apply to this to yield an item which wants to combine with an S|NP or an S^{NP} and whose meaning is:

(19) $\lambda P_{<e,t>}[\lambda Z_{<e,<t,t>>}[\lambda x [[[also]] (P(x))(Z(x))]]$

We are now ready to consider a relative clause like *(who) BILL also voted for* which we will conveniently represent as *(who) also BILL voted for*. The apparatus above gives the right result when **g**(*also*) (i.e., 19) combines with *BILL voted for*. Thus this takes as input the set that Bill voted for and the function Z which maps individuals into sets of propositions about various people voting for that individual. It returns something which maps an individual to true if Bill did vote for them, and if the function Z applied to them yields a set which contains a proposition (about someone other than Bill voting for them) which is true in the discourse context. In short, then, *(who) also BILL voted for* maps an individual x to true if Bill voted for that individual and we can assume that someone else did, false if Bill didn't but someone else did, and is undefined for all other individuals.

Our task is to explain why (10a) is fine, even with no prior context. Assume that the set taken as argument of *every* or any other determiner must be non-empty for the DP to be defined (this assumption is not actually crucial, as far as I can tell, but it makes the exposition much simpler). Thus in (10a), the set *boy that BILL also voted for* must be non-empty. Let x be in that set, then it follows that it must be in the set *[[(that) BILL also voted for]]*. As noted above, it can be in that set only if both Bill voted for that person and the context supplies the information that someone else did. But in virtue of the meaning of the entire sentence, it follows that for any such x, Mary voted for that x. Granted, there is a very interesting question about how the full computation proceeds in that the presupposition is satisfied in virtue of the meaning of the entire sentence. (In short, there is a true antecedent containment puzzle with respect to the interaction of the presupposition and the computation of the relative clause.) How exactly to allow the presupposition generated by the matrix to be satisfied within the relative clause will be left open here. But it is clear that this problem is not some artifact of this analysis.[5]

The same sort of point will hold for (15b). There must be some individuals that Bill voted for, in order for the entire sentence to be defined. But for at least one such individual, the global semantics insures that Mary voted for that individual, hence the use of *also* in the relative clause is such that the relative clause will be defined for at least one individual, and so nothing is amiss.

Now consider instead (15c), where the determiner is *no*. Assume that there are individuals that Bill voted for. Are we guaranteed (in virtue of this sentence alone, with no prior context) that there is any such individual that someone else voted for, such that the conditions for *also* are met? Indeed not, which is why this sentence would be good only with additional context. Note that an interesting case is supplied by about (20) (pointed out to me by Chris Barker) which is somewhat intermediate:

---

[5] Hans Kamp points out to me that exactly the same questions arise with respect to a case like *I'll go if you'll go too*. Notice that this case (and the corresponding case discussed in the text) does not reduce to the simple case of the antecedent of the conditional supplying the presupposition (as in *If John has a son, his son is bald*); in the conditional case here the presupposition is satisfied by the entire clause and is relevant to the well-formedness of the antecedent. And this is parallel to the case of the matrix supplying the presupposition relevant to the well-formedness of the relative clause.

(20) ?Mary voted for few boys that BILL also voted for.

Here the presupposition comes from the implicature of *few*.

Let us now return to our key case which was parallel to the Kennedy puzzle case:

(10) b. *Mary voted for every boy that lives next door to a boy that BILL also voted for.

Let x be a boy that Bill voted for. Can we conclude on the basis of this sentence alone that someone else voted for that boy? Of course not. Thus there is no guarantee that there is any x such that the relative clause would be defined for that x. With no additional context, then, *that BILL also voted for* is not guaranteed to be defined for anyone, which makes the entire sentence undefined.

The important point is that this all follows purely semantically, with no reference to representational properties of subparts of these sentences. Of course we do need a way to talk about the effect of *also* when it combines with a sentence with a "gap" in it (as in these relative clauses) and about the focus values of such sentences, but as we saw above this is not difficult to do under a variable-free account.

4.5 Back to the ACD case

In light of the striking similarity in the paradigms in (6) (the ACD cases) and (10) (the "antecedent contained *also*" cases), it is natural to wonder whether the lesson from *also* can help us in the analysis of the ACD case. The answer, not surprisingly, is that it can: we need only realize that in ACD (and in ellipsis in general), the meaning which contrasts with that of C_{ELL} (in Rooth's terms) need not be the meaning of anything overt. The requirement is simply that it be salient in the discourse context. With that, we can use most of the mechanisms already in place for *also* to account for the contrast between, e.g, (6a) and (6b).

Before continuing, I will state at the outset that the analysis here is not complete. There are pieces which remain stipulative or not fully worked out, and perhaps the most frustrating part is my inability at this point to give a completely general and formalized definition of what it means to be "salient". But I do think that many of these loose ends apply equally well to any corresponding "standard" account and thus in need of an answer on any theory. In particular, I think that some of the loose ends here derive simply from an incomplete understanding of *why* something like the focus condition (or the analogue of it which will be proposed below) should hold.

To work out a sketch of the analysis, we will begin by making use of a "silent" operator $\sim$ to indicate the scope of contrastive focus. The use of $\sim$ is, of course, based on the operator in Rooth (1992a), although my $\sim$ and his are not exactly the same. (I will not have space to discuss the detailed differences.) Note that one might immediately object that the use of a silent "operator" or lexical item seems to violate at least the spirit of a direct compositional analysis. But I will return to this below, to show that one can always recast such a creature as a meaning shift rule (though the recasting does have some interesting implications). For now, then, let us adopt $\sim$ as a silent lexical item which at some level combines with an expression that contains an occurrence of contrastive focus (and hence has a non-singleton focus value). The system will be set up in some way as to require this to combine with such an expression at some level; its job is to make sure that focus "does something" and it makes undefined any expression that contains contrastive focal stress within it but where there is no actual salient alternative in the discourse context. Thus—again taking some liberties with Rooth (1992a)—we can for the moment adopt (21) as the interpretation of $\sim$ (as with our first version of *also*, we are giving an interpretation of the structure [$\sim$ C]; later we will come back and pack all of the work directly into the meaning of $\sim$):

(21) $[[\sim C]] = [[C]]$ if there is another expression C′ in the discourse context such that $[[C']]\ \varepsilon\ [[C]]^{FOC}$ and $[[C']] \neq [[C]]$.
$[[\sim C]]$ is undefined otherwise

Thus $\sim$ will ensure that there is some salient proper alternative to C in the discourse context. Recall Rooth's focus condition on VP Ellipsis, which we restate here as (22):

(22) VP$_{ELL}$ must be contained within a constituent C$_{ELL}$ such that there is a C$_{ANT}$ which contains VP$_{ANT}$ and which is such that $[[C_{ANT}]]$ *or something which follows (possibly pragmatically) from* $[[C_{ANT}]]$ is a member of $[[C_{ELL}]]^{FOC}$ and is not identical to $[[C_{ELL}]]$.

In other words, ignoring the material in italics for the moment, $[[C_{ANT}]]$ must be a proper alternative to $[[C_{ELL}]]$.

But given that the definition of $\sim$ in (11) ensures that there is a linguistically overt expression whose meaning is a proper alternative to the expression that $\sim$ combines with, we could (essentially) recast (22) as simply (23):

(23) Ellipsis is licensed only if it is in the scope of $\sim$.

This is not a completely faithful translation of (22) in two respects (a) it leaves out the italicized material in (23), a fact to which I will return, and (b) it does not enforce any connection between VP_{ANT} and C_{ANT}. But I see no harm done by this and no reason to do this (especially since in the end we are actually not requiring there to be any VP_{ANT}).[6] So this says that ellipsis is licensed only when contained within some expression C which is such that there is another expression in the discourse context whose meaning is a proper alternative to C. (Thus C will have to have focal stress somewhere in order to have a non-singleton set of alternatives.)

Alarm bells should be ringing here for any serious direct compositionalist—for (23) is not at all the kind of statement that could be stated under such a theory. Indeed, I consider (23) simply to be a placeholder for a more adequate account, in at least three respects. First, "~" should probably be recast as directly as a meaning shift rule, but as noted above, this will be done later. Second, grammars have no notion of things like "ellipsis" and cannot refer to such a notion. In fact we are assuming that "VP ellipsis" (including ACD) is simply the occurrence of a VP (or, VP with a gap) anaphor. So what does it mean to "license" it in a particular place? I will not only leave this open for now, but will in fact flesh out the analysis under a view in which there is actual (silent)_ material in the ellipsis site (rather than having

---

[6]A referee objects that there is still a generalization missed by having no enforced connection between VP_{AND} and C_{ANT}. Thus the referee claims that: "Certainly the following descriptive generalization seems systematic enough to require an explanation:

> Whenever the C_ant that is relevant for the focus condition corresponds to an overt clause, there is a VP_ant within the C_ant that provides the content of the elided VP."

I am sympathetic with this worry, but I am not sure that there is any problem here. Except in those cases where the overt C_{ANT} supplies the relevant contrasting indirectly, it will follow that it has to contain a VP which is identical to that of the content of the elided VP, simply because everything within C_{ANT} will be parallel to everything within C_{ELL}, except for the focussed constituent in C_{ELL}. The place to look for a problem would be the case where C_{ANT} provides the requisite contrast indirectly. But in fact many of the cases where there is no overt antecedent are of just this type: we can construct a contrast indirectly from some antecedent expression in the discourse, but this does not directly supply a VP whose meaning is that of the elided material. Take, for example, the famous examples from Webber (1978):

(i) John wants to go to Paris and Mary wants to go to Berlin, but neither of them WILL.

C_{ANT} is presumably the conjunction *John wants to go to Paris and Mary wants to go to Berlin* which taken together sets up the contrasting relevant proposition "at issue" which is the proposition both of John and Mary go to the place that s/he wants to go to; the contrasting proposition C_{ELL} is that both of them in fact do not go to the place that s/he wants to go to. Thus there is an overt C_{ANT} here which supplies the contrast indirectly, but it does not contain an overt VP_{ANT} which supplies the content of the ellipsis site.

the auxiliary be a proform). That is, I will represent the compositional semantics of what I will be calling "C_{ELL}" (the constituent containing the "ellipsis site" or anaphor) as if there really were material in that site. I have already said that I am actually rejecting this. so this move should not be taken as the final analysis here. It does, however, simplify the exposition—but the reader should be aware that ultimately the analysis will need to be fine-tuned to remove this aspect. And third,—and of most relevance to the project of direct compositionality—there is no way under such a theory to say that "ellipsis" (whatever it may be) must be "in the scope" of something else. How can the presence of an anaphor (or even silent material) know anything about what it is contained in? So that too will need to ultimately be answered. I suspect, however, that both the second and the third problems here are really just part and parcel of a bigger question: *why* does any analogue of the focus condition hold? My hope is that the real story will lie in a better understanding of how it is that the listener picks up contextually salient meanings when they are properties (or two-place relations), and that these themselves are made salient by appropriate contrasts. This would be the beginning of an explanation of the relationship between the kind of anaphora found here and the need for it to be within a larger expression which has a salient contrasting object. But I will have nothing more concrete to say about this at this point. Note, though, that the need to explain more fully the "focus condition" arises under any account. Rooth's condition itself (which we will be revising) is also purely stipulative and should obviously follow (regardless of one's theory) from something else.

With these caveats, we can return to our recasting of the focus condition so as to seriously consider the italicized portion in (22). Recall that $[[C_{ANT}]]$ need not actually <u>be</u> a proper alternative to $[[C_{ELL}]]$, it can just "imply" it (possibly pragmatically—that is, in conjunction with other assumptions). Rather than build a change into the focus condition itself, we can instead assume that the culprit is $\sim$, and that the $\sim$ should be revised. To get at this result, we could revise the interpretation of $\sim$ as follows:

(24) $[[\sim C]] = [[C]]$ if there is another expression C' in the discourse context such that $[[C']]$ or some other meaning (i.e., model-theoretic object) X which follows from $[[C']]$ (either by entailment or other assumptions) ε $[[C]]^{FOC}$ and X $\neq$ $[[C]]$.
      $[[\sim C]]$ is undefined otherwise

But now (partly recalling the earlier discussion about *also*) the question arises: do we really want to require there to be an overt C'? The answer is most certainly not. In the first place, even given the rest of the assumptions in Rooth this would make little sense. After all, to say that the proper alternative X can follow from $[[C']]$ plus other background assumptions makes the role of C' almost vacuous. Given enough background, anything can follow from $[[C']]$—which means that the role of requiring an overt C' does nothing except to say that there must be something overt somewhere, which is an unlikely condition on VP Ellipsis. Second, we've seen that VP Ellipsis does not in fact require an overt antecedent. So if there does not need to be an actual VP_{ANT} there certainly cannot be a requirement on the existence of a C_{ANT} since the latter is defined in terms of the former. And third, even independently of the role of $\sim$ in VP Ellipsis, the fact is that contrastive focus can be licensed by non-overt material. I could watch my dog Kolya wildly rolling in the snow and turn to you and, with no prior linguistic material, say "MITKA [my other dog] doesn't do that".

We can thus give one more revision of $\sim$, as follows:

(25) $[[\sim C]] = [[C]]$ if there is a contextually salient X (i.e., some model-theoretic object) such that $X \varepsilon [[C]]^{FOC}$ and $X \neq C$.
   $[[\sim C]]$ is undefined otherwise.

Thus the role of $\sim$ is to filter out the interpretation of expressions which have this but where there is no proper alternative which is "salient".

There is, then, one final piece of all this which needs to be made more precise: what do we mean by "contextually salient"? This is particularly pressing in view of the fact that $\sim$ can combine with a variety of expressions (and hence of semantic types), and so salience will need to be defined rather generally. Here, however, we are concerned only with cases where $\sim$ combines with sentential type constituents (including Ss with pronouns or gaps), and hence the basic case concerns cases where propositions are salient. As a first pass, then, let us say that a proposition p is salient in the discourse context if its truth or falsity is, minimally, a question under discussion. Undoubtedly there are other ways in which a proposition can be salient, but I think that this will serve for the present purposes.

Given this, we have the ingredients to give an account of the ACD paradigm in (6) in a way parallel to what we did with *also*. The trick is simply that we are looking for a salient alternative rather than a true alternative. But the rest of the analysis will be the same. First, as we did earlier with *also*, we will give the definition of $\sim$ itself, where we will take it as a Curry'ed function which takes a pair of a regular meaning and a focus value (and again ignore the focus output).

(26) $[[\sim]] = \lambda Z_a \ [\lambda W_{<a,t>}$ [Z if there is a contextually salient X such that $W(X)$, and undefined otherwise]]

We will be concerned here only with the case where $\sim$ occurs with something basically sentential (including a sentence with an extraction gap or a pronoun), and so its arguments will (like those of *also*) be a proposition and a set of propositions. Thus in the case where it combines with an S with an extraction gap or an S with a pronoun, it undergoes the generalized **g** rule, and is, therefore (27)

(27) $\mathbf{g}(\sim) = \lambda A_{<e,t>} \ [\ \lambda K_{<e,<t,t>>} \ [\lambda x \sim (A(x))(K(x))]]$

Thus consider $\sim$ *(that) BILL voted for*. Here $\sim$ applies to the following pair: <set of individuals that Bill voted for; function from individuals x to propositions that of the form a voted for x, for all (relevant) a>. Thus the second member of the pair is a function which maps Tom into a set of propositions Mary voted for Tom, Sue voted for Tom, Bill voted for Tom, ... and so forth for each other individual. Applying $\mathbf{g}(\sim)$ to such a pair has the effect that the set denoted by the relative clause must contain a member that Bill voted for, and must also be an individual for whom there is some question under discussion as to whether or not someone else did.

Let us take each of the following sentences in turn:

(28) a. Mary voted for every candidate that BILL did ~~vote for~~.
      b. Mary voted for no candidate that BILL did ~~vote for~~.
      c. Mary voted for exactly half of the candidates that BILL did ~~vote for~~.
      d. Mary voted for some candidate that BILL did ~~vote for~~.

In (a) through (c) it is obvious that for each candidate that Bill voted for, it matters whether or not Mary did (since Mary's voting for such a candidate is crucial to the truth of the whole sentence). In (d) the situation is a little bit more complex, but it is obvious that for the sentence to be true it must be the case that there is some candidate that Bill voted for and that it is salient that Mary did. (This does present some difficulty in formalizing, since if Mary and Bill voted for three of the same candidates then for any single candidate one could argue that it is not crucial and hence not relevant that Mary voted for that candidate. But I take this problem to simply show that we need to formalize this better: it is quite obvious that what is going on in (d) is that candidate-by-candidate that Bill voted for, Mary's voting or not for that candidate is potentially relevant.) Essentially the same story could be told for any determiner here, since they all denote a relation between the Mary-vote-for set and the Bill-vote-for set, and since they can all be defined in terms of the intersection of these sets. Thus in all of these cases *(that)* $\sim$ *(BILL voted for)* will be defined, and needs no prior contextual assumptions in order to be defined. Of course again this is like the case with *also*: the salient alternative allowing the presupposition of $\sim$ within the relative clause to be satisfied comes from the matrix, posing an interesting problem about presupposition (downward) projection. But this is independent of the framework here.

But now take a bad ACD case like (10b):

(10) b. *Mary voted for every boy that lived next door to a girl that
           BILL did ~~vote for~~.

We are looking at the set *that* $\sim$ *BILL did vote for*. This will be defined only for those individuals for whom there is some question under discussion as to whether or not someone else voted for them. But—without additional context—there are no individuals for whom it is guaranteed that anything hinges on whether or not anyone else voted for them. The difference between this and (10a) is precisely the intuition that the individuals are the "same" in (10a) and not in (10b). In both cases, each individual that Bill voted for gets to "count" for the definition of *that* $\sim$ *BILL voted for* only if the matrix supplies information about someone else voting for that person. In (10a) it does. In (10b) it doesn't; it supplies information about who Mary voted for but there is no claim made about any connection between Mary's votees and Bill's votees. (Note that the same fact holds if we substituted *boy* for *girl* as head of the relative clause in (10b). In fact, Sauerland (2004) claims that this substitution crucially redeems (10b). While it does improve it, it does not make it perfect; for much more extensive discussion of this see Jacobson (2004)).

The claim, then, is that Heim's intuition about the difference between (10a) and (10b) is exactly right. But the way to "track" the individuals is not through the use of variable names, since this succeeds only if we adopt a complex constraint on the representations which blocks "accidental" reuse of the variable names. If, instead, we directly track the individuals—and consider the focus value of the relative clause to be function from individuals to alternative propositions, we can directly check the individuals and see whether or not there is some salient alternative proposition of relevance to that individual.

Finally, let me conclude with a brief remark about the use of $\sim$. One can always trade in a "silent" lexical item for a shift rule, and here one could instead recast the meaning of $\sim$ as such a rule. What is interesting about this is that we have made use of applying a further shift to $\sim$; crucially this underwent the **g** rule. If the effect of $\sim$ were instead taken to be a shift rule, this would mean we would need a system in which the operations themselves were mapped into other operations. This, I believe, actually is probably warranted anyway within this (and related) systems, but I will leave this here for future investigation.

References

Chomsky, Noam. 1976. Conditions on Rules of Grammar. *Linguistic Analysis* 2(4):303–351.

Cormack, Annabel. 1984. VP Anaphora: Variables and Scope. In F. Landman and F. Veltman, eds., *Varieties of Formal Semantics*, pages 81–102. Dordrecht: Reidel.

Dalrymple, Mary, Stuart M. Shieber, and Fernando C. N. Pereira. 1991. Ellipsis and Higher Order Unification. *Linguistics and Philosophy* 14(4):399–452.

Evans, Frederic. 1988. Binding into Anaphoric Verb Phrases. In J. Powers and K. de Jong, eds., *Proceedings of ESCOL 5*, pages 122–129. Columbus: Ohio State University.

Fox, Danny. 1999. Focus, Parallelism, and Accommodation. In T. Matthews and D. Strolovitch, eds., *Proceedings of the Ninth Conference on Semantics and Linguistic Theory*. Cornell: CLC Publications.

Hankamer, Jorge and Ivan Sag. 1976. Deep and Surface Anaphora. *Linguistic Inquiry* 7:391–426.

Hardt, Daniel. 1993. *VP Ellipsis: Form, Meaning, and Processing*. Ph.D. thesis, University of Pennsylvania.

Heim, Irene. 1997. Predicates or Formulas? Evidence from Ellipsis. In A. Lawson and E. Cho, eds., *Proceedings of the Seventh Conference on Semantics and Linguistic Theory*. Cornell: CLC Publications.

Heim, Irene and Angelika Kratzer. 1998. *Semantic Interpretation in Generative Grammar*. Malden: Blackwell.

Jacobson, Pauline. 1992. Antecedent Contained Deletion in a Variable-Free Semantics. In C. Barker and D. Dowty, eds., *Proceedings of the Second Conference on Semantics and Linguistic Theory*, pages 193–213. Columbus: Ohio State Working Papers in Linguistics.

Jacobson, Pauline. 1999. Towards a Variable-Free Semantics. *Linguistics and Philosophy* 22:117–184.

Jacobson, Pauline. 2003. Binding without pronouns (and pronouns without binding). In G.-J. Kruiff and R. Oehrle, eds., *Binding and Resource Sensitivity*. Dordrecht: Kluwer Academic Publishers.

Jacobson, Pauline. 2004. Kennedy's Puzzle: What I'm Named or Who I Am? In R. Young, ed., *Proceedings of the Fourteenth Conference on Semantics and Linguistic Theory*. Cornell: CLC Publications.

Jacobson, Pauline. 2007. Direct Compositionality and Variable Free Semantics: The Case of Antecedent Contained Ellipsis. In K. Johnson, ed., *Topics in Ellipsis*. Cambridge: Cambridge University Press.

Kennedy, Chris. 1994. Argument Contained Ellipsis. *Linguistic Research Center Report LRC 94-03*. Santa Cruz: UC Santa Cruz.

Kennedy, Chris. 2004. Argument Contained Ellipsis Revisited. Unpublished MS, University of Chicago.

Kennedy, Chris. 2007. Argument Contained Ellipsis. In K. Johnson, ed., *Topics in Ellipsis*. Cambridge University Press.

Merchant, Jason. 2000. *The Syntax of Silence*. Oxford: Oxford University Press.

Montague, Richard. 1974. The Proper Treatment of Quantification in Ordinary English. In R. Thomason, ed., *Formal Philosophy: Selected Papers of Richard Montague*. New Haven: Yale University Press.

Partee, Barbara and Mats Rooth. 1983. Generalized Conjunction and Type Ambiguity. In R. Bäuerle, C. Schwarze, and A. von Stechow, eds., *Meaning, Use, and the Interpretation of Language*, pages 361–383. Berlin: de Gruyter.

Rooth, Mats. 1985. *Association with Focus*. Ph.D. thesis, University of Massachusetts.

Rooth, Mats. 1992a. A Theory of Focus Interpretation. *Natural Language Semantics* 1:75–116.

Rooth, Mats. 1992b. Ellipsis Redundancy and Reduction Redundancy. In S. Berman and A. Hestvik, eds., *Proceedings of the Stuttgart Ellipsis Workshop*. Stuttgart: University of Stuttgart.

Sag, Ivan. 1976. *Deletion and Logical Form*. Ph.D. thesis, MIT.

Sauerland, Uli. 2004. The Interpretation of Traces. *Natural Language Semantics* 12:63–127.

Steedman, Mark. 1987. Combinatory Grammars and Parasitic Gaps. *Natural Language and Linguistic Theory* 5:403–439.

Webber, Bonnie. 1978. *A Formal Approach to Discourse Anaphora*. Ph.D. thesis, Harvard University.

5

Approximate Interpretations of Number Words: A Case for Strategic Communication*

MANFRED KRIFKA

5.1 Round Numbers and Round Interpretations

In Switzerland, one can find street signs like the one near Zürich airport that tells the car driver that there is a stop sign 103 meters down the road. Visitors are struck by this and consider it typical for the land of bankers and watchmakers because it appears so ridiculously precise. But why? Why would a sign that says that there is a stop sign 100 meters down the road be considered unremarkable? Why is *100 meters* interpreted less precise than *103 meters*?

In the United States, one occasionally finds street signs that give distances in miles and in kilometers, in an effort to make the public familiar with the metric system. A sign of this type might read: *Eagle*

---

*I had the opportunity to present various precursors of this paper at a number of conferences, including *Sinn & Bedeutung* 2001 in Amsterdam, the annual meeting of the *Deutsche Gesellschaft für Sprachwissenschaft* in Munich 2002, the Workshop on *Cognitive Foundations of Interpretation* at the Royal Academy of Science of the Netherlands (KNAW) in 2004, and the *West Coast Conference in Formal Lingustics* in Berkeley in 2007. A version of this paper was published at the proceedings of the KNAW conference, see Krifka (2007). I would like to express my thanks to numerous suggestions and critiques that helped me to develop the points presented here, in particular by David Beaver, Anton Benz, Reinhard Blutner, Peter Bosch, Regine Eckardt, Gerhard Jäger, Jason Mattausch, Robert van Rooy, Philippe Schlenker, Uli Sauerland, Torgrim Solstad, Theo Vennemann, Henk Zeevat and three anonymous reviewers.

Pass. 7 miles. 11.265 kilometers. Evidently, the educational effect of such signs is limited because they suggest that the metric system might be suitable for scientists, but not for ordinary folks. But why? Why is *7 miles* interpreted as less precise than *11.265 kilometers*?

The phenomenon illustrated by these examples is well known. In Krifka (2002) I called this the Round Numbers Round Interpretation (RNRI) principle:

(1) RNRI principle:
Round number words tend to have a round interpretation in measuring contexts.

The RNRI principle is far too specific to be an irreducible axiom of language use. How can we derive it from more general principles?

In Krifka (2002) I tried to show that this is possible within the framework of Bidirectional Optimality Theory. In the present article, I will point out various problems with this account and propose a more convincing explanation. But first I will turn to my previous theory.

5.2 A General Preference for Approximate Interpretations?

The explanation of the RNRI phenomenon in Krifka (2002) runs as follows:

First, there is a well-known pragmatic principle of economy that prefers simple expression over complex ones. This principle has been identified by numerous researchers, and is most prominently expressed in the Principle of Least Effort in Zipf (1929). In the Neo-Gricean theories of Horn (1984) and Levinson (2000), it has been captured by the R-Principle and I-Principle, respectively. These principles express that the speaker should say only as much as necessary in order to be understood, as the hearer will fill in information that is not expressed. In the Swiss street sign example, this will lead to a preference of the simple number term *one hundred* over *one hundred and three*, provided that *one hundred* can be interpreted in an approximate way.

Secondly, I assumed a principle that prefers approximate interpretations over precise ones. Something like this principle has been proposed before occasionally, and can be motivated in various ways. For example, Duhem (1904) speaks of a balance between precision and certainty; if one wants to increase the latter, one has to decrease the former, and so it might be prudent to be imprecise. Ochs Keenan (1976) has argued, quite similarly, that speakers (in her case, the population of rural Madagascar) might prefer vagueness over precision in order to save face in case what they said turns out to be not true. We also can argue that a more coarse-grained representation of information might be cognitively less costly than a more fine-grained one. It is easier to remember that the speed of light is 300,000 kilometers per second than to remember that it is 299,792,458 meters per second. Also, digital watches met with less than total success, partly because they present too much information, compared to analog ones. In general, I argued, we have the following pragmatic preferences, one for linguistic forms and one for their interpretation.

(2) SIMPEXP: simple expression > complex expression

(3) APPRINT: approximate interpretation > precise interpretation

These two pragmatic principles interact in the way proposed in Bidirectional Optimality Theory, cf. Blutner (2000) and Jäger (2002). That is, pairs of expressions and interpretations, or forms and meanings $\langle F, M \rangle$, are compared, and among various candidates the optimal pairs are selected according to the following rule:

(4) A form-meaning pair $\langle F, M \rangle$ is optimal iff
    a. there is no optimal pair $\langle F', M \rangle$ such that $\langle F', M \rangle > \langle F, M \rangle$
    b. there is no optimal pair $\langle F, M' \rangle$ such that $\langle F, M' \rangle > \langle F, M \rangle$

This type of interaction has been invoked to explain so-called M(arkedness)-implicatures (cf. Levinson 2000), according to which a marked expression receives a marked interpretation.

The RNRI phenomenon can be explained in the following way. Consider the following four form-meaning pairs as candidates to be evaluated by the constraints SIMPEXP and APPRINT:

(5) ⟨*one hundred*, precise⟩
    ⟨*one hundred*, approximate⟩
    ⟨*one hundred and three*, precise⟩
    ⟨*one hundred and three*, approximate⟩

Clearly, ⟨*one hundred*, approximate⟩ is an optimal pair because there is no other pair that is better, hence there is no other **optimal** pair that is better:

(6) a. ⟨*one hundred*, approximate⟩ > ⟨*one hundred*, precise⟩,
        due to APPRINT
    b. ⟨*one hundred*, approximate⟩ > ⟨*one hundred and three*, approximate⟩,
        due to SIMPEXP

From (6) it follows that ⟨*one hundred,* precise⟩ and ⟨*one hundred and three*, approximate⟩ are not optimal. But then ⟨*one hundred and three*, precise⟩ is an optimal pair, as it does not compete with any optimal pair: It does not compete with ⟨*one hundred,* approximate⟩, and the pairs it does compete with, ⟨*one hundred*, precise⟩ and ⟨*one hundred and three*, approximate⟩, are not optimal.

We can summarize the preference structure in the following diagram:

	Simple Expression	Complex Expression
Approximate Interpretation	⟨*Simple, Approx*⟩ ←	⟨*Complex, Approx*⟩
Precise Interpretation	⟨*Simple, Precise*⟩ ←	⟨*Complex, Precise*⟩

TABLE 1

The pair ⟨Complex, Precise⟩ is an optimal pair because the two competing pairs ⟨Simple, Precise⟩ and ⟨Complex, Approx⟩ are preferred, but they are themselves not optimal.

5.3 A Conditional Preference for Simple Expressions?

In this section I will address two arguments against the theory developed in Krifka (2002), by showing that they can be countered by another theory that accounts for the RNRI phenomenon.

The first objection is that one of the four form/interpretation pairs in (5) should be out of consideration. There is no situation in which the pairs ⟨*one hundred*, precise⟩ and ⟨*one hundred and three,* precise⟩ can compete with each other from the perspective of the speaker, as the two pairs are not applicable in the same situation. If the actual distance is 103 meters, we would have to remove the pair ⟨*one hundred,* precise⟩ from the optimization process. The algorithm in (4) still would identify ⟨*one hundred*, approximate⟩ and ⟨*one hundred and three*, precise⟩ as the optimal pairings of forms and interpretations. But the argument points to a more general problem: We did not distinguish between the perspective of the speaker and the perspective of the hearer. The speaker might know that the two mentioned pairs do not compete with each other, but the addressee does not.

A more important objection is concerned with the preference for approximate interpretations. Why should there be such a general preference? There are many situations in which the speaker wants to be interpreted in a precise way. For example, if someone offers to sell a car for *one thousand euros*, then he would not be satisfied if the buyer offers him less than that, with the excuse that approximate interpretations are preferred.

The basic idea for an improved explanation of the RNRI phenomenon is that the two constraints SIMPEXP and APPRINT in (2) and (3) are not independent of each other. The constraint that prefers simple expressions over complex ones, SIMPEXP, can be operative only if there is a choice between simpler and more complex expressions. Such a choice exists only under the approximate interpretation; under the precise interpretation, we are bound to one value only.

If precise and approximate interpretation are not ordered with respect to each other, then they cannot be used to evaluate candidates of forms and interpretations. Rather, precise interpretation and approximate interpretation should be candidates themselves from which one or the other can be selected, according to pragmatic principles.

This can be made clear as follows. Let us assume a principle IN-RANGE, a consequence of the Gricean maxim of Quality, which says that assertions must be truthful:

(7) INRANGE:
The true value of a measure must be in the range of interpretation of the measure term.

Let us consider a simple example. Assume that an integer in the interval [1, 2, ... 100] is to be reported as the result of a measurement. This can be done in a precise way, or in an approximate way, where the latter means that if the value i is reported, it may stand for the range [i-2...i+2]. For example, reporting the value by *forty* stands for the range [38...42] under the approximate interpretation, and for [40] under the precise interpretation. We now can construct tableaus like the following, in which pairs of form and interpretation and the actual value constitute the input:

	Form / Interpretation Pairs	ActualValue	INRANGE	SIMPEXP
☞	$\langle forty, [38...42]\rangle$	39		
	$\langle forty, [40]\rangle$	39	*	
	$\langle thirty\text{-}nine, [37...41]\rangle$	39		*
☞	$\langle thirty\text{-}nine, [39]\rangle$	39		
☞	$\langle forty, [38...42]\rangle$	40		
☞	$\langle forty, [40]\rangle$	40		
	$\langle thirty\text{-}nine, [37...41]\rangle$	40		*
	$\langle thirty\text{-}nine, [39]\rangle$	40	*	

TABLE 2

If the actual value is 39, then two winners emerge: *forty* under an approximate interpretation, and *thirty-nine* under a precise interpretation. This is certainly a desired result, as it corresponds to the RNRI principle. In particular, it shows that the approximate interpretation of *thirty-nine* is ruled out, even if it would result in a true statement, because it violates SimpExp.

If the true value is 40, then again two winners emerge: *forty* under an approximate interpretation, and *forty* under a precise interpretation. This is not quite the desired result, as in this case the approximate interpretation of *forty* is preferred. It seems that we still need a general preference for approximate interpretations to model preference for *forty* here.

A more general problem of the tableau in Table 2 is that it assumes that the actual value of the reported measurement is known, as the candidates consist of an expression and an interpretation. But this is usually not the case for the addressee (except perhaps in answers to exam questions), and it is often not even the case for the speaker either, who might be uncertain about the precise actual value. I will show in the following section how these intrinsic problems can be solved within a framework of strategic communication.

5.4 Conditional Preferences in Strategic Communication

Let us assume a game-theoretic setting of strategic communication, as developed by Parikh (2001). This is not alien to the bidirectional approach to pragmatic tendencies of interpretation; in fact, Dekker and van Rooy (2000) have given a game-theoretic formulation in terms of Nash equilibria for cases like the one depicted in Table 1. In this setting, the preference for approximate interpretations of simple measure terms can be derived under the assumption that addressees hypothesize about the coding strategies of speakers, and speakers make use of this hypothesizing in their coding.

Parikh investigated the coding of information in a setting in which the probability or utility of a message is taken into consideration, an idea already put forward by Shannon (1948). For example, if an expression F is ambiguous between two meanings M, M', where M is, in the given context, much more likely than M', then a speaker can safely encode the meaning M by F. If the meaning M is less likely, then the speaker better refers to it by a more complex expression F* that denotes M but not M'. For example, *mother* is usually applied to biological mothers, but also to step mothers, foster mothers, etc. In many cases, there is no need for further specification, but if there is, expressions like *biological mother* can be used (cf. Horn 1993). We see a similar phenomenon at work when a round number is typically interpreted as vague.

In the case at hand, the idea of economical encoding allows us to explain the RNRI phenomenon without a general bias towards approximate or precise interpretation. The only bias we have to assume is the uncontroversial one towards simple expressions.

Assume as before that measurements may be reported in precise or approximate ways, where reporting in an approximate way means that a reported value stands for range of possible values. For example, if *thirty-nine* is reported in an approximate way, it would optimally represent 39, less optimally 38 and 40, still less optimally 37 and 41, and so on. This could be captured by using normal distributions as measures of fit, but here I will just use intervals like [39 ±2], that is, [37...41] for the range of admissible interpretations of a number word like *thirty-nine*. I will talk of the precision level as a real number r that determines the level of precision at which a number word is interpreted. If the number word strictly denotes i, and the level of precision is r, then the number word under this level of precision denotes the interval [i ±ir]. For example, for the precision level r = 1/15 the numeral *thirty-nine* is interpreted as [39 ±2.6], that is, [36.4...41.6]. At a precision level of 0, numbers are interpreted in a precise way. Cf. Dehaene (1997) for further discussion of approximation levels and their relation to the Weber-Fechner law of discriminability of stimuli.

Two expressions that are interpreted in an approximate way may be indistinguishable with respect to each other for a given value. For example, the expressions *thirty-nine* and *forty* are indistinguishable for values like 38, 39, 40 and 41 if reported under a precision level of 1/15, as they would report the intervals [39 ±2.6] and [40 ±2.7], respectively, which overlap for these values. In everyday conversation, the information carried by *thirty-nine* and *forty* is equivalent under this precision level if the given values are to be reported. This does not apply for reporting measurement values with a margin of error in physics, where 39 ±2.6 and 40 ±2.7 may mean something different. But then reporting values with margin of errors is not an indication of a coarse-grained representation, but rather a hallmark of high precision.

Consider now the same task as before, in the following setting. A result of a measuring has to be reported that is an integer in the interval [1 ... 100]. The addressee has no initial hypothesis about the value of the measurement, so he assumes an a priori likelihood of p = 0.01 for each of the integers. Let us assume two possible interpretations, an approximate one with level of approximation of 1/15, and a precise one with level of approximation 0. Let us furthermore assume that both precision levels are equally likely.

Let us first consider the case the speaker reports *thirty-nine*. There are two possible interpretations. We first consider the approximate interpretation, under which the expression reports the interval [39 ±2.6]. This interpretation is indistinguishable from a number of alternative utterances, in particular *forty*. The speaker could have uttered any of these alternative utterances to convey the message. But if he had this choice, he would have uttered *forty*, which is the preferred utterance among the alternatives, as it is the shortest. The speaker has not done so; he uttered *thirty-nine*. Consequently, the premise that the speaker intended the approximate interpretation must be false. The speaker must have intended the precise interpretation.

Under the precise interpretation, no problem arises. *Thirty-nine* is interpreted as 39, there are no indistinguishable alternative utterances. The utterance is consistent with the assumption that the speaker intended a precise interpretation.

Consider now the case that the speaker utters *forty*. Again, there are two possible interpretations. Under the approximate interpretation, the utterance reports the interval [40 ±2.7]. This is indistinguishable from the interpretations of the alternative utterances like *thirty-nine*. But among the alternative utterances, *forty* is the shortest and would have been chosen. Hence the utterance is consistent with the assumption of the approximate interpretation.

Of course, the utterance *forty* is also consistent with the precise interpretation, as before. But now we can make an argument that overall the approximate interpretation is preferred, following Parikh's reasoning about the a priori likelihood of the message. Under the precise interpretation, *forty* would report the value 40, which has an a priori likelihood of 0.01. Under the approximate interpretation, *forty* would report the integer values in [40 ±2.7], that is, [38, 39, 40, 41, 42], which together have a likelihood of 0.05. Hence the more conservative assumption is that the speaker had in mind the approximate interpretation, as it would report a value of a greater a priori likelihood. If the speaker wants to block this inference, some indication like the adverb *exactly* would have to be applied.

We can summarize the computation of overall probabilities in these two cases in the following diagrams, where we assume that the a priori probability of each value is 0.01, and that the a priori probability of precision level 0 and precision level 0.15 is 0.5 in either case. We see that for *thirty-nine*, only a precise interpretation is possible, whereas for *forty*, the approximate interpretation is selected because the reported values have a greater a priori likelihood.

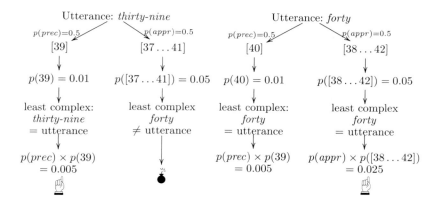

FIGURE 1

I have stressed that speaker and addressee know about each other's knowledge concerning the communicative situation. This means that by using a round number word, like *forty*, a speaker can signal a round interpretation, provided that the context is not skewed towards a precise one (as e.g. in arithmetic class, when the sum of $13 + 26$ is requested).

In the *gedankenexperiment* above, we have assumed that all measurement values have the same a priori likelihood. This is a simplifying assumption which turns out to be unnecessary. Even if e.g. 40 is more likely to be reported than 38, 39, 41 and 42, the cumulative likelihood of [38..42] is still greater than the likelihood of 40, and this is all that is necessary for the argument to get through. Furthermore, if the context is such that a precise interpretation is a priori more likely (as e.g. when in arithmetic class the sum of $13 + 26$ is requested), then this can override any other interpretation tendency when *forty* is uttered.

5.5 Simplicity of Expressions vs. Simplicity of Representations

In Krifka (2002) I pointed out that simplicity of expression is not always the decisive factor for an approximate interpretation. A bias for simple expressions cannot explain all interpretation preferences, as in the following examples:

(8) a. I wrote this article in twenty-four hours. (approx.)
    b. I wrote this article in twenty-three hours. (precise)

(9) a. The house was built in twelve months. (approx.)

      b. The house was built in eleven months. (precise)

Even in our original example concerning Swiss street signs, it might be difficult to argue that complexity of expression is the reason if we consider the fact that the distance is given in Arabic numbers; after all, *100* and *103* consist of the same number of digits.

Worse yet, the idea that simple expressions lead to approximate interpretations sometimes is plain wrong. Consider the following minimal pairs:

(10) a. Mary waited for forty-five minutes. (approx.)

      b. Mary waited for forty minutes.   (precise)

(11) a. The wheel turned one hundred and eighty degrees. (approx.)

      b. The wheel turned two hundred degrees.   (precise)

(12) a. Her child is eighteen months. (approx.)

      b. Her child is twenty months. (precise)

(13) a. John owns one hundred sheep. (approx.)

      b. John owns ninety sheep.   (precise)

I would like to argue that such examples show that speakers do not (just) prefer simple expressions, but rather simple representations. When speaking of time intervals, 24 hours is simpler than 23 hours because it denotes the length of a day, a prominent conceptual unit. The same holds for the other examples mentioned above: 12 months correspond to a year, 45 minutes to three quarters of an hour, 180 degrees to half of a complete turn, 18 months to one and a half years, and 100 is not just a multiple of ten, but a power of 10. The expressions that have a more approximate interpretation all refer to more salient units on their scales.

It is easy to replace the argumentation of the previous sections by postulating, instead of a bias for short expressions, a bias for simple representations. This bias for simple representations is, more specifically, one for coarse-grained representations, in the sense of Curtin (1995). The basic idea is this: The results of measuring can be reported with respect to various levels of granularity, which differ from each other in the density of representation points. For example, a distance can be specified on scales listing hundreds of kilometers, tens of kilometers, kilometers, etc. In a rather transparent way, scales are optimal if the points are distributed in an equidistant fashion (or sometimes according in other regular ways, e.g. logarithmically, cf. Hobbs 2000).

Furthermore, scales of different granularity levels should align, which simplifies conversion from one granularity level to the other. The most frequent type in our culture is the one based on the powers of ten, as illustrated in (14):

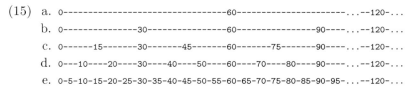

(14) a. -30-------------------------40-----------------------------50- ...

  b. -30-31-32-33-34-35-36-37-38-39-40-41-42-43-44-45-46-47-48-49-50- ...
                                                       o

The more coarse-grained scale (14.a) has fewer values for representing measurements than the more fine-grained scale (b). For example, any measurement between 35 and 45 is represented by a single value on the scale, 40. Results of counting or measuring have to be reported using the value that is closest, at the chosen granularity level. In the indicated example, the small circle in (14) will be represented by 43 on the fine-grained level (b), and by 40 on the coarse-grained level (a).

The scale hierarchy in (14) can be refined by introducing an intermediate scale. The optimal choice appears to be the one that adds the numbers 25, 35, 45 etc., thus creating scale points with a distance of five. This refinement is optimal insofar as it allows for the best overall representation of random measure values. On this scale, the circle in (14) would be represented by the number 45, as this is closer than 40.

In examples (8) to (13), the scales of different granularity are not based on the powers of ten, but on some other principle that is merely translated into the decimal system. As an example, take the minute scale (10). The relevant scales are the scale that counts the hours; then the scale that counts half-hours; then the scale that counts quarter hours; then the scale that counts ten minutes, then the scale that counts in 5 minute intervals. I will not represent even more fine-grained scales here, like the scale that counts single minutes, half minutes, quarter minutes, etc.

(15) a. 0---------------------------------60-----------------------...--120-...

  b. 0---------------30----------------60---------------90----...--120-...

  c. 0------15-------30-------45-------60-------75-------90----...--120-...

  d. 0---10----20----30----40----50----60----70----80----90----...--120-...

  e. 0-5-10-15-20-25-30-35-40-45-50-55-60-65-70-75-80-85-90-95-...--120-...

We can now explain why (10.a), *forty-five minutes*, is interpreted in a less precise way than (10.b), *forty minutes*. It follows from the following principle:

(16) The Coarsest Scale Principle:
        If a measure expression α occurs on scales that differ in granular-

ity, then uttering α implicates that the most coarse-grained scale on which α occurs is used.

For example, the most coarse-grained scale of *forty-five minutes* is (15.c), and for *forty minutes*, this is scale (15.d). As scale (c) is coarser than scale (e), *forty-five minutes* is interpreted in a more approximate way than *forty minutes*.

Why are measure expressions interpreted at the coarsest scale? Consider *forty-five minutes*. This term is represented only on scales (c) and (e), hence we can disregard the other scales. With respect to scale (c), the scale point 45 represents the times in $[38 \ldots 52]$; with respect to scale (e), the scale point 45 represents the times in $[43 \ldots 47]$. Let the a priori probability that the measured time is any particular minute within the range to be considered be r. Then the probability that the measured time is in $[43 \ldots 47]$ is 5r, and the probability that the measured time is in $[38 \ldots 42]$ is 10r. Let the a priori probability on hearing *forty-five minutes* that one of the scales (c) or (e) be used be the same, say s. Then on hearing *forty-five minutes* the probability that the more fine-grained scale (e) is used is 5rs, and the probability that the more coarse-grained scale (c) is used is twice that value, 10rs. Hence the hearer will assume the more coarse-grained scale.

Let me illustrate this with the help of a diagram. Assume that for each scale the a priori probability for using the scale is 0.2. Assume also that the a priori likelihood that the measured event is n minutes to be 0.01, for each n in the range under consideration. We then have the situation in Figure 2 (see page 121).

We see that the most coarse-grained scale on which the measure expression occurs is the winner. This is the case if the a priori likelihood of each scale is the same. As before, we can assume that the context changes this probability, e.g. by increasing the a priori likelihood of more fine-grained scales, which might tip the balance towards the other solution.

We might also factor in a context-dependent utility function that penalizes coarse-grained representations to greater or lesser degree— see Jäger (2007) for a suggestion that builds on the proposal discussed here. One can integrate this by assuming a function on the total probability in the last line of Figure 2 that multiplies this value with a factor 1 if the real value is represented by the precise interpretation of the number word, and by factors that decrease to 0 the farther removed the real value is from the precise interpretation. The best representation, then, is one that maximizes the resulting value. To illustrate, consider the utterance of *thirty minutes* with respect to the

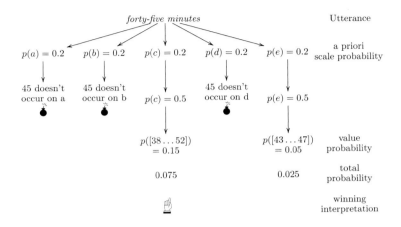

FIGURE 2

scales in (15). We get the following:

(17) Utterance *thirty minutes*

      Scale (a):   excluded

      Scale (b):   Scale probability 0.25,
                    value probability p([15...45]) = 0.30,
                    total: 0.075

      Scale (c):   Scale probability 0.25,
                    value probability p([23...37]) = 0.14,
                    total: 0.035

      Scale (d):   Scale probability 0.25,
                    value probability p([35...45]) = 0.10,
                    total: 0.025

      Scale (e):   Scale probability 0.25,
                    value probability p([37...42]) = 0.05,
                    total: 0.0125

As before, the most coarse-grain scale (b) is selected. Now assume a factor that gives a penalty in case the actual number differs from the precise interpretation of the measure expressions. For concreteness, we can assume the following function:

(18) penalty for misrepresentation: $\pi_r(v, u) = (1 + r)^{-(v-u)^2}$

      where   v: actual value,
               u: precise value of utterance,
               r: value ≥ 1 specifying severeness of penalty

In case $r = 0$ we have a constant penalty factor of 1, that is, no penalty ensues. In case $r = 0.1$ we have the following penalty factor, where the x axis indicates the difference between v and u.

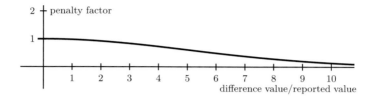

FIGURE 3

For example, if the utterance value differs from the actual value by 8, the probability that the scale is used decreases by 0.5. When we apply the penalty factor $\pi_{0.1}$ to the probabilities of the scales (15.b) and (c), we get the following picture:

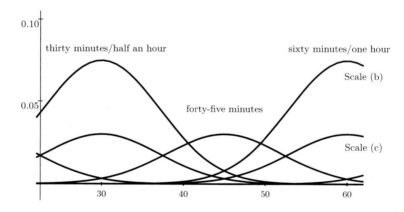

FIGURE 4

We see that for most of the values in the given interval (between 20 and 60), scale (b) is preferred over scale (c), in line with what we have argued so far. However, for reporting values between 40 and 50, the more fine-grained scale (c) is better, and we expect *forty-five minutes* for reported values within this range. The net effect of this competition between scales is that for values in the middle between the scale points of coarse-grained scale that otherwise is preferred, a more fine-grained scale will be used.

This example also shows an important principle that governs scale refinement. If there is a scale of equidistant points $[n, 2n, 3n, 4n, \ldots]$, then the optimal refinement of this scale will be one with equidistant points that contains intermediary points, $[0.5n, n, 1.5n, 2n, 2.5n, \ldots]$. The reason is that at exactly these intermediary points, the penalty for expressing values by coarse-grained scales is highest. We will return to this principle of scale refinement below.

The penalty function in Figure 3 is symmetric, that is, values that are higher or lower than the expressed value are penalized in the same way. Penalty functions don't have to be that way. If I tell someone that the train leaves in half an hour (or 30 minutes), then this is a bad choice of wording if the train actually leaves in 28 minutes, because the addressee might blame me if he missed the train. It would be more appropriate here to say that it leaves in 25 minutes, or even in 20 minutes. This can be modeled with a penalty function that is asymmetric, penalizing higher values more than lower values.

5.6 From Simplicity of Representation to Simplicity of Expression

Optimal scale selection, as discussed in the last section, can explain everything that we have tried to explain by selection of shortest expressions, and more. We can apply exactly the same reasoning for the preference of *forty* over *thirty-nine* by assuming that the coarse-grained scale $[\ldots, 30, 40, 50, \ldots]$ is preferred over the fine-grained scale $[\ldots, 38, 39, 40, 41, \ldots]$. An additional advantage of optimal scale selection seems to be that we do not have to apply the concept of indistinguishable reported values (cf. (9)). The attentive reader might have questioned this concept—at least, an anonymous referee did. For example, the relation of being indistinguishable is not transitive: if expressions α and β are indistinguishable, and expressions β and γ, then α and β need not be indistinguishable).

Yet the explanation of the RNRI phenomenon by a preference for simple expressions works in the majority of cases as well, and this hardly can be an accident. For the most part, the two explanations yield the same result. This is so because the number words of more coarse-grained scales are, in general, shorter than the number words of less coarse-grained scales. For example, the following scale hierarchy, while satisfying the requirement of equidistance of scale points, would be decidedly odd:

(19) a. ...-30-31-32-33-34-35-36-37-38-39-40-41-42-43-44-45-46-47-48-49-50-...

  b. ...-30-------33-------36-------39-------42-------45-------48-------...

The scale (19.b) is odd because the expressions that denote the scale points do not make use of the scale points for which the decimal system offers simple expressions. It neither is motivated as a translation of another system into the decimal one.

We can measure simplicity of expressions on a specific scale in various ways. One is by counting syllables. I have computed the following average numbers of syllables for the number words at the three following scales, from one to one hundred:

(20)
a. *one, two, three, four, ... one hundred:*
$273/100 = \textbf{2.73}$ syllables per word

b. *one, five, ten, fifteen, ... one hundred:*
$46/20 = \textbf{2.3}$ syllables per word

c. *one, ten, twenty, thirty, ... one hundred:*
$21/10 = \textbf{2.1}$ syllables per word

In contrast, the scale suggested in (19.b) does not show any such decrease of expression complexity when compared to the basic scale (20.b)—quite to the contrary:

(21) *three, six, nine, twelve, ... ninety-nine:*
$92/33 = \textbf{2.79}$ syllables per word

Hence we can assume the following general principle which relates Simplicity of Expressions and Simplicity of Representations.

(22) SER:
If S_1 is a more fine-grained scale than S_2, then
the average complexity of expressions of the values of S_1
tends to be greater than
the average complexity of expressions of the values of S_2
(measured over a reasonably large interval).

SER is not without exceptions. For example, consider the following scales of reporting the ages of young kids in months:

(23) a. 1-2-3-4-5-6-7-8-9-10-11-12-13-14-15-16-17-18-19-20-21-22-23-24
b. 1---3-----6-----9-------12-------15-------18-------21-------24

The average complexity of English number words at the scale (23.a) is $44/24 = 1.83$, the average complexity of the more coarse-grained scale is $25/9 = 2.78$, a clear violation of SER. However, granularity hierarchies like this one are quite rare. Furthermore, the age of children is more often given by expressions like *one year, one and half years, two years,* etc.

One indication that SER is an important principle of language is that in case simplicity of expressions and simplicity of representations diverge, there is evolutionary pressure to realign them. One example of this is the expression of amounts of money, e. g. in the US: *quarter* instead of *twenty-five cents*. For similar reasons, Dutch had expressions like *kvartje* for 25 cents and *rijksdaler* for 2,50 guilders in pre-Euro times. A particular curious case of translation from one system to another happened in German when the duodecimal system of *12 Pfennig = 1 Groschen* got replaced by a decimal system; now *Groschen* was used for 10 Pfennig, and the already established term *Sechser* (literally, 'sixer') for half that value, 5 Pfennig.

A more subtle influence of this evolutionary force can be seen in the way how the number 5 is expressed in certain combinations. The number 5 is special in the decimal system because it allows for an optimal refinement of granularity by the factor $1/2$, as illustrated:

(24) a. 10----20----30----40----50----60----70----80----90----100

   b. 10-15-20-25-30-35-40-45-50-55-60-65-70-75-80-85-90-95-100

This is the reason why the expression of this number is sometimes special. In English and in colloquial German, we have phonological irregularities for the number words of 15 and 50. We also find a special, shortened form for $1\frac{1}{2}$ in German.

(25) a. *fifteen* [fɪftiːn], instead of regular *fiveteen [faɪftiːn]

   b. *fifty* [fɪfti], instead of regular *fivety [faɪfti]

(26) a. colloquial form *fuffzehn* [fʊtˢeːn], standard form *fünfzehn* [fynftˢeːn]

   b. colloquial form *fuffzig* [fʊftˢɪg], standard form [fynftˢɪg]

(27) *eineinhalb* (long form), *anderthalb* (short form) for $1\frac{1}{2}$.

Notice that the irregular forms are phonologically simpler: The stem *fif*- has a monophthong in place of a diphthong. The stem *fuff*- exhibits a loss of rounding, and a loss of the nasal. The form *eineinhalb* has three heavy syllables, resulting in an unusual molossus foot; the form *anderthalb* has a light second syllable, resulting in a more usual cretic foot (heavy-light-heavy).

We can see this as evidence for the simplification of expressions that invite an approximate interpretation for conceptual reasons. In the case of English, the Old English stem *fīf* [fiːf] was reduced to *fif* [fɪf] in these environments, while undergoing regular development to *five* [faɪf] during the Great Vowel Shift in others. Notice that *five / fifteen / fifty* developed differently from the phonologically similar *nine / nineteen / ninety*. The most likely reason for the distinct development of *fifteen* and *fifty* is that these numbers occurred more frequently due to the fact that they occur on coarse-grained scales, and that increased use resulted in phonological simplification.

In this connection, it is also interesting to note the special encoding of the numbers 5, 50 and 500 in Roman numerals, which always are shorter than their immediate neighbors on the same granularity scale. This is, of course, not a result of evolution but of design, also motivated by the iconic representation of the hand. Nevertheless, it gives evidence of the special function of 5.

(28)	4--5--6:	IV--V--VI
	40--50--60:	XL--L--LX
	400-500-600:	CD--D--DC

Certain irregularities of numbers bear witness of the shaping effect of scales that are not operative anymore. One case in point is English *twelve* (Germanic *twa-libi* 'two+remnant'), which translates the basic unit of an older duodecimal system based on the number 12. Another is the suppletive form of the number word for 40 and 90 in Russian and other East-Slavonic languages:

(29)	'10'	*desjat'*	'60'	*šestdesjat'*
	'20'	*dvadcat'*	'70'	*sem'desjat'*
	'30'	*tridtcat'*	'80'	*vosem'desjat'*
	'40'	*sorok*	'90'	*devyanosto*
	'50'	*pjatdesjat'*	'100'	*sto*

According to Comrie (1992), the form *sorok* has replaced a regular Slavonic form; it is either a Greek loan or a classifier. The form *devyanosto* has been analyzed as a subtractive numeral or as evidence of an older nonal system. There is a way to connect these two oddballs by assuming that they represent remnants of an ancient octal subsystem, where 90 is the first multiple of 10 beyond 80, and 40 specifies $1/2$ times 80. There are various other indications that have been adduced to argue for an octal, or quaternary system (cf. Winter 1992).

Another irregularity can be found in the different complexity of multiples of 10 up to 60 and beyond 60 in older Germanic languages, e.g. Anglo-Saxon *sixtig* '60' vs. *hund-seofontig* '70', which again might point to the role that 60 played since Babylonian times (cf. Menninger 1962).

Returning from such speculative excursions, it should be mentioned that there is evidence form linguistic corpora that the number words for 12 and 15 are indeed more frequent than other number words denoting 11–19 (cf. Dehaene and Mehler (1992) for English, French, Japanese, Kannada, Dutch, Catalan and Spanish). Also, there is evidence that between 10 and 100, the number words denoting the powers of ten are far more frequent than other numbers (cf. Sigurd 1988). Jansen and Pollmann (2001) define a notion of roundness in which multiples of 10, of 2 and of 5 play a special role. The special role of 10 is, of course, due to the accidental fact that humans have ten fingers, thus providing the basis for a popular type of number system. The special role of 2 is motivated by the prominent operation of doubling or a quantity, or dividing it in half.

5.7 Avoidance of Complexity?

Not all number systems are based on ten, and we might ask what will happen in systems with different base. In particular, vigesimal systems are of interest here, that is, systems based on twenty, as there are a number of European languages that have vestiges of it, even if sometimes only in part, as in Standard French. European vigesimal systems are mixed, at least in the sense that 100 is a simple number word (this does not hold for all vigesimal systems, e.g. for Nahuatl). This creates a tension between optimal scale geometry and complexity of expressions: If we want to refine the scale based on multiples of 100 minimally (cf. (30.a)), we arrive at one that also adds the scale item 50 (cf. b). But in vigesimal systems, this is denoted by a relatively complex number word ("two scores and ten"), in any case more complex than the number words for 40 ("two scores") and 60 ("three scores"). Also, the number words for 30, 70 and 90 are more complex than their decimal counterparts.

```
(30)   a.  0---------------------------------100
       b.  0-----------------50-----------------100
       c.  0------20------40------60------80------100      vigesimal
       d.  0--10--20--30--40--50--60--70--80--90--100      decimal
```

I have looked into the frequency of number words in three languages: First, Norwegian, a decimal system, and Danish, a partially vigesimal system (partial insofar as e.g. the number 51 will be represented as *en og halvtreds* 'one and fifty', not as "eleven and forty"). I selected Norwegian and Danish as a pair of languages that are spoken by culturally similar communities, in an attempt to exclude cultural biases. Second, I also looked at Basque, which has a full vigesimal system (e.g., the number 51 is *berrogei ta hamaika* 'forty (= twice twenty) and eleven'). For Norwegian and Danish the Google web sites restricted to those languages could be used; the search was done on March 4, 2005. For Basque, restricted searches like that are not possible, all that one can do is to restrict searches to Spanish web sites. But sample inspections revealed that the words nearly exclusively occurred on Basque web sites.

This search was done on November 20, 2007. I made sure that the number words did not have homonyms (for this reason, Basque *hogei* '20' had to be excluded, as this sequence occurs in other languages as well). One should be aware of the fact that the number words also occur as part of complex numbers, as e.g. the number 41 in the Norwegian spelling *førti en*, in addition to *førtien*, or in Danish *en og fyrre*, in addition to *enogfyrre*. For Basque, I made sure that the occurrences of, e.g., *berrogei* excluded complex numbers like *berrogei ta bat* '41' by subtracting the number of occurrences of the string *berrogei ta*. It should be stressed that these are still preliminary results that need to be done more carefully by language experts; the results could be influenced, e.g., by a big Danish company with many web sites that has the word *tres* in its title. Also, the reader should be warned that Hammarström (2004), who looked at (presumably much smaller) Danish and Welsh corpora did not find a difference between languages with decimal number system and languages with vigesimal number system.

Number	Norwegian		Danish		Basque	
	Numeral	#	Numeral	#	Numeral	#
20	*tjue*	61300	*tyve*	121000		
30	*tretti*	43700	*tredive*	25400	*hogei ta hamar*	892
40	*frti*	**39200**	*fyrre*	**26800**	*berrogei*	**85000**
50	*femti*	**81200**	*halvtreds*	**15500**	*berrogei ta hamar*	**213**
60	*seksti*	**19400**	*tres*	**36400**	*hirurogei*	**34000**
70	*sytti*	10200	*halvfjerds*	581	*hirurogei ta hamar*	69
80	*tti*	13100	*firs*	3740	*larogei*	9000
90	*nitti*	13500	*halvfems*	540	*larogei ta hamar*	7

TABLE 3

Let us first consider Norwegian and Danish. We find for Norwegian the predicted relative (and even absolute) maximum for *femti* '50'; for Danish, we find the opposite, a relative minimum for *halvtreds* in comparison to *fyrre* and *tres*. This picture does not change when we consider the complete form *halvtredsind-s-tyve* '50', literally 'half-third-times-of-twenty', which has only 1180 occurrences. There also exists a form *femti* '50', mostly for monetary purposes, which occurred only 988 times on Danish web pages. The table also shows sharp local minima in Danish for the complex forms *halvfjerds* '70' and *halvfems* '90', which are absent in Norwegian. Interestingly, *tres* '60' even occurs considerably more often than the longer number words *tredive* '30' and *fyrre* '40', which might be seen as further evidence of the influence of simplicity on use.

In the case of Basque, the numbers are even more extreme. In particular, it is stunning how rare the number word *berrogei ta hamar* '50' occurs, compared to *berrogei* '40' and *hirurogei* '60'. Yet within its immediate neighbors, it forms a local maximum, with 213 occurrences, as shown in Table 4. It is unclear whether this reflects the cognitive status of 50 or is a result of translations from a language with a decimal number system like Spanish. There are also local maxima at '45' and '55'. The very low number of occurrences above '50' is remarkable; in fact, most of these occurrences just stem from web sites that list all Basque number words.

Numeral	'41'	'42'	'43'	'44'	'45'	'46'	'47'	'48'	'49'
Occurr.	37	151	40	118	147	72	70	109	54
'50'	'51'	'52'	'53'	'54'	'55'	'56'	'57'	'58'	'59'
213	29	10	7	6	50	5	3	3	7

TABLE 4

There are, I think, two possible explanations for these differences between languages with decimal and with vigesimal number systems. One is that the scale hierarchy of vigesimal languages is the same as the scale hierarchy with decimal languages, but that number words for numbers meaning '50', '70' and '90' are underused due to their complexity, as complex expressions are avoided. In written language, writers may resort to Arabic numbers, something that could be checked with more careful corpus research. The second explanation is that the scale hierarchy of vigesimal languages itself is different, insofar as these languages also have a prominent scale based on multiples of 20, which—in the case of Basque—appears to be more prominent than the scale based on multiples of 10. Of course, these two explanations do not exclude each other. In particular, the complexity of expressions can obviously be an obstacle against switching from one scale system to another, in the case at hand, from switching from a state with a prominent scale based on multiples of 20 to a state with a prominent scale based on multiples of 10.

5.8 Conclusion

In this paper I have argued that the fact that round numbers are interpreted in an approximate way can be explained by general pragmatic principles, even in the absence of an a priori preference for approximate interpretations. The crucial argument was that the approximate interpretation is more likely because it is compatible with a wider range of possible meanings. This reasoning is blocked with non-round numbers as under the approximate interpretations, round numbers would be selected, as short expressions are preferred. We have discussed limitations of this motivation, and have argued that it should be generalized to a principle that predicts that the most coarse-grained scale compatible with the selected expression should be chosen. Simplicity of expressions then appears as a secondary phenomenon, as coarse-grained scales tend to have simpler expressions to denote their scale points. We have finally seen that there are interesting differences between languages based on different number systems. In particular, languages with an vigesimal number systems seem to make use of a scale based on multiples of 20, which is reflected in the frequency of use of number words.

This point is perhaps the most interesting one: According to a well-known phrase by DuBois (1987) that has been used to motivate frequency-based explanations in linguistics, grammars do best what speakers do most. It might very well be the case that sometimes the reverse is true: Speakers do most what grammars do best. A grammar that offers simple coding of multiples of 20 will motivate speakers to use multiples of 20 more often than other numbers. So far, pragmatics is mostly concerned with the role of simplicity or complexity of coding a particular message; we should perhaps also pay attention to the role of simplicity and complexity of coding in selecting what is said in the first place.

References

Blutner, Reinhard. 2000. Some Aspects of Optimality in Natural Language Interpretation. *Journal of Semantics* 17:189–216.

Comrie, Bernard. 1992. Balto-Slavonic. In J. Gvozdanović, ed., *Indo-European Numerals*, pages 717–834. Berlin: Mouton de Gruyter.

Curtin, Paul. 1995. *Prolegomena To a Theory of Granularity*. Master's thesis, University of Texas at Austin.

Dehaene, Stanislas. 1997. *The Number Sense: How the Mind Creates Mathematics*. Oxford: Oxford University Press.

Dehaene, Stanislas and Jacques Mehler. 1992. Cross-linguistic regularities in the frequency of number words. *Cognition* 43:1–29.

Dekker, Paul and Robert van Rooy. 2000. Bi-directional Optimality Theory: An application of game theory. *Journal of Semantics* 17:217–242.

DuBois, John. 1987. The discourse basis of ergativity. *Language* 63:805–855.

Duhem, Paul. 1904. *La théorie physique, son objét et sa structure*. Paris: Chevalier et Rivière.

Hammarström, Harald. 2004. Number bases, frequencies and lengths cross-linguistically. Abstract accepted at the conference *Linguistic perspectives on numerical expressions*. Utrecht, Netherlands. Article (draft) see http://www.cs.chalmers.se/~harald2/.

Hobbs, Jerry. R. 2000. Half orders of magnitude. In L. Obrst and I. Mani, eds., *Workshop on Semantic Approximation, Granularity, and Vagueness*, pages 28–38.

Horn, Laurence R. 1984. Towards a new taxonomy of pragmatic inference: Q-based and R-based implicature. In D. Schiffrin, ed., *Meaning, form, and use in context: Linguistic applications*, pages 11–89. Washington D.C.: Georgetown University Press.

Horn, Laurence R. 1993. Economy and redundancy in a dualistic model of natural language. In S. Shore and M. Vilkuna, eds., *SKY 1993: 1993 Yearbook of the Linguistic Association of Finland*, pages 33–72.

Jäger, Gerhard. 2002. Some notes on the formal properties of bidirectional Optimality Theory. *Journal of Logic, Language and Information* 11:427–451.

Jäger, Gerhard. 2007. Communication about similarity spaces. Talk given in Amsterdam, KNAW Academy colloquium, *New perspectives on games and interaction*. http://wwwhomes.uni-bielefeld.de/gjaeger/talks/slidesKnawGames.pdf.

Jansen, C. J. M. and M. M. W. Pollmann. 2001. On round numbers: Pragmatic aspects of numerical expressions. *Journal of Quantitative Linguistics* 8:187–201.

Krifka, Manfred. 2002. Be brief and vague! And how bidirectional optimality theory allows for Verbosity and Precision. In D. Restle and D. Zaefferer, eds., *Sounds and Systems. Studies in Structure and Change. A Festschrift for Theo Vennemann*, pages 439–458. Berlin: Mouton de Gruyter.

Krifka, Manfred. 2007. Approximate interpretations of number words: A case for strategic communication. In G. Bouma, I. Krämer, and J. Zwarts, eds., *Cognitive Foundations of Interpretation*, pages 111–126. Amsterdam: Royal Netherlands Academy of Arts and Sciences.

Levinson, Stephen. 2000. *Presumptive Meanings*. Cambridge, Mass.: MIT Press.

Menninger, Karl. 1962. *Number Words and Number Symbols: A Cultural History of Numbers*. Dover Publications.

Ochs Keenan, Elinor. 1976. The universality of conversational postulates. *Language in Society* 5:67–80.

Parikh, Prashant. 2001. Communication, meaning, and interpretation. *Linguistics and Philosophy* 23:141–183.

Shannon, Claude E. 1948. A mathematical theory of communication. *Bell Systems Technical Journal* 27:379–432, 623–656.

Sigurd, Bengt. 1988. Round numbers. *Language in Society* 17(2):243–252.

Winter, Werner. 1992. Some thoughts about Indo-European numerals. In J. Gvozdanović, ed., *Indo-European Numerals*, vol. 57 of *Trends in Linguistics: Studies and Monographs*, pages 11–28. Berlin: Mouton de Gruyter.

Zipf, George K. 1929. Relative frequency as a determinant of phonetic change. *Harvard Studies in Classical Philology* 40:1–95.

6

Compositional Interpretation in Which the Meanings of Complex Expressions are not Computable from the Meanings of their Parts[*]

Peter N. Lasersohn

6.1 Introduction

The title of this paper should sound paradoxical. Isn't it a matter of *definition* that in a compositional interpretation, the meanings of complex expressions are computed from the meanings of their parts?

Certainly this would seem to be what many authors mean by the term *compositional*. In introductory textbooks, the idea of compositionality is often introduced by pointing out that if there weren't some systematic way of calculating the meanings of complex expressions from the meanings of their parts, we could not explain how speakers understand novel sentences, or indefinitely many sentences. The following passage from Larson and Segal (1995, pp. 11–12) is representative; similar passages may be found in many other textbooks:

> The hypothesis that we know a set of compositional semantic rules and principles is a highly attractive one having a great deal of explanatory power. In particular, it accounts for three notable and closely related features of linguistic competence. First, it explains why *our*

[*]Thanks to Chris Barker, Theo Janssen, Dag Westerståhl, and the audience at the symposium, particularly Gertjan van Noord, for helpful discussion. Errors are my own, of course.

Theory and Evidence in Semantics.
Erhard Hinrichs and John Nerbonne (eds.).

understanding of sentences is systematic—why there are definite, predictable patterns among the sentences we understand... Second, the hypothesis accounts for the obvious but important fact that *we can understand new sentences*, sentences we have never come across before... Third, the hypothesis accounts for the slightly less obvious but equally important fact that *we have the capacity to understand each of an indefinitely large number of sentences...*

Similar points are often made in more advanced or technical discussions of compositionality as well. Dowty (2007, pp. 23–24) asks us to consider several points:

- Linguists agree that the set of English sentences is at least recursive in size, that English speakers produce sentences virtually every day that they have never spoken before, and that they successfully parse sentences they have never heard before.
- If we accept the idealization that they do understand the meanings of the sentences they hear, obtaining the same meanings from them that others do, then:
- Since the meanings of all sentences obviously cannot be memorized individually, there must be some finitely characterizable procedure for determining these meanings, one shared by all English speakers.
- As the sentences themselves can only be enumerated via derivations in the grammar of the language, then inevitably, the procedure for interpreting them must be determined, in some way or other, by their syntactic structures as generated by this grammar (plus of course the meanings of the individual words in them).

Dowty goes on to suggest that in light of these points, the primary empirical issue regarding compositionality is not *whether* natural language semantics is compositional, but rather *how* it is compositional.

Given the frequency with which semanticists justify the principle of compositionality by appealing to the ability of language users to understand novel sentences (or indefinitely many sentences), it is striking to realize that in more mathematically-oriented work on compositionality, often very little is done to preserve the idea that the meaning of a complex expression may be computed from the meanings of its parts.

For example, in the system of Montague (1970), which I think represents the most standard approach to the mathematical representation of compositional interpretation, the central idea is that meaning is assigned homomorphically, not that it be assigned computably. The homomorphism requirement does nothing to guarantee computability, as we will see from a simple example.

In this paper, I will explore several issues regarding the relation between the principle that interpretation is assigned homomorphically and the idea that meanings can be systematically computed. Since language users presumably must have some way of computing the meanings of the expressions they use and understand, it might seem natural simply to impose a computability requirement on a system of homomorphic interpretation like Montague's. However, I will argue that there are good reasons not to do so. Rather, I claim, psychological computation of meanings may be done on an entirely separate basis from homomorphic interpretation; this will be illustrated using a second example, in which sentences in a small, artificial language may be easily understood, despite being assigned a non-computable homomorphic interpretation.

If psychological understanding of meanings is not done by computing a homomorphic interpretation function, then the claim that interpretation is assigned homomorphically can only be motivated on grounds other than explaining speakers' ability to understand novel sentences. I will argue that such motivation may be found by noting that the principle of homomorphic interpretation is equivalent to familiar principles licensing the substitution of synonyms or coreferring terms for one another. To the extent that we observe languages to respect such substitution patterns, then, a principle of homomorphic interpretation is well supported, regardless of its relation to the psychological computation of meaning.

6.2 Background Notions

As background to our first example, and to some of the points to be made later in the paper, we begin by reviewing the major features of Montague's system, as well as some basic definitions. Central to Montague's approach is the idea that complex expressions are derived from more basic expressions through successive application of syntactic operations. If we close the set of basic expressions under all the syntactic operations, the result is the *syntactic algebra* for the language, which we may notate $\mathfrak{A} = \langle A, F_1, \ldots, F_i \rangle$.[1]

We assume that each expression is assigned a "meaning" from some set B. Although Montague made specific proposals about what "meanings" are, those proposals are largely independent of this part of the theory; for the purposes of defining compositionality, the elements of B may be anything whatsoever.

Although there are no requirements on what meanings *are*, we do require that they relate to each other in specific ways. In particular

---

[1] Here $F_1, \ldots, F_i$ are the syntactic operations, and A is the set obtained by closing the set of basic expressions under these operations. Montague's notation is a little more general, and avoids the inexplicitness of the three dots, but I think the current notation is easier to read and should be clear enough for our present purposes.

B must be closed under a series of operations $G_1, \ldots, G_i$, which have the same numbers of argument places as $F_1, \ldots, F_i$, respectively. Thus $\mathfrak{B} = \langle B, G_1, \ldots, G_i \rangle$ must be a "similar" algebra to $\mathfrak{A}$. We can think of $G_1, \ldots, G_i$ as operations for deriving meanings of complex expressions from the meanings of their parts. Each semantic operation $G_n (1 \leq n \leq i)$ corresponds to a syntactic operation F_n and is used to assign meanings to the expressions which F_n derives.

Now we require that the meanings of expressions in A be assigned by a homomorphism h from $\mathfrak{A}$ to $\mathfrak{B}$. That is, for each of our syntactic operations F_n and its corresponding semantic operation G_n, we require:

(1) $h(F_n(\alpha_1, \ldots, \alpha_m)) = G_n(h(\alpha_1), \ldots, h(\alpha_m))$

It is perhaps worth noting that Montague himself did not use the term *compositionality* for this requirement; but the idea that this homomorphism requirement is a formalization of the intuitive idea of compositionality seems quite widespread (see, e.g., Partee et al. (1990, p. 334); Janssen (1997, p. 450); Westerståhl (1998, pp. 635–636)). The intuition behind it is pretty straightforward: If you derive an expression syntactically from more basic expressions $\alpha_1, \ldots, \alpha_m$, its meaning should be derived from the meanings of $\alpha_1, \ldots, \alpha_m$.

This does not guarantee that the meanings of complex expressions can be computed from the meanings of their parts, for the very simple reason that there is nothing in this picture to require that the semantic operations $G_1, \ldots, G_i$ or the homomorphism h be computable functions.

A *computable function* is one which can be represented as a recursively enumerable set of ordered pairs. Mathematically, there is no reason to suspect that the homomorphism requirement would force the semantic operations to be computable, and in fact it is easy to show that it does not.

6.3 A Simple Example

As an example of homomorphic interpretation in which the semantic operations are not computable, consider the following simple artificial language L_1:

(2) *Formation Rules:*
    a. 0 is a term
    b. 1 is a term
    c. If α is a term and β is a term, then $[\alpha\beta]$ is a term
    d. If α is a term, then $\#\alpha$ is a sentence

In this language, sentences consist of any number of 0's and 1's (bracketed to show their derivational history) preceded by #.

Given these rules, we may define our syntactic operations as F_1 and F_2, where:

(3) *Syntactic Operations:*
    a. $F_1(\alpha, \beta) = [\alpha\beta]$
    b. $F_2(\alpha) = \#\alpha$

So, our set A will be the closure of $\{0, 1\}$ under F_1 and F_2; our syntactic algebra is $\mathfrak{A} = \langle A, F_1, F_2 \rangle$.

To interpret this language, we use as "meanings" the set of natural numbers $\mathbb{N}$, the strings of a second language L_{NR}, which is not recursively enumerable, and a "dummy" object † to serve as the meaning of ill-formed expressions.[2] That is, $B = \mathbb{N} \cup L_{NR} \cup \{\dagger\}$.

Although L_{NR} is not recursively enumerable, we do make the standard assumption that it is a set of finite strings over a finite vocabulary, hence that it is denumerably infinite. Therefore, there is a function putting it in 1-1 correspondence with $\mathbb{N}$. Call this function f.

Even though f might do something as simple as arrange the sentences of L_{NR} in alphabetical order, or sort them by length, it is not a computable function. (If f were computable, it would be representable as a recursively enumerable set of ordered pairs. Then you could easily recursively enumerate L_{NR} just by stripping off the first element of each pair. But we have stipulated that L_{NR} is not recursively enumerable. Therefore f is not computable.)[3]

Now, we interpret L_1 by letting each term have a natural number as its meaning, and letting each sentence have a string of L_{NR} as its meaning. If a term is of the form $[\alpha\beta]$, its meaning will be the sum of the meaning of α and the meaning of β. Each sentence is of the form $\#\alpha$, and will have as its meaning the string of L_{NR} which f assigns to the number which serves as the meaning of α. Since the operation deriving the meanings of sentences from the meanings of terms appeals to this non-computable function, there will be no general procedure for

---

[2]Because our operations are total and A is closed under them, A will contain strings such as #0#0 which are not well-formed according to the rules in (2). For ease of presentation, I follow Montague (1970) in allowing such expressions into A and using a set of syntactic rules to identify which elements of A are well-formed, rather than using a partial algebra in which the operations are undefined for arguments which would yield ill-formed values.

[3]Some people find it paradoxical that something as systematic as alphabetization or length-sorting could be non-computable. Of course, *if we had a list* of all the strings in L_{NR}, we could construct an algorithm for alphabetizing them or sorting them by length; the problem is that there is no way to construct such a list.

computing the meanings of sentences from the meanings of their parts. More formally, let the semantic operations be G_1 and G_2, where:

(4) *Semantic Operations:*

    a. If $x, y \in \mathbb{N}$, then $G_1(x, y) = x + y$.
       (If $x \notin \mathbb{N}$ or $y \notin \mathbb{N}$, then $G_1(x, y) = \dagger$.)
    b. If $x \in \mathbb{N}$, then $G_2(x) = f(x)$.
       (If $x \notin \mathbb{N}$, then $G_2(x) = \dagger$.)

Note that $B = \mathbb{N} \cup L_{NR} \cup \{\dagger\}$ is closed under G_1, G_2. We let our semantic algebra be $\mathfrak{B} = \langle B, G_1, G_2 \rangle$.

Now let the meaning assignment be $h : A \to B$, where:

(5) *Meaning Assignment:*

    a. $h(0) = 0$
    b. $h(1) = 1$
    c. If $h(\alpha), h(\beta) \in \mathbb{N}$, then $h([\alpha\beta]) = h(\alpha) + h(\beta)$
       (If $h(\alpha) \notin \mathbb{N}$ or $h(\beta) \notin \mathbb{N}$, then $h([\alpha\beta]) = \dagger$.)
    d. If $h(\alpha) \in \mathbb{N}$, then $h(\#\alpha) = f(h(\alpha))$.
       (If $h(\alpha) \notin \mathbb{N}$, then $h(\alpha) = \dagger$.)

Now it is easy to see that $h(F_1(\alpha, \beta)) = G_1(h(\alpha), h(\beta))$, and that $h(F_2(\alpha)) = G_2(h(\alpha))$; so h is a homomorphism from $\mathfrak{A}$ to $\mathfrak{B}$.

Note also that for every $n \in \mathbb{N}$, there is some term α such that $h(\alpha) = n$. Hence the function mapping $h(\alpha)$ onto $h(\#\alpha)$ for each term α is f, and not some proper subset of f.[4] But f is non-computable. Since sentences in this language are of the form $\#\alpha$, there is no general procedure in this language for calculating the meanings of sentences from the meanings of their parts.

From a mathematical point of view this is not at all surprising. But it does show that if the idea we are trying to capture in formulating a principle of compositionality is that the meanings of complex expressions can be computed from the meanings of their parts, we don't get that result just by imposing a Montagovian requirement of homomorphic meaning assignment.

Now a natural reaction at this point might be to see this as a shortcoming—but a fairly trivial and easily fixed shortcoming—of the Montagovian conception of compositionality. After all, for any natural language, or even any useful language, we must be able to compute

---

[4]Of course our semantic operation is G_2, which is an extension of f, not f itself. (G_2 differs from f in that it is defined for objects which are not the meanings of terms; it maps these onto $\dagger$.) But G_2 must also be non-computable; otherwise we could compute f by computing G_2, then stripping off all pairs with $\dagger$ as their second element.

the meanings. So it might seem that the obvious thing to do would be to impose an additional constraint on our system, requiring that the meaning assignment h and/or the semantic operations $G_1, \ldots, G_i$ be computable functions. And in fact, those few discussions of this issue that I've been able to find in the literature seem to favor exactly this (Muskens (1995, p. 89); Kracht (2003, p. 186)).

What I'd like to suggest is that we *don't* need to impose such a requirement in order to explain the fact that people can comprehend novel utterances, and that in fact there might be good reasons for *not* requiring semantic operations to be computable. In fact I think we can have a perfectly reasonable, comprehensible language with interpretations assigned in a semantic algebra with non-computable operations.

6.4 Non-Computable Reference Assignment

The idea of non-computable semantic operations might be easiest to accept if we consider it first in the context of compositionality of *reference*, rather than compositionality of *meaning* or *sense*. In a Fregean semantics, it is the sense of an expression, not the referent, which serves as the expression's "cognitive value"; it is the sense, not the referent, which is mentally "grasped" when one understands the expression. So if our main reason for believing that semantic operations must be computable is that this assumption is necessary for a psychological explanation of how people understand novel utterances, it is perhaps not quite so obvious that we must assume computability of reference as it is that we must assume computability of sense.

Here it is worth recognizing that Montague's system draws a three-way distinction between "meaning," "sense" and "denotation" (or reference),[5] and it is only at the level of meaning that the homomorphism requirement is imposed. In other words, there is no compositionality of reference (or even sense) in Montague's system.

But compositionality of reference is quite crucial to some semantic theories, including—I would claim—that of Frege (1892/1970). Of course there has been some dispute whether Frege believed in compositionality,[6] and it may be that his views on this changed over his

---

[5]The "meaning" of an expression is analogous to its *character* in the sense of Kaplan (1989)—it determines its sense relative to a range of contexts. "Sense" and "denotation" are the familiar notions of intension and extension.

[6]The main evidence against the idea that Frege believed in compositionality appears to be his dictum "it is only in the context of a proposition that words have any meaning" (Frege (1884/1980) S 62; see also the Introduction, S 60, S 106). As I read him, however, Frege is not arguing for a theoretical principle that words are meaningless in isolation, but for a methodological strategy of identifying the meaning of a word by considering what it contributes to sentences in which it

lifetime; but I think it is clear that some of his most famous arguments only make sense against a background assumption of compositionality, and specifically of compositionality of reference.

For example, Frege argued that sentences denote truth values, by noting that the truth value is what is guaranteed not to change if a constituent of the sentence is replaced by a different expression with the same reference. This argument is compelling only if we assume that the referent of the sentence is determined by the referents of its constituent parts. Without this assumption, we would have no reason to expect that the referent of the sentence *should* remain constant across the substitution.

Likewise, Frege argued that all expressions shift their reference in indirect quotation and similar contexts, where they refer instead to what would customarily be their sense. The reason is that in such contexts, substitution of a constituent by an expression with the same customary reference will not preserve truth value—that is, will not preserve the referent of the sentence as a whole. Again, this argument is only compelling if one assumes that the referent of the whole sentence is determined by the referents of the parts.

So I'd like to assume for the sake of discussion that reference is determined compositionally. Now if we take this to mean it is assigned homomorphically, we can ask whether it is reasonable to require the operations in the semantic algebra—that is, the reference algebra—to be computable. I think the answer is clearly *no*, because we can refer to specific strings in a non-recursively-enumerable set (and apply predicates to them, make true or false claims about them, etc.) using mechanisms like those in our previous example.

To see this, consider a language L_2 like L_1, but with a few changes: All terms of L_1 will be "number terms" of L_2. All sentences of L_1 will be "string terms" of L_2. We will continue to map the number terms onto natural numbers, and the string terms onto strings in a non-recursively-enumerable language L_{NR}; but we regard this mapping as an assignment of referents, not of meanings. L_2 will also have predicates, including a designated predicate **TL**. Formulas will consist of a predicate followed by a string term in parentheses. More formally:

(6) a. 0 is a number term.

    b. 1 is a number term.

    c. If α is a number term and β is a number term, then $[\alpha\beta]$ is a number term.

---

appears (as opposed to simply contemplating the word in isolation). Frege scholars may disagree; see Pelletier (2001), Janssen (2001) for more discussion.

    d. If α is a number term, then $\#\alpha$ is a string term.

    e. $\mathbf{TL}, P_1, P_2, P_3, \ldots$ are predicates.

    f. If α is a predicate and β is a string term, then $\alpha(\beta)$ is a formula.

Our syntactic operations include F_1 and F_2 as in our previous example,[7] as well as F_3, where $F_3(\alpha, \beta) = \alpha(\beta)$. A will now be the closure of $\{0, 1, \mathbf{TL}, P_1, P_2, P_3, \ldots\}$ under F_1, F_2, F_3; the syntactic algebra $\mathfrak{A}$ will be $\langle A, F_1, F_2, F_3 \rangle$.

As in L_1, we will need to make use of a 1-1 correspondence f from $\mathbb{N}$ to L_{NR}. In our previous example, it did not matter which function this was, as long it was a 1-1 correspondence. For the interpretation of L_2, however, let us assume more specifically that f is a function which arranges the strings of L_{NR} in order of increasing length, mapping the smallest numbers onto the shortest strings, and larger numbers onto longer strings. Strings of the same length may be arranged alphabetically.

Let us further assume that L_{NR} is a language over a 26-letter alphabet.

Number terms will be assigned elements of $\mathbb{N}$ as their referents, and string terms will be assigned elements of L_{NR}. Predicates will be assigned subsets of L_{NR} (that is, elements of $pow(L_{NR})$), and formulas will be assigned elements of $\{\mathbf{true}, \mathbf{false}\}$. So referents in general are drawn from $\mathbb{N} \cup L_{NR} \cup pow(L_{NR}) \cup \{\mathbf{true}, \mathbf{false}\} \cup \{\dagger\}$; we now call this set B.

With this in mind, we may now define our semantic operations as follows. G_1 and G_2 are the same as before (but extended to deal with our expanded set B); G_3 simply checks to see if its second argument is a member of its first argument:

(7) a. If $x, y \in \mathbb{N}$, then $G_1(x, y) = x + y$.
       (If $x \notin \mathbb{N}$ or $y \notin \mathbb{N}$, then $G_1(x, y) = \dagger$.)
    b. If $x \in \mathbb{N}$, then $G_2(x) = f(x)$.
       (If $x \notin \mathbb{N}$, then $G_2(x) = \dagger$.)
    c. If $x \subseteq L_{NR}$ and $y \in L_{NR}$, then $G_3(x, y) = \mathbf{true}$ if $y \in x$ and $G_3(x, y) = \mathbf{false}$ if $y \notin x$.
       (If $x \not\subseteq L_{NR}$ or $y \notin L_{NR}$, then $G_3(x, y) = \dagger$.)

B is closed under these operations, so we let our semantic algebra $\mathfrak{B}$ be $\langle B, G_1, G_2, G_3 \rangle$.

---

[7]Technically, these are not quite the same functions as F_1, F_2 from L_1, since they must be defined for a broader set of expressions; but they work in intuitively the same way: $F_1(\alpha, \beta) = [\alpha\beta]$ and $F_2(\alpha) = \#\alpha$.

We assign referents via a function h, much like the one from L_1, but extended to deal with predicates and formulas:

(8) a. $h(0) = 0$

b. $h(1) = 1$

c. If α is a predicate, then $h(\alpha) \subseteq L_{NR}$.

d. $h(\mathbf{TL}) = \{x \in L_{NR} | x$ consists of at least two letters$\}$

e. If $h(\alpha), h(\beta) \in \mathbb{N}$, then $h([\alpha\beta]) = h(\alpha) + h(\beta)$.
(If $h(\alpha) \notin \mathbb{N}$ or $h(\beta) \notin \mathbb{N}$, then $h([\alpha\beta]) = \dagger$.)

f. If $h(\alpha) \in \mathbb{N}$, then $h(\#\alpha) = f(h(\alpha))$.
(If $h(\alpha) \notin \mathbb{N}$, then $h(\alpha) = \dagger$.)

g. If $h(\alpha) \subseteq L_{NR}$ and $h(\beta) \in L_{NR}$, then $h(\alpha(\beta)) = \mathbf{true}$ if $h(\beta) \in h(\alpha)$, and $h(\alpha(\beta)) = \mathbf{false}$ if $h(\beta) \notin h(\alpha)$.
(If $h(\alpha) \not\subseteq L_{NR}$ or $h(\beta) \notin L_{NR}$, then $h(\alpha(\beta)) = \dagger$.)

It should be evident that h is a homomorphism from $\mathfrak{A}$ to $\mathfrak{B}$. And just as in L_1, where the meanings of sentences were derived by a non-computable function, here in L_2, the referents of string terms are derived by a non-computable function.

Now consider the following sentence of L_2:

(9) $\mathbf{TL}(\#[[[[[[[[[[[[[[[[[[[[[[[[[[[11]1]1]1]1]1]1]1]1]1]1]1]1]1]1]1]1]1]1]1]1]1]1]1]1]1]1])$

This sentence consists of the predicate $\mathbf{TL}$ followed in parentheses by $\#$ and 28 occurrences of 1 (with brackets).

This sentence makes a perfectly sensible and easily comprehensible claim, namely that the 28th string of L_{NR} (when the strings of L_{NR} are arranged in order of increasing length) consists of at least two letters. In fact it is clear from the rules above what *all* sentences of the form $\mathbf{TL}(\#\alpha)$ mean: any such sentence means that the nth string of L_{NR} (in order of increasing length) consists of at least two letters, where n is the number of 1's in α. So despite our use of a non-computable operation in the reference algebra, we can understand the meanings of sentences. It appears that a limitation to computable functions is not a necessary prerequisite to comprehensibility, at least if we are considering compositionality of reference.

Moreover, it is apparent that sentence (9) is *true*, because L_{NR} was stipulated to be a language over a 26-letter alphabet. There are at most 27 strings of length less than 2: the empty string, and the 26 one-letter strings. The 28th string must contain at least two letters.

So here we have an example of a language which uses a non-computable semantic operation in its reference algebra, and of a sentence in that language whose truth value is derived in part via that non-computable operation—but where the sentence is not only comprehensible, but easily truth evaluable.

Does this mean that natural languages must have non-computable operations in their reference algebras? Of course it is only in very specialized contexts that we refer to specific strings in non-recursively-enumerable languages, but it does happen—for example, I've been doing it all through this paper—so we need to take some account of it. Whether or not we need non-computable semantic operations for this is more debatable, but is not, I think, completely implausible. Consider the English sentence in (10):

(10) Number twenty-eight consists of at least two letters.

A phrase like *Number twenty-eight* refers to different things in different pragmatic contexts. It seems to me that we must regard each context in which this phrase may be felicitously used as providing a domain of objects from which this reference is drawn, and a sequential ordering on those objects. Now relative to a given context, this phrase will refer to the 28th item in the ordering. In a context which provides L_{NR} as the relevant domain and f as the relevant ordering, this phrase will refer to 28th string of L_{NR} according to f, and sentence (10) will be true. But we also presumably want to claim that the name *twenty-eight* refers to the number 28 (in all contexts), and since this is a constituent of the phrase *number twenty-eight*, we will presumably have to apply this non-computable function f to 28 in deriving the referent of the whole phrase from the referents of its parts.

Whether this is done in the application of a semantic operation, or instead, we regard f as the referent (in context) of the word *number*, or of some phonologically empty constituent, is less clear.[8] In the latter case, the non-computability is all in the denotations and not in the operations, which we could maintain to be computable. But an analysis that uses a non-computable semantic operation in its reference algebra is, I think, at least a reasonable competitor among the other candidate analyses; and most importantly, it cannot be ruled out on the grounds that sentences derived using non-computable semantic operations are necessarily incomprehensible.

---

[8]Note that in L_1 and L_2, I was free to simply stipulate what the semantic operations were, since these were artificial languages; no one can complain that in the "right" analysis, '#' should be treated as denoting f rather than as syncategorematic. But in English, the right syntactic analysis must presumably be discovered rather than stipulated.

6.5   C-Compositionality and H-Compositionality

In the preceding section, we considered compositionality of reference rather than meaning, because the referent of an expression is not generally a psychological object, and it therefore seemed less clear with reference than with meaning that there is a psychological reason for assuming that the operations of the semantic algebra must be computable. As we saw, it is possible to have a language in which the referents of complex expressions are derived via a non-computable operation from the referents of their parts; and that sentences whose truth values are assigned in part via such non-computable operations may nonetheless make sense, and be easily comprehensible—and even truth evaluable. But if we were able to evaluate the truth value of such sentences ((9), for example), we presumably did so through some sort of psychological computation. This shows that psychological issues are not irrelevant to compositionality of reference after all! But now we have a little paradox: We can easily see that sentence (9) is true—so we must have some way of calculating its truth value. But the semantic operations involved in deriving this truth value included one which was non-computable. How, then, was it possible to figure out the truth value?

Readers who view this primarily as a mathematical problem might point out that I have not proved that the referent of any particular string term in L_2 is non-computable—only that function f, taken as a whole, is non-computable. The first twenty-eight pairs of f form only a finite set and are therefore trivially computable. So in fact there *is* a computable function assigning a referent to the string term in (9), and one could easily give a computational procedure for deriving the truth value of (9).[9]

But this response misses a crucial point, namely that we can easily see that (9) is true *without* figuring out what the referent of its string term is. In fact we can do this even though I have not even specified what the alphabet of L_{NR} is—I haven't given enough information to

---

[9]In fact, one could assign truth values to all the sentences of L_2 using computable functions by replacing G_2 with an infinite series of operations $G_2^1, G_2^2, \ldots$, each of which encoded only the first n pairs of f for some n. But presumably a system with this sort of infinite series of operations is no more psychologically plausible than one with non-computable operations.

It is also worth noting that the set of sentences of L_2 whose truth values we can figure out are those containing string terms denoting *all but* the first 27 strings of L_{NR}—there is an infinite number of sentences whose truth values we can figure out, and only a small finite number whose truth values we can't. The truth evaluable sentences of L_2 thus do not correspond to a recursively enumerable sublanguage of L_{NR}.

figure out what the referent is even if all our operations *were* computable.

I think it is obvious, then, that we were able to compute the truth value of (9) because we were *not* computing it by first computing the referents of its parts. All we needed in order to compute the truth value were certain crucial pieces of background information (L_{NR} is over a 26-letter alphabet; f arranges strings by length), and some very limited information about the referents of the parts (the referent of the string term comes 28th in the ordering; the members of the referent of **TL** are all strings consisting of at least two letters).

I would suggest that this is actually typical of the way we calculate the truth values of sentences, when we do so in real, practical situations. We rarely if ever calculate the referent of each constituent, deriving each from the referents of its immediate constituents; but instead figure out the truth value from relevant background knowledge combined with very limited, possibly non-identifying information about the referents of the parts.

This point will not be controversial, I think; and although it is made particularly vividly by examples involving non-computable operations, it is obvious enough just from ordinary subject-predicate sentences. The most standard analysis of a sentence like *John smokes*, for example, treats *smokes* as denoting the set of things that smoke. No one would claim that people have to identify this set in any meaningful sense in order to evaluate whether the sentence is true. But if we don't even know what the referents of the parts of a sentence are, how can we calculate the truth value of the sentence by applying semantic operations to them? This is the sort of question that students ask in introductory semantics classes all the time, and I think most of us who teach such classes probably respond by making the correct and elementary point that you don't *need* to know the referent of *smokes* to calculate the truth value; all you need to know is whether John is member of it. But if this is right, then we are *not* calculating the truth value by starting from the referents of the parts and successively applying semantic operations; we start instead from very limited, potentially non-identifying information about the referents of the parts, and calculate the truth value from that, together with any relevant background knowledge.[10]

A defender of the view that the truth values of verifiable or falsifiable sentences are computed from the referents of their parts might respond

---

[10]The introduction of "witness sets" in Barwise and Cooper (1981) provides a classic discussion of a different kind of case in which truth values may be calculated in ways other than applying semantic operations directly to the denotations of the immediate constituents of the sentence.

as follows: In semantic analysis, we are free to posit as the referents of expressions any objects which do the work we theoretically require of referents. If there is a way to compute the truth value of a sentence, we may assign as the referents of its parts whatever objects are used in the computation. Then the truth value is guaranteed to be computable from the referents of its parts.

For example, one could computably assign truth values to all those L_2 sentences of the form $\mathbf{TL}(\#\alpha)$, where α contains at least 28 occurrences of 1, simply by letting $h(\alpha) = h(\#\alpha) = h(\mathbf{TL}(\#\alpha)) = \mathbf{true}$. Or, one could assign truth values to sentences like *John smokes* by letting *smokes* denote, not the set of things that actually smoke, but a representation of some language user's mentally encoded information about who smokes.

It is reasonable to expect that in any case where we have the psychological ability to verify or falsify a sentence, it will be possible to recast its semantics in a computable fashion by reassigning referents in this way—choosing as "referents" whatever is needed to make the computation work. Whether the objects assigned in this way really deserve to be called "referents," however, seems debatable. It seems to me that this technique gives a theory of something rather different from what we usually mean by reference and truth.

First, one should note that this approach is a kind of verificationism, since it yields truth values only for those sentences whose truth values can be computed. But intuitively, sentences may be true or false even if we have no way of discovering the truth value. Moreover, if the motivation for this move is to explain people's psychological abilities to verify sentences, it leads immediately to a mentalistic conception of reference, since any computation we do is presumably done on psychological representations. But intuitively, reference is normally to the mind-independent entities we talk about and make claims about.

It is clear that we do have psychological procedures for computing the truth values of sentences, and presumably any step in these procedures must be representable as a computable function. But it also seems clear that this computation is not necessarily done directly from the referents of the parts of the sentence—at least if we understand "referents" in the usual way—but rather from potentially very limited information about those referents, and from other relevant background information.

If we want to motivate the idea that truth values are assigned "compositionally" based on the psychological fact that people are able to figure out the truth values of novel sentences, then the principle of compositionality amounts to a claim that this kind of procedure exists.

Let us call this conception of compositionality *C-compositionality* (C for "computable"). To say that truth values are assigned C-compositionally is to say that there is a way of computing them. If people can assign truth values to novel sentences, this shows that they must be employing some sort of C-compositional system. But to say that reference is assigned C-compositionally does *not* mean that it is possible to compute the reference of a complex expression from the referents of its parts— only that there is some way of computing the referents of complex expressions; and this may well be on the basis of information which is insufficient to identify the referents of the parts.

On the other hand, the formal notion of compositionality which we have from Montague requires that "compositionally" assigned values be derivable by operations from the values of their parts, but makes no claims that these operations correspond to any sort of computational procedure. Let us call this conception of compositionality *H-compositionality* (H for "homomorphic"). To say that reference is assigned H-compositionally is to say that the referent of a complex expression is determined by the referents of its (immediate) parts.

6.6 H-Compositionality, Substitution, and Intensionality

If C-compositionality explains people's psychological abilities,[11] is there still any reason for maintaining a principle of H-compositionality? For the moment, let us continue to limit ourselves to reference assignment in considering this question. We will return to the issue of compositionality of *meaning* below.

I suspect many semanticists might justify H-compositionality by claiming that people employ the C-compositional system only because they know it will give the same results as an H-compositional system whose principles form a more basic part of their semantic knowledge. This view is reinforced by the fact that I presented the semantics of L_2 in H-compositional format, and did not specify a C-compositional procedure for it at all, yet we were able to compute the truth value of (9). We must have figured out some sort of C-compositional procedure for doing so, presumably based on the H-compositional semantics which was presented in (8)—since this was the only information about L_2 we had.

---

[11]Of course I have not given an actual theory of C-compositionality here, so I do not claim to have explained people's psychological abilities to understand novel sentences or evaluate their truth values. But *some* theory must explain such abilities, and such a theory is, by definition, a theory of C-compositionality.

But to a skeptic, this kind of argument will probably not be compelling. This example really shows only that a C-compositional procedure can sometimes be constructed to match an antecedently given H-compositional semantics; it does not show that language users must have such an antecedently given H-compositional semantics in order to construct a C-compositional procedure. To make a convincing case for H-compositionality, we need to find something which H-compositionality explains but C-compositionality does not—and I hope it is by now clear that the ability of language users to deal with novel sentences will not serve this purpose.

I think the explanatory value of H-compositionality becomes clear if we recognize that it is equivalent to a familiar substitutivity principle. Specifically, reference is assigned homomorphically if and only if one expression may always be substituted for another expression with the same reference without altering the reference of any larger expression of which it is a part.[12] (A proof is given in the appendix.)

We should maintain the principle of H-compositionality of reference, then, precisely if we hold that reference is preserved under substitution of coreferring parts—regardless of any considerations having to do with language users' ability to understand novel sentences. It is on this basis, I suggest, that any principle of H-compositionality must be justified.

As a corollary to this equivalence, we can see that any counterexample to H-compositionality of reference must take the form of some context where coreferring expressions cannot be substituted for one another without altering the reference of a larger expression containing them. But this is just the standard definition of an intensional context, so it follows immediately that *any counterexample to H-compositionality of reference must involve an intensional context.*

In fact, *all* intensional contexts are prima facie counterexamples to H-compositionality of reference. But there are familiar ways of maintaining the principle in the face of such counterexamples: we may claim that what appear to be coreferring expressions do not really corefer after all, at least in the contexts in question; or we may claim that what appears to be the result of substituting one expression for another re-

---

[12]Essentially this same mathematical point was made with a short proof-sketch by Muskens (1995, p. 89), though in a non-algebraic context, and in a discussion of compositionality of meaning and substitution of synonyms rather than compositionality of reference and substitution of coreferring terms. As Muskens notes, if we impose the further restriction that all semantic operations must be computable, the equivalence fails. Westerståhl (1998) and Janssen (2001) sketch essentially the same result, in an algebraic framework. Hodges (2001) gives a more detailed proof, also in an algebraic framework, and explores the relation between compositionality and substitutivity in detail.

ally isn't. The first strategy is Frege's—expressions in intensional contexts are analyzed as referring to something other than their customary reference. The second strategy is Russell's—sentences are analyzed as having an abstract logical form of which the apparently coreferring expressions are not really constituent parts, or do not really occupy the same structural position, so that the substitution is not well-defined.

Both approaches come with some cost. Davidson (1968) famously suggested that "if we could but recover our pre-Fregean semantic innocence," it would seem implausible to us to claim that expressions in intensional contexts refer to anything different than they do elsewhere. But if the Fregean strategy involves a loss of semantic innocence, the Russellian strategy involves just as much a loss of *syntactic* innocence— which, if recovered, would make it seem implausible to claim that the sentence *Scott is the author of Waverly* has a radically different syntactic structure from *Scott is Scott*. Either way, we do some violence to our innocent (or perhaps one should say "naive") intuitions.

Despite these concerns, I think that H-compositionality of reference is an intuitively sound principle, which we should try to maintain. The intuition behind it—or really, behind the substitutivity principle to which it is equivalent—is just that (for any x, y) if you can say something truthfully about x, and x is the very same thing as y, then you can say the same thing truthfully about y. If you say something true, then swap out some part of the sentence and wind up saying something false, you must not have been talking about the same thing in the substituted part as you were in the original. This intuition seems at least as secure as those underlying the "innocent" perspectives, and is sufficient in my view to render something like a Fregean theory of indirect reference plausible. Any analysis which tries to maintain both semantic and syntactic innocence at the cost of H-compositionality of reference must either reconcile itself with this intuition, or explain why it should be abandoned.

That having been said, both the Fregean strategy and the Russellian strategy, if left completely unconstrained, seem likely to rob the principle of H-compositionality of reference of all content. One suspects that if we are free to assign whatever structure we like to the expressions we are analyzing, an H-compositional reference assignment will always be possible; and likewise, that if we are free to use any arbitrary object as the indirect referent of an expression in intensional contexts, an H-compositional reference assignment will always be possible even if the syntax is antecedently given.[13] If we are to regard H-compositionality

---

[13] Janssen (1986, pp. 74–75) proves that, given a recursively enumerable language

of reference as a real issue, then, it should probably be in the context of a theory which places specific constraints both on syntactic analysis and on indirect reference.

6.7 Compositionality, Computability and Meaning

Having seen that the use of non-computable semantic operations does not necessarily render sentences incomprehensible, and having separated C-compositionality from H-compositionality, and found at least some motivation for H-compositionality of reference, it is now worth returning to the issue of compositionality of *meaning*. Could the use of non-computable operations be called for here as well? More importantly, does H-compositionality of meaning have any conceptual or empirical motivation, or is it only C-compositionality which is motivated?

These issues are complicated by the fact that the term *meaning* is imprecise, coming as it does from our pretheoretic, non-technical vocabulary; we need to be more explicit about what we mean by it before we can expect to make much headway.

Obviously, if we simply *define* meaning as something which language users calculate in understanding each other's utterances, meaning will be C-compositional by definition; and there will be no obvious reason to suspect a role for non-computable operations, or to expect that meaning assignment will be H-compositional. But if, in developing a technical notion of meaning, we focus instead on the role meaning plays in the determination of truth and falsity, the issue appears in a rather different light.

Intuitively, there are two factors which go into determining the truth value of a sentence: what it means, and what the world is like. The study of indexicality has shown the usefulness of considering the context of use separately from other aspects of "what the world is like," so we get a conception of the meaning of a sentence as something which, in combination with a context and a world, determines a truth value. Generalizing, the meanings of other expressions will be things which, again in combination with a context and a world, determine a referent. Meanings, then should correspond to, or be representable as, or identified with, functions from contexts and worlds to referents. In fact,

---

and a function assigning interpretations to its sentences, a grammar and semantic algebra can always be given for which a homomorphic interpretation is possible; Janssen (1997, pp. 455–456) additionally shows that if the interpretation function is computable, the resulting semantic operations will be too. Janssen's technique involves an unintuitive assignment of interpretations to non-sentential expressions, and therefore is available only if we allow ourselves a good deal of freedom both in assigning syntactic structure and assigning interpretations to the "parts" of a sentence.

this is precisely the position taken in Montague (1970), and it bears an obviously close relation to the notion of *character*, from Kaplan (1989).

If this is what we mean by *meaning*, we should note immediately that if the set of contexts or worlds is sufficiently large, then the set of functions from context-world pairs to possible denotations will be non-denumerable, and operations on this set will be non-computable by reasons of cardinality alone. But assuming there are only denumerably many expressions in a language, we really only need denumerably many meanings for them, so we need not regard all functions from context-world pairs to possible denotations as meanings. We may always limit the set B in our semantic algebra to the range of the meaning assignment h; then B will be no larger than the set A from our syntactic algebra.

If meaning determines reference, and the reference algebra requires non-computable operations, does this mean the meaning algebra will too? It turns out the answer is *no*—in some cases, we can locate the non-computability in the context, rather than the operations.

To see this, recall the analysis mentioned above for the English noun phrase *number twenty-eight*: we regard the context as providing a domain of relevant individuals, and a sequential ordering relation on that domain. Relative to a context c, the noun phrase will denote the 28th element of the domain, according to the ordering. Let us suppose for the sake of argument that the phrase *number twenty-eight* is derived from *twenty-eight* by a syntactic operation which prefixes the word *number*, and consider what the corresponding operation in the meaning algebra might be like.

In pursuing this line of analysis, we might represent each context c as an ordered pair consisting of a non-empty set D and a sequential ordering σ on D. The meaning of *twenty-eight* should be the constant function mapping each such pair (and a possible world) onto the number 28—in other words a set of pairs of the form $\langle \langle \langle D, \sigma \rangle , w \rangle , 28 \rangle$. Note that σ itself is a set of ordered pairs.[14] The meaning of *number twenty-eight* should be the function mapping each pair $\langle D, \sigma \rangle$ (and world w) onto $\sigma(28)$; that is, a set of pairs of the form $\langle \langle \langle D, \sigma \rangle , w \rangle , \sigma(28) \rangle$. Each pair in the latter function corresponds directly to a pair in the former function, and there is a straightforward procedure for deriving it from the pair it corresponds to: just scan the pairs in σ to find the one whose left-hand member is the number 28, then pair $\langle \langle D, \sigma \rangle , w \rangle$ with the right-hand member. As long as the number of contexts and

---

[14] By a *sequential ordering* on D I mean a function from the set of natural numbers, or an initial segment of the natural numbers, into D.

worlds is at most denumerably infinite,[15] we may use this procedure to compute the meaning of *number twenty-eight* from the meaning of *twenty-eight*, even if in some cases σ is non-computable. The semantic operation is computable, even though in a context which provides L_{NR} and a length-sorting function f as the values of D and σ, the corresponding operation in the reference algebra is non-computable.

On the other hand, we can also imagine a language in which reference to a non-computable function is built directly into an operation of the meaning algebra. Suppose for example that pragmatic contexts are not pairs $\langle D, \sigma \rangle$ as above, but just arbitrary objects. Now for each expression α in L_2, assign as its meaning the constant function which maps every context c and world w onto the referent assigned to it by the rules in (8) above. Now the relativization to worlds and contexts is vacuous (every expression is a non-indexical rigid designator), and the operation deriving the meanings of string terms from number terms must appeal to the non-computable function f which sorts L_{NR} by length.

It seems unlikely that a natural language could work this way, but not because a language with such an operation must be incomprehensible; on the contrary, this interpretation of L_2 is perfectly intelligible. What is implausible is that a natural language might have a dedicated grammatical construction for talking about strings in some other specific non-recursively-enumerable language. This pragmatic function is simply too specialized and comes up too rarely to get grammaticized.

I would suggest, then, that concerns about the ability of language users to understand novel sentences should not lead us to impose a computability constraint on meaning algebras any more than on reference algebras—at least if by *meaning* we mean something like functions from contexts and worlds to denotations. And just as with H-compositionality of reference, we should motivate H-compositionality of meaning on grounds other than this ability.

Just as H-compositionality of reference turned out to be equivalent to the principle that one expression can always be substituted for another with the same reference without altering the reference of any larger expression of which it is a part, H-compositionality of meaning is equivalent to the principle that one expression can always be substituted for another with the same meaning without altering the meaning of any larger expression of which it is a part. (The same proof will show this; see the appendix.) And just as with reference, we should maintain

---

[15]Of course it might not be, but this does not affect the mathematical point—that a non-computable operation in the reference algebra can correspond to a computable operation in the meaning algebra.

the principle of H-compositionality of meaning precisely if we accept this substitutivity principle, regardless of any considerations having to do with language users' abilities to understand novel sentences.

An interesting corollary of this equivalence is that in a language with no perfect synonyms, an H-compositional meaning assignment is always possible. This follows immediately, because in a language with no perfect synonyms, the substitutivity principle is vacuously satisfied.[16] It is inconsistent to maintain as a point of doctrine that there are no perfect synonyms, while denying that meaning is H-compositional.

It also follows that any counterexample to H-compositionality of meaning must take the form of a context where synonymous expressions cannot be substituted for one another without altering the meaning of a larger expression containing them. As with H-compositionality of reference, intensional contexts would appear to be the primary source of apparent counterexamples: it might be true that John believes there is a woodchuck in his yard, but false that he believes a groundhog is in his yard, if he does not know that *woodchuck* and *groundhog* are synonyms. Our strategies for trying to maintain H-compositionality of meaning in the face of such examples are basically the same as the strategies for trying to maintain H-compositionality of reference: we may claim that in such contexts, words don't mean what they customarily mean, but instead express some special meaning (a metalinguistic meaning, for example[17]); or we may claim that the syntactic structure is different from how it appears, so that the substitution is not legitimate. And just as before, H-compositionality of meaning would seem to impose a significant constraint only if both these strategies are also significantly constrained.

H-compositionality of meaning is motivated in precisely the same way as H-compositionality of reference. If two expressions have the same meaning (correspond to the same function from world-context pairs to referents), but substituting one for the other results in change of meaning for the sentence as a whole (that is, a different function from world-context pairs to truth values), then there must be some world-

---

[16]We must construe *synonym* broadly enough here to include complex expressions with the same meaning, not just lexical items. Westerståhl (1998) also points out that compositionality is automatic in a language with no synonyms.

[17]Consider how odd it would be to say of a dog, for example, that it believed that a woodchuck was in the yard but not that a groundhog was in the yard. This sort of assertion seems to imply a knowledge of English, implying a metalinguistic component to the belief. Note that the oddity disappears if no contrast between the synonyms is asserted; it is not at all strange to say of a dog simply that it believes a woodchuck is in the yard—suggesting the metalinguistic interpretation is not systematically present in all belief ascriptions.

context pair at which *reference* is determined non-H-compositionally. H-compositionality of reference thus commits us to H-compositionality of meaning (if we understand meanings to be functions from indices to referents). If the intuition underlying substitutivity for reference seems legitimate, we must accept it for meaning as well.

6.8 Conclusion

We have seen that a principle of homomorphic interpretation will not explain the ability of language users to compute the meanings of novel sentences. However, I argued that we should not resolve this issue by placing a computability requirement on the semantic algebras used in homomorphic interpretation. Even if non-computable operations are used in the derivation of sentences, these sentences may be comprehensible and even truth evaluable.

The important point here is *not* that we need non-computable operations in an adequate semantic theory. After all, the examples discussed in this paper are mainly from artificial languages, and have interpretations which could be used only in highly specialized technical contexts. Rather, the point is that we need to separate the issue of how people compute meanings, referents, truth values, etc.—essentially a processing question—from the issue of whether the interpretations of complex expressions are functionally determined by the interpretations of their immediate parts—essentially a structural question. Considering these issues separately leads to two separate principles corresponding to the traditional idea of compositionality: a principle of computable interpretation, or "C-compositionality," and a principle of homomorphic interpretation, or "H-compositionality."

If we motivate the "Principle of Compositionality" by pointing out the ability of language users to understand an indefinite number of novel sentences, and then take the central issue to be one of how this ability relates to syntactic structure (as suggested by Dowty (2007), for example), the theory we construct will most naturally be construed as a theory of C-compositionality. This line of investigation will not, I have suggested, lead naturally to a theory of H-compositionality—and might, in fact, cause us to miss the very real motivation that exists for such a theory.

The principle of homomorphic interpretation turns out to be equivalent to a familiar substitutivity principle: one expression may be substituted for another with the same interpretation without altering the interpretation of any complex expression of which it is a part. We should maintain the principle of homomorphic interpretation precisely to the degree that we accept this substitutivity principle, regardless of any psychological considerations.

The equivalence of the H-compositionality to substitutivity entails that counterexamples to H-compositionality of reference must come from intensional contexts, and that H-compositionality of meaning will always hold in a language with no perfect synonyms.

6.9 Appendix: Proof that interpretation is homomorphic if and only if the substitutivity principle holds

If by "interpretation" we mean reference assignment, this proof will show that reference is assigned homomorphically if and only if one expression may be substituted for another with the same reference without altering the reference of any larger expression of which it is a part. If by "interpretation" we mean meaning assignment, it will show that meaning is assigned homomorphically if and only if one synonym may be substituted for another without altering the meaning of any expression of which it is a part.

To prove these claims, we must first make them a little more precise. Given a syntactic algebra $\mathfrak{A} = \langle A, F_1, \ldots, F_i \rangle$, set B, and interpretation function $h : A \to B$, let us say that interpretation is homomorphic iff there are operations $G_1, \ldots, G_i$ on B such that $\mathfrak{B} = \langle B, G_1, \ldots, G_i \rangle$ is an algebra similar to $\mathfrak{A}$ and h is a homomorphism from $\mathfrak{A}$ to $\mathfrak{B}$.

When h is construed as assigning referents, we understand α and β to corefer iff $h(\alpha) = h(\beta)$. When h is construed as assigning meanings, we understand α and β to be synonyms iff $h(\alpha) = h(\beta)$.

Where $\mathfrak{A} = \langle A, F_1, \ldots, F_i \rangle$ and $\alpha, \gamma \in A$, let us say that α is a *first level part* of γ iff $\gamma = F_n(\alpha_1, \ldots, \alpha, \ldots, \alpha_m)$ for some syntactic operation F_n. We will say that α is a *second level part* of γ iff α is a first level part of a first level part of γ; and more generally that α is a $(j+1)^{th}$ *level part* of γ iff α is a jth level part of a first level part of γ. We say that α is a *part* of γ iff α is a jth level part of γ for some j.

If α is a first level part of γ (that is, if $\gamma = F_n(\alpha_1, \ldots, \alpha, \ldots, \alpha_m)$ for some F_n), then γ' is a result of substituting β for α in γ iff $\gamma' = F_n(\alpha_1, \ldots, \beta, \ldots, \alpha_m)$. If α is a jth level part of γ ($j \geq 2$), then γ' is a result of substituting β for α in γ iff $\gamma = F_n(\delta_1, \ldots, \delta, \ldots, \delta_m)$ (for some F_n), $\gamma' = F_n(\delta_1, \ldots, \delta', \ldots, \delta_m)$, and δ' is a result of substituting β for α in δ.

By the *substitutivity principle* let us mean the claim that if α is a part of γ, and $h(\alpha) = h(\beta)$, and γ' is a result of substituting β for α in γ, then $h(\gamma) = h(\gamma')$.

An m-place *operation* on B is a set G of ordered $(m+1)$-tuples of elements of B, such that for any $x_1, \ldots, x_m \in B$, there is exactly one $y \in B$ such that $\langle x_1, \ldots, x_m, y \rangle \in G$. If this condition is met we may also write $y = G(x_1, \ldots, x_m)$.

Now we show that given a syntactic algebra $\mathfrak{A} = \langle A, F_1, \ldots, F_i \rangle$, set B, and interpretation function $h : A \to B$, interpretation is homomorphic iff the substitutivity principle holds.

Left to right (If interpretation is assigned homomorphically, an expression β may always be substituted for an expression α with the same interpretation, without altering the interpretation of any expression of which α is a part):

Assume interpretation is assigned homomorphically. This means there is a semantic algebra $\mathfrak{B} = \langle B, G_1, \ldots, G_i \rangle$ similar to our syntactic algebra $\mathfrak{A} = \langle A, F_1, \ldots, F_i \rangle$, and h is a homomorphism from $\mathfrak{A}$ to $\mathfrak{B}$.

First we show that substituting β for α will not affect the interpretation of any expression γ of which α forms a first level part, then we show that if substituting β for α does not affect the interpretation of any expression of which α is a jth level part, it will not affect the interpretation of any expression of which it forms a $(j+1)^{th}$ level part.

Suppose that γ has α as first level part; that is, that $\gamma = F_n(\alpha_1, \ldots, \alpha, \ldots, \alpha_m)$ for some F_n. Let γ' be a result of substituting β for α in γ; that is, $\gamma' = F_n(\alpha_1, \ldots, \beta, \ldots, \alpha_m)$. Because h is a homomorphism, $h(\gamma) = G_n(h(\alpha_1), \ldots, h(\alpha), \ldots, h(\alpha_m))$, and $h(\gamma') = G_n(h(\alpha_1), \ldots, h(\beta), \ldots, h(\alpha_m))$. But since $h(\alpha) = h(\beta)$, it follows that $h(\gamma) = h(\gamma')$. That is, substituting β for α will not affect the interpretation of any expression of which α is a first level part.

Now suppose that substituting β for α does not affect the interpretation of any expression of which α is a jth level part. Assume α is a $(j+1)^{th}$ level part of γ. Then $\gamma = F_n(\delta_1, \ldots, \delta, \ldots, \delta_m)$, for some δ of which α is a jth level part (and some F_n). Because α is a jth level part of δ, $h(\delta) = h(\delta')$, where δ' is any result of substituting β for α in δ. Let γ' be the result of substituting δ' for δ in γ. This means that γ' is also a result of substituting β for α in γ. Because h is a homomorphism, $h(\gamma) = G_n(h(\delta_1), \ldots, h(\delta), \ldots, h(\delta_m))$, and $h(\gamma') = G_n(h(\delta_1), \ldots, h(\delta'), \ldots, h(\delta_m))$. But since $h(\delta) = h(\delta')$, it follows that $h(\gamma) = h(\gamma')$. That is, if substituting β for α does not affect the interpretation of any expression of which α is a jth level part, it will not affect the interpretation of any expression of which α is a $(j+1)^{th}$ level part.

Right-to-Left (If one expression may always be substituted for another with the same interpretation without affecting the interpretation of complex expressions of which it is a part, then interpretation is assigned homomorphically):

Assume that one expression may always be substituted for another with the same interpretation without affecting the interpretation of any complex expression of which it is a part.

Now for each m and each m-place syntactic operation F_n, let G_n be the smallest set of $(m+1)$-tuples such that if $\gamma = F_n(\alpha_1, \ldots, \alpha_m)$, then $\langle h(\alpha_1), \ldots, h(\alpha_m), h(\gamma) \rangle \in G_n$.

We show that G_n is an operation: If G_n were not an operation, there would be some α, β, x, y such that $h(\alpha) = h(\beta)$ and $x \neq y$, but $\langle h(\alpha_1), \ldots, h(\alpha), \ldots, h(\alpha_m), x \rangle \in G_n$ and $\langle h(\alpha_1), \ldots, h(\beta), \ldots, h(\alpha_m), y \rangle \in G_n$. By the definition of G_n, $x = h(\gamma)$ where $\gamma = F_n(\alpha_1, \ldots, \alpha, \ldots, \alpha_m)$, and $y = h(\gamma')$, where $\gamma' = F_n(\alpha_1, \ldots, \beta, \ldots, \alpha_m)$. But since substitution of one expression for another with the same interpretation will not affect the interpretation of expressions of which it is a part, $h(\gamma) = h(\gamma')$; that is, $x = y$. We now have $x = y$ and $x \neq y$; this is a contradiction, so G_n must be an operation.

By the definition of G_n, if $\gamma = F_n(\alpha_1, \ldots, \alpha_m)$, then $\langle h(\alpha_1), \ldots, h(\alpha_m), h(\gamma) \rangle \in G_n$. Since G_n is an operation, we may write this as $h(\gamma) = G_n(h(\alpha_1), \ldots, h(\alpha_m))$. That is, $h(F_n(\alpha_1, \ldots, \alpha_m)) = G_n(h(\alpha_1), \ldots, h(\alpha_m))$. This is the relevant condition to make h a homomorphism; simply let $\mathfrak{B} = \langle B, G_1, \ldots, G_i \rangle$ and it immediately follows that h is a homomorphism from $\mathfrak{A}$ to $\mathfrak{B}$.

References

Barwise, Jon and Robin Cooper. 1981. Generalized Quantifiers and Natural Language. *Linguistics and Philosophy* 4:159–219.

Davidson, Donald. 1968. On Saying That. *Synthese* 19:130–146.

Dowty, David. 2007. Compositionality as an Empirical Problem. In C. Barker and P. Jacobson, eds., *Direct Compositionality*. Oxford: Oxford University Press.

Frege, Gottlob. 1884/1980. *The Foundations of Arithmetic*. Evanston, Illinois: Northwestern University Press, 2nd edn.

Frege, Gottlob. 1892/1970. On Sense and Reference. In P. Geach and M. Black, eds., *Translations from the Philosophical Writings of Gottlob Frege*. Oxford: Basil Blackwell, 2nd edn.

Hodges, Wilfrid. 2001. Formal Features of Compositionality. *Journal of Logic, Language and Information* 10:7–28.

Janssen, Theo. 1986. *Foundations and Applications of Montague Grammar, Part 1: Philosophy, Framework, Computer Science*. No. 19 in CWI Tracts. Amsterdam: Stichting Mathematisch Centrum.

Janssen, Theo. 1997. Compositionality. In J. van Benthem and A. ter Meulen, eds., *Handbook of Logic and Language*, pages 417–473. Cambridge, Massachusetts: MIT Press.

Janssen, Theo. 2001. Frege, Contextuality and Compositionality. *Journal of Logic, Language and Information* 10:115–136.

Kaplan, David. 1989. Demonstratives. In J. P. Joseph Almog and H. Wettstein, eds., *Themes from Kaplan*, pages 481–563. Oxford: Oxford University Press.

Kracht, Marcus. 2003. *Mathematics of Language*. Berlin: Mouton de Gruyter.

Larson, Richard and Gabriel Segal. 1995. *Knowledge of Meaning: An Introduction to Semantic Theory*. Cambridge, Massachusetts: MIT Press.

Montague, Richard. 1970. Universal Grammar. *Theoria* 36:373–398.

Muskens, Reinhard. 1995. *Meaning and Partiality*. Stanford, California: CSLI Publications.

Partee, Barbara, Alice ter Meulen, and Robert Wall. 1990. *Mathematical Methods in Linguistics*. Dordrecht: Kluwer Academic Publishers.

Pelletier, Francis Jeffry. 2001. Did Frege believe in Frege's principle? *Journal of Logic, Language and Information* 10:87–114.

Westerståhl, Dag. 1998. On Mathematical Proofs of the Vacuity of Compositionality. *Linguistics and Philosophy* 21:635–643.

7

Quantitatively Detecting Semantic Relations: The Case of Aspectual Affinity

JOHN NERBONNE AND TIM VAN DE CRUYS

7.1 Introduction

The explosion in the creation of text corpora in recent years suggests that the opportunity may be ripe to examine quantitative techniques for their value in semantics.[1] The present paper aims to explore one quantitative technique with an eye toward its potential value in illuminating questions of semantic theory. It is exploratory in nature, and it will not offer definite conclusions or specific advice.

To exploit large text corpora—of a size of the order of magnitude of 10^9 words, we need to employ automatic procedures of analysis. It is unthinkable to work through such volumes of material except by using computer programs. This leads to a difficulty when one's analytical ambitions are semantic, since the semantics of texts is not immediately accessible to automatic procedures.

Perhaps in some glorious future there will be data annotated for semantics to an extent that makes the direct application of quantitative analyses straightforward. But at present we do not have such resources, only fairly large corpora of texts. This means in turn that we need to operationalize our semantic concepts in a way that is amenable to automatic processing. Naturally this has an impact on the sorts of

---

[1] We have benefited from discussions with the computational linguistics group at the University of Groningen and from astute comments by two anonymous referees.

Theory and Evidence in Semantics.
Erhard Hinrichs and John Nerbonne (eds.).
Copyright © 2009, CSLI Publications.

phenomena that can be studied.

In the present study we concentrate on aspect and on the affinities different sorts of adverbials have with some aspectual categories as opposed to others. We operationalize the inherent aspect of verb phrases by noting the verb heading the phrase, and the class of the durative adverbial by noting the preposition heading the durative adverbial. Both of these steps are subject to some error, but fortunately, quantitative techniques also tolerate noise in characterizations as long as the statistical strength of the association between the category and its operationalization is sufficient, and as long as the "noise" does not systematically favor some analyses over others. We still need to be on guard against using procedures that bias search routines and ultimately, the results of analysis.

7.2 Background

We discuss computational semantics in this section as well as the statistical background needed for detecting aspectual affinities in large corpora.

7.2.1 Computational Semantics

Work in COMPUTATIONAL LINGUISTICS has frequently implemented and applied work from SEMANTIC THEORY, often with special interest for issues concerning disambiguation (Nerbonne, 1996). Since the quantitative turn in computational linguistics, lexical classification and lexical semantics have been the focus of attention in computational work. Schulte im Walde (to appear) reviews a large number of papers which classify verbs using corpus evidence. The focus is on recognizing subcategorization frames, but there has also been work on detecting selectional preferences, semantic roles and diathesis alternations.

It is difficult to collect the statistical information that is useful to lexical semantics, but many quantitative techniques have nonetheless been proposed with an eye toward detecting semantic properties. In addition to the work on semantic roles mentioned above, there has been a substantial number of papers aimed at distinguishing regular semantic combination from the irregular sorts of combination found in multi-word expressions, idioms, and non-compositional constructions (Villavicencio et al., 2005, Deane, 2005, Villada Moirón, 2005).

A second area of focus in quantitative work on semantics has been LEXICAL SEMANTIC SIMILARITY. Automatically acquiring a relative measure of how semantically similar a word is to known words is much easier than determining what the actual meaning is, as Manning and Schütze (2000, chap. 8.5) point out. Manning and Schütze's textbook refer to a number of works in which the detection of lexical semantic similarity is central.

Brent (1991) shows that one can distinguish stative verbs from others using the presence of progressive variants as well as adverbials expressing rates of speed (e.g., *quickly*), essentially using frequencies of combination as a cue. Siegel (1998) extends Brent's work, using several more cues, including durative adverbials, which we focus on below. He applied three techniques from statistics and machine learning (logistic regression, decision trees and genetic algorithms) with the goal of classifying the aspectual predication of the clause. Since we attempt to detect the relations between the verbal heads and the durative adverbials, we effectively attempt to classify these simultaneously, and also to gauge the strength of the association between subtypes of these.

Mehler (2007) analyzes semantics from a quantitative perspective and recognizes the need for structural sensitivity in quantitative semantics. He allows for structural effects by viewing semantic combination as a HIERARCHICAL CONSTRAINT SATISFACTION PROBLEM (HCSP). In principle Mehler thus allows that semantic combination be dependent on "syntactic dependency and text coherence relations" (p. 147), even if the specific constraints he handles are discourse based rather than grammatical. Like Mehler, we shall be concerned to rise above the lexical level, but where his focus is on the theoretical underpinnings of the relation between quantitative work and semantic theory, we shall try to develop an experimental technique.

In this paper we try to extend the techniques used in computational linguistics to address questions in semantic theory. Since it is an early effort we will try to be alert for signals that we are detecting semantic structure and to be open for opportunities to exploit the information that large corpora, processed automatically, might offer.

7.2.2 Vector Space Model

The VECTOR SPACE MODEL is one of the most widely used models to investigate lexical semantic similarity in textual data, mainly because it is easy to understand, and it allows one to express 'semantic proximity' between entities in terms of spatial distance (Manning and Schütze, 2000). It is particularly popular in Information Retrieval, where it is used to create term-document matrices. We introduce the vector space model via an example. Consider two documents, one about *Belgium* (B) and one about the *Netherlands* (NL).

- Belgium is a kingdom in the middle of Europe, and **Brussels** is its capital. **Brussels** has a Dutch-speaking and a French-speaking university, but the largest student city is **Leuven**. **Leuven** has 31,000 students.

- The Netherlands is a country in Western Europe, located next to the North Sea. The Netherlands's capital is **Amsterdam**. **Amsterdam** has two universities. **Groningen** is another important student city. In **Groningen**, there are 37,000 students.

The documents can easily be transformed into a term-document matrix, in which each document is represented by a vector. Each dimension in the vector corresponds to a term (a word or fixed expression), where the frequencies of the terms (in this case, cities) in each of the documents are indicated. The resulting matrix is shown in Figure 1.

$$
\begin{bmatrix}
 & B & NL \\
Groningen & 0 & 2 \\
Leuven & 2 & 0 \\
Amsterdam & 0 & 2 \\
Brussel & 2 & 0
\end{bmatrix}
$$

FIGURE 1   A term-document matrix

To term-document matrices like this one, SIMILARITY MEASURES can be applied,[2] to assay how similar documents are to each other, or to a query entered by the user. Note that the *Belgian* document is represented in the term-document matrix as vector of city-reference frequencies, viz. $< 0, 2, 0, 2 >$, the first column in Figure 1. Similarly, words are represented as document-occurrence frequencies, so that *Groningen* is just $< 0, 2 >$. Vector spaces are immediately amenable to the application of distance metrics, which is one reason why they are popular. These distance metrics are used to assay the similarity between words. The two words for which the semantic similarity is to be calculated are represented as vectors in a multi-dimensional feature space.

The co-occurrence information that can be captured by such matrices is not limited to words and documents. If we add grammatical analysis, we can straightforwardly record the dependency relations of a particular word. In that case, the dimensions of the vectors correspond to the dependency relations that the word occurs in together with the lexical head to which it is related. Dependency relations that might be suitable for a word like *apple* could e.g. be 'object of verb *eat*'

---

[2]The COSINE is a natural choice when dealing with vectors, but one may also use the inverse of distance measures such as Euclidean distance or MANHATTAN DISTANCE, or set-based measures such as JACCARD.

and 'modified by adjective *red*'. Similarly, such matrices can capture the co-occurrence information that is the subject of this research, viz. verbs and the adpositional heads of modifiers modifying those verbs. Figure 2 gives an example of two adpositions represented as vectors, with some verbs as features. We read '5' in the (*leave, at*) cell of the matrix, indicating that, in our example corpus, *at* occurred five times as the prepositional head of a modifier modifying a verb phrase headed by *leave*.

$$\begin{bmatrix} & leave & start & work & live \\ at & 5 & 7 & 0 & 0 \\ during & 0 & 0 & 7 & 6 \end{bmatrix}$$

FIGURE 2   A preposition by verb matrix

The matrix shows that—in our sample corpus—the preposition *at* collocates with the verbs *leave* and *start*, while *during* only collocates with *work* and *live*. A matrix of this kind is the basic input for subsequent statistical techniques (see below). A more detailed explanation about the construction of our co-occurrence matrix can be found in subsection 7.3.4.

Semantic classification based on co-occurrence frequencies improves significantly when more informative collocations are weighted more heavily. Some features, such as co-occurrences with the verbs *have* and *be*, are less informative because they occur with many words. Other features only occur with a limited number of words, and are thus more informative. To account for these distributional differences, we use POINTWISE MUTUAL INFORMATION (Church and Hanks, 1990). Intuitively, PMI assigns a high value when the frequency of two events co-occurring is much higher than would be expected on the basis of the individual events' frequencies. The formula is given as equation 7.1.

$$I(x, y) = log \frac{p(x, y)}{p(x)p(y)} \qquad (7.1)$$

7.2.3   Singular Value Decomposition

SINGULAR VALUE DECOMPOSITION (SVD) is a technique that is used to calculate a so-called *low-rank approximation* of a matrix. It is often used as a dimensionality reduction technique in applications that involve large-scale matrix computations.

Technique: SVD originates from linear algebra: a rectangular matrix is decomposed into three other matrices of specific forms so that the product of these three matrices is equal to the original matrix.

$$A = TSD^T \qquad (7.2)$$

where A is the original matrix. The first component matrix, T, contains the same number of rows as the original matrix, but has m columns, corresponding to new, especially derived variables. The second component matrix D has the same number of columns as in the original matrix A, but m rows of derived vectors. These specially derived variables are respectively called left-singular vectors and right-singular vectors. The third matrix S is a diagonal matrix: it is a square $m \times m$ matrix with non-zero entries only along the diagonal. This matrix contains derived constants called SINGULAR VALUES, and these are ordered with respect to their significance in contributing to the product that approximates the original matrix. If one or more of the least significant singular values are omitted, then the reconstructed matrix will be the best possible approximation of the original matrix in the lower dimensional space.

One key property of the derived matrices is that all dimensions are linearly independent: they are *orthogonal* to each other. This is an aid to the interpretation of the results.

Thorough understanding of singular value decomposition requires a firm background in linear algebra. Below we will try to sketch the idea behind SVD intuitively. The interested reader may consult a good introduction on linear algebra (e.g. Strang 2003) for more information. Landauer and Dumais (1997) also contains a brief but illuminating appendix on SVD.

Example: We will now look at a small, made-up example to see how SVD might be able to detect latent semantic structure present in the data. Figure 3 shows the SVD of the matrix in Figure 1.

$$A \begin{bmatrix} & B & NL \\ Groningen & 0 & 2 \\ Leuven & 2 & 0 \\ Amsterdam & 0 & 2 \\ Brussel & 2 & 0 \end{bmatrix} =$$

$$T \begin{bmatrix} 0.00 & 0.71 \\ -0.71 & 0.00 \\ 0.00 & 0.71 \\ -0.71 & 0.00 \end{bmatrix} * S \begin{bmatrix} 2.83 & 0 \\ 0 & 2.83 \end{bmatrix} * D^T \begin{bmatrix} -1 & 0 \\ 0 & 1 \end{bmatrix}$$

FIGURE 3 SINGULAR VALUE DECOMPOSITION of a term-document matrix

The original matrix A is decomposed into three other matrices T, S and D^T. The singular values in S show that two equally important dimensions are found; furthermore, the left- and right-singular vectors show that the frequencies are evenly divided among terms as well as among documents.

Figure 4 shows what happens when we add another document about Belgium, with a slightly different frequency distribution of terms: the Belgian dimension becomes the most important (i.e. captures the most variation, 2.92), while the Dutch dimension remains the same (2.83). The third dimension (0.68) captures the remaining variation (the fact that the third document only talks about Brussels).

$$
\begin{bmatrix}
 & B & NL & B \\
Groningen & 0 & 2 & 0 \\
Leuven & 2 & 0 & 0 \\
Amsterdam & 0 & 2 & 0 \\
Brussel & 2 & 0 & 1
\end{bmatrix} =
$$

$$
T \begin{bmatrix}
0.00 & -0.71 & 0.00 \\
-0.66 & 0.00 & 0.75 \\
0.00 & -0.71 & 0.00 \\
-0.75 & 0.00 & -0.66
\end{bmatrix} * S \begin{bmatrix}
2.92 & 0.00 & 0.00 \\
0.00 & 2.83 & 0.00 \\
0.00 & 0.00 & 0.68
\end{bmatrix} *
$$

$$
D^T \begin{bmatrix}
-0.97 & 0.00 & 0.26 \\
0.00 & -1.00 & 0.00 \\
-0.26 & 0.00 & -0.97
\end{bmatrix} \cong A' \begin{bmatrix}
0.00 & 2.00 & 0.00 \\
1.87 & 0.00 & 0.50 \\
0.00 & 2.00 & 0.00 \\
2.12 & 0.00 & 0.56
\end{bmatrix}
$$

FIGURE 4   Truncated Singular Value Decomposition

If we now truncate the SVD by keeping only the two most important dimensions, and then reconstruct our original matrix, we get matrix A', which is the best possible reconstruction from only two dimensions. Note that matrix A' resembles matrix A, except for the numbers of the third document: instead of assigning all frequency mass to the term *Brussel*, the mass is almost evenly divided among the Belgian terms *Brussel* and *Leuven*. When keeping only two dimensions, the SVD "guesses" the best possible distribution. This is an example of how the technique is used to obtain more succinct models.

Applications: While rooted in linear algebra, singular value decomposition has proven to be a useful tool in statistical applications. In this respect, it is akin to statistical methods such as factor analysis, correspondence analysis and principal components analysis. The technique can easily be interpreted statistically: the left-singular and right-singular vector linked to the highest singular value represent the most important dimensions in the data (i.e. the derived dimension—independent of other dimensions—that explains the most variance of the matrix). The singular vectors linked to the second highest value represent the second principal component (orthogonal to the first one), and so on. Typically, one uses only the first n principal components, stripping off the remaining singular values and singular vectors. Intuitively, SVD is able to transform the original matrix—with an abundance of overlapping dimensions—into a new, many times smaller matrix that is able to describe the data in terms of the principal components. Due to this dimension reduction, a more succinct and more general representation of the data is obtained. Redundancy is filtered out, and data sparseness is reduced.

SVD has achieved good results in INFORMATION RETRIEVAL (IR), where it is applied in the framework of LATENT SEMANTIC ANALYSIS (LSA, Landauer and Dumais 1997, Landauer et al. 1998). In LSA, a singular value decomposition is applied to a fairly large term-document matrix (on the order of 30K terms by 30K documents). According to its proponents LSA finds actual lexical tendencies in the data. The technique is applied in order to obtain a small number of semantic dimensions in terms of which words are characterized for retrieval purposes. This allows researchers (and practitioners) in IR to ignore many other characteristics of individual noun distributions.

The fact that LSA is able to discover some kind of latent structure is shown by its performance on a synonymy test, which is part of a Test of English as a Foreign Language (TOEFL). This is a test given to foreign applicants to American universities. If one applies LSA to determine the closest synonym in a word-pair test in multiple choice format, the algorithm scores as well as the average non-English speaking participant in the test (Landauer et al., 1998).

The calculation of SVD involves iteratively solving a number of eigenvalue problems, which we will not discuss. A number of programs are available that can handle the kind of large-scale singular value decompositions that are necessary for linguistic data sets. In this research, SVDPACK (Berry, 1992) has been used. SVDPACK is a program that is able to handle sparse matrices efficiently and quickly (depending on the number of singular values one wants to retain). Most decompositions can easily be computed on ordinary Unix workstations, in a reasonable amount of time.

7.3 Aspectual Affinity

We turn to the linguistic phenomenon which is the focus of our experiments, viz., the affinity in combination that is seen in English, Dutch and other languages between different verbal aspects (aka aspectual classes or *Aktionsarten*) on the one hand and two different sorts of durative adverbial on the other.

7.3.1 Background

Vendler (1967), building on Aristotelian concepts and twentieth century work by Ryle and Kenny, distinguished four classes of verbs (or verb phrases) based on their logical and grammatical properties: states, activities, achievements and accomplishments. We do not attempt to summarize all of this work, but suggest the sorts of properties that are appealed to. We suggest Dowty (1979), Moens and Steedman (1988) and Egg (2005) for more comprehensive discussion of the differences in linguistic and inferential behavior among the aspectual classes. For example, states such as *be tired* do not normally occur in the progressive **be being tired*, while activities such as *sing* easily can. Accomplishments such as *draw a box* and achievements such as *die* or *notice* are associated with implicit completions or end points, which leads to striking differences compared to activities. For example, someone who stopped drawing a house at a certain time, did not draw one, while someone who stops being tired or stops singing certainly was tired and did sing at an immediately prior time.

States and activities do not have implicit completions or end points and are therefore referred to as ATELIC; both combine with adverbials of duration headed by *for*, unlike the TELIC classes of achievements and accomplishments, which combine with adverbials of duration headed by *in*. While all achievements and accomplishments combine felicitously with *in*-adverbials, if one attempts to combine them with durative adverbials headed by *for*, the resulting phrase is usually understood iteratively. Thus someone who is said to have drawn a box for an hour, is normally understood to have drawn the box repeatedly, not a single time lasting an hour. Compare the combination with *notice* as well.

Some accomplishments combine with adverbials headed by *for* without being understood iteratively, namely those with a clearly associated resulting state. Thus if someone opened a channel for several weeks, we might understand either that it was repeatedly opened (as noted above) or that it was opened once and remained open. The adverbial indicates the length of time it stayed open in that case.

Let's dwell on the parenthetical mention of "verb phrases" in the first paragraph because its ramifications will influence our chances of finding distributional traces of the distinction. We can illustrate the importance aspect of this extension from verbs to verb phrases with a simple example. *Drink a glass of juice* is a telic predicate with a clearly defined end point, while *drink juice, drink liters of juice* and *drink* used without a direct object, in at least one of its uses, are all atelic. This illustrates why we prefer to speak of telic vs. atelic verb phrases, rather than telic vs. atelic verbs *simpliciter*. If we are to detect signals of telicity among verb phrases in full generality, we need to incorporate information about the object as well (as well as other adverbials the verb phrase is modified by). In fact we will find it necessary below to ignore the presence of objects and other modifiers for reasons we discuss there.

Dowty (1979, chap. 2) is the *locus classicus* for modern discussion of these topics, where he reviews and discusses the classification as well as the distinctions in logical and grammatical behavior that motivate the classification. He goes on then to suggest underlying differences in temporal reference that help to explain why the distinctions exists, proposing an "aspectual calculus" (Dowty, 1979, sec. 2.3) to account for the limited range of combinations and their meanings. Krifka (1987) proposes an axiomatic characterization of the distinction.

7.3.2 Mixed Affinities

We could not hope to do justice to all of the work done in Dowty's *Word Meaning and Montague Grammar* (and following this) on the telic/atelic distinction, but we shall focus on this distinction below as we seek distributional traces of it in a very large corpus. We review a discussion about the strictness of the combinatorial restrictions since this bears directly on the chances of finding distributional traces of the distinction in corpora.

As Dowty (1979, subsec. 2.2.5) notes, one cannot apply the test of adverbial modification to partition verbs (or verb phrases) into distinct classes. It is natural to say that someone *read an article in an hour*, but not ill-formed to say that someone *read an article for an hour*. Thus it is possible to construe naturally telic phrases such as *read a book* as atelic in some circumstances. Similarly, normally atelic verbs such as *swim* can also be construed telically. Dowty (1979, p. 61) notes that, if interlocutors know that John swims a certain distance daily, it can be natural to say that *John swam today in an hour*, for example, to indicate how long it took him to swim his normal distance. Dowty (1979) notes that the other linguistic tests indicating telicity likewise apply, but we do not repeat these here.

These sorts of considerations led Moens and Steedman (1987) to construe aspectual classes as types and to investigate the role of various temporal operators as type-changing. The progressive aspect, seen from this perspective, maps a telic accomplishment such as *write a book* to an atelic activity capable of combining with an atelic-seeking durative such as *for a year* to obtain the felicitous *was writing a book for a year*, which indeed does not imply that the book was completed.

Moens and Steedman (1987) note that applying an adverbial of an inappropriate type such as *in an hour* to a verb such as *swim* might be viewed as TYPE COERCION, an analytical possibility examined at length by Egg (2005), who rejects type coercion as a general account, appealing instead to LANDING SITE COERCION to explain the (most accessible) reading of *She left for an hour* as meaning 'she left and stayed away for an hour'.

7.3.3 Distributional Expectations

The basic generalization is very simple, namely that atelic verbs (and verb phrases) combine with durative adverbials headed by *for* and telics with adverbials headed by *in*, but as we have seen there are a number of necessary qualifications. First, for many verbs the nature of the grammatical direct object influences whether it refers to a telic or atelic event. Second, our knowledge of the expected length of an event may likewise influence our judgment as to whether the event should be understood telically or atelically. For example, *read a book* refers to a telic event, but if one hears that *Sue read 'War and Peace' this morning*, one is inclined to understand it atelically, given what one knows of the book's length, and limits on reading speeds. Third, some adverbials, e.g., *this morning*, can combine with both telic and atelic verb phrases. The research literature does not suggest distributional restrictions that are hard and fast.

On the other hand, the basic generalization sounds at first quite convincing, and the exceptions often sound a bit strange. Adverbials headed by the preposition *in* or, alternatively, by the preposition *for*, combine to form telic and atelic verb phrases respectively, sometimes "coercing" the verb phrases they combine with into the right aspect. This suggests that the relative affinities of the two types of adverbial for the different verbs ought to be reflected in the relative frequency with which combinations are founded, and that the frequency of combinations respecting the affinity ought to outpace that of exceptions. We have additional reasons for ignoring the presence of objects (of particular sorts that influence aspect) in verb phrases, namely first that it is difficult to recognize the relevant range of objects automatically, and second that including verb-object combinations would increase the number of categories greatly, reducing the frequencies with which classes are instantiated and thereby the reliability of the analysis.

Furthermore, since our primary aim in this paper is to explore the possibility of applying quantitative techniques in order to detect semantic structures, we wish to forge ahead in spite of the potential exceptions. We wish to verify whether such an affinity is reflected in the very large corpora we examine; whether we can detect aspectual classes among the verbs heading verb phrases in construction with specific durative adverbials; whether we can detect classes of temporal adverbials with aspectual affinities like those of adverbials headed by *in* and *for*, respectively (and what those prepositions in fact are); and, finally, whether there are other conditioning factors on telicity. It will be interesting if it turns out that some adverbials prefer to combine with the one or the other aspectual class, even though there is no straightforward aspectual requirement that they do so. This putative phenomenon has not received theoretical attention, but the quantitative approach we apply lends itself naturally to the question.

7.3.4 Methodology

In order to explore semantic distinctions among verbs and temporal adverbials in a quantitative way, the required frequency information needs to be extracted from a corpus. First of all, a set of 22 adpositions that occur as head of temporal adverbial PPs was manually selected. These adpositions and their translations are shown in Table 1.

adposition	translation	adposition	translation
in	'in'	*geleden*	'ago'
na	'after'	*later*	'later'
over	'in'	*lang*	'for'
binnen	'within'	*op*	'in'
sinds	'since'	*voor*	'for'
om	'at'	*tot*	'until'
eerder	'before'	*vanaf*	'from'
gedurende	'during'	*terug*	'ago'
door	'during'	*rond*	'around'
halverwege	'half way'	*tijdens*	'during'
tegen	'around'	*achtereen*	'in a row'

TABLE 1 Manually selected adpositions that head time adverbials

Many of these adpositions also appear in PPs that are not temporal

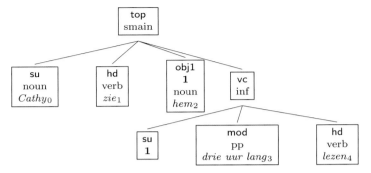

FIGURE 5 Example of dependency structure for the sentence *Cathy zag hem drie uur lang lezen* 'Cathy saw him read for three hours'

adverbials. To make sure that only temporal adverbials are extracted, we only take into account PPs that contain an NP headed by nouns that express a time quantity, namely *minuut* 'minute', *uur* 'hour', *dag*, day', *week* 'week', *maand* 'month' or *jaar* 'year'.

The combinations of verbs and modifying time adverbials were automatically extracted from the *Twente Nieuws Corpus*,[3] a large corpus of Dutch newspaper texts (500 million words), which has been automatically parsed by the Dutch dependency parser Alpino (van Noord, 2006). Alpino reaches an accuracy of up to 90% per grammatical dependency. An example parse is shown in Figure 5. Alpino's output parses are saved in XML. An XSL-style-sheet was developed to extract the required information, viz. the adposition and the verb (in this example the postposition *lang* and the verb *lezen*).

Next, a matrix is created of the occurrences of the 22 temporal adpositions cross-classified by the 5,000 most frequent verbs. The matrix contains the frequency of each co-occurrence. Each value is weighted with pointwise mutual information (see above), so that more informative features get a higher weight.

As a last step, singular value decomposition is applied, reducing the matrix to two dimensions. This dimensionality reduction exposes the two most important dimensions that are present in the data. Additionally, using two dimensions has the advantage that the results can easily be visualized. We should note that other dimensions can, in principle, be interesting as long as they contribute significantly to the explanation of variance. But we found it difficult to interpret the third and following dimensions, whose importance naturally decreases as well.

---

[3]http://www.vf.utwente.nl/~druid/TwNC/TwNC-main.html

Since the parsing method is fully automatic, our input may contain erroneous parses. However, our statistical techniques are robust with regard to random noise. Only systematic noise (introduced by the parser's grammar or disambiguation model) can cause problems in the analysis. A random evaluation of the parsing results turned up no indication of systematic error.[4]

7.3.5 Results

From the inspection of the results, we conjecture that the first SVD dimension gives an indication of the (a)telicity of the clause, and the second dimension of the duration of the timespan (introduced by the durative adverbial). We will concentrate on the first dimension in examining the data.

Adverbials: Figure 6 gives a graphical representation of the adverbials in the reduced dimensionality space; the x-axis shows the first dimension, and the y-axis shows the second dimension. The first dimension captures approximately 9.5% of the variance present in the original matrix, the two first dimensions together account for approx. 15.5%.

Due to the application of the SVD, a continuum emerges between atelic modifiers (*lang* 'for') and telic modifiers (*om* 'at [3 o'clock]', *rond, tegen* 'around [3 o'clock]', and *geleden* '[several hours] ago'). We note that *binnen* 'within [an hour]' is also correctly classified toward the telic end of the spectrum, as is *over* 'in [a week]'. But we also note three examples which do not seem immediately plausible, given our interpretation of the first dimension as (a)telicity. We shall examine *achtereen* '[three days] in a row', *tijdens* 'during', and *geleden* 'ago'. *Achtereen* seems as if it should be used iteratively and therefore atelically just by virtue of its meaning.[5] *Tijdens* can be crucially used both with an event specification, e.g. *tijdens de oorlog* 'during the war', and also with a specification of temporal durations, e.g. *tijdens drie dagen* 'for a period of three days'. The latter should be atelic, and the former might be compatible with either telic or atelic propositions. Both of the prepositions are found fairly far to the left on the x-axis, among predominantly telic prepositions.

Finally we shall examine *geleden* 'ago', which combines with expres-

---

[4]As parsing experts are well aware, the attachment of prepositional phrases is subject to more error than other parse decisions. But we know of no tendency for parsers to err more in attaching telic durative adverbials than in attaching atelic duratives, for example.

[5]In fact *achtereen* can also be used with no hint of iterativity. *Hij werkte hier drie jaar achtereen* 'He worked here for three years in a row'. But we suspect that iterative uses predominate.

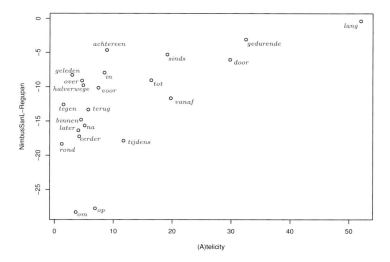

FIGURE 6 The classification of the heads of temporal adverbials according
to the two most significant dimensions of the SVD applied to the frequency
co-occurrence matrix between such heads of adverbials and heads of verb
phrases in 400 million words of Dutch newspaper text.

sions of duration such as *drie jaar* 'three year(s)' to form frame adverbials. Since there is no logical constraint restricting the combinations
of frame adverbials with either telic or atelic verb phrases, we expect
frame adverbials to be relatively insensitive to aspect—both *lived in
Columbus a decade ago* but also *ran a mile a week ago* are well-formed.
It is therefore surprising to see *geleden* classified as having such a strong
affinity with telicity (see Fig. 6). Similarly *op* heads frame adverbials
once combined with an expression denoting a day: *op zondag* 'on Sun-
day', or *op Pasen* 'at Easter'. It should likewise be expected to be
somewhat neutral with respect to telicity, but it too is classified much
more closely to the telic extreme.

   To test whether these interpretations are plausible, we decided to
examine a random sample of twenty sentences for each of the prepositional or postpositional heads from the material that the SVD is based
on. We shall not present all twenty sentences, but only the verbs and
arguments that are crucial for the category telic/atelic.

   We first examine twenty random sentences involving adverbials
headed by the preposition *tijdens* 'during'. The adverbials, the verb

verb phrase	argument
suffered pain in her abdomen	during an au-pair year
168 rebels were killed	during the first six days
aim at a number of subscribers	during the first year
warm air was introduced	during the first week
compose music	during his Paris years
contract a cold	during the last few days
drop marines off	during the first day of [...]
what goes on	during a moment of silence
fill the auditorium	during the first three days
grow	[during] the most recent days
spend time	during his last [work]days
play great tennis	during the last two weeks
remain the same	during your 12 years as [...]
not function well	during the last years
record stories	during the days in [...]
[this] wine was bottled	during the last year of [...]
promote sport	during their days
work with [...]	during this hectic month
get lost	during the longest and hardest day
maintenance costs are low	during the first two years

TABLE 2 Crucial verb-argument combinations in randomly sampled sentences (from twenty million) involving aspectual adverbials headed by *tijdens* 'during'. Most of the predications ought to be classified as atelic, with, however, exceptions such as 'contract a cold', 'be bottled (of (a specific quantity of) wine)', and 'get lost'.

and the relevant arguments are listed in Table 2. The table (as well as the full examples, not shown) seem to bear out the linguistic intuition that adverbials formed with *tijdens* combine primarily with atelic predications. This means in turn that, if our hypothesis about this first dimension is correct, i.e., if the x-axis in Fig. 6 does correspond with telicity, then the boundary for adverbial heads that combine with telics lies to the left of this point.

We turn now to the examination of twenty random sentences involving adverbials headed by the postposition *achtereen* '[three days] in a row'. We note that only one of the twenty sentences was crucially misparsed. In that case a temporal adverbial that modified a noun phrase was parsed as modifying the verb. We found the combinations shown in Table 3.

verb phrase	argument
production fell	three years in a row
won the championship	three years in a row
'enjoy' a high salary	for many consecutive years
repel everything [every attempted goal]	for 908 consecutive minutes
jog a quarter hour	for three days in a row
show low growth	for months on end
cast his fishing rod	for many years in a row
wear the yellow jersey for several days	three years in a row
be clear to me	four days in a row
presents [herself] as hotel slut	five days in a row
cost the company sales	five years in a row
participate in the championships	four years in a row
watch TV ads	for four hours in a row
sing it	three years in a row
fall 2,75% in purchasing power	four years in a row
sit in the car	for 48 hours in a row
read	for several hours in a row

TABLE 3 Crucial verb-argument combinations in nineteen randomly sampled sentences (from twenty million) involving aspectual adverbials headed by *achtereen*. It is striking that many are telic predications used iteratively, and therefore atelically, while others are atelic by virtue of plural arguments ('watch ads'). At the same time, it is clear that some examples are simply atelic and misclassified ('read').

The range of examples in Table 3 illustrate how difficult it is to deal with input that has not been selected for its clarity with respect to theoretical issues. 'Fill the auditorium' seemed to be used atelically in the sentence in the example. Several examples involve clearly telic predications which, probably because of appearing in construction with the postposition *achtereen*, are nonetheless understood atelically. This suggests that SVD is classifying the postposition as telic due to the fact that most of the material it combines with is at base telic. Other examples are more complicated, involving potential telics in construction with quantified arguments, leading to an atelic reading (e.g., 'repel everything', 'cost sales', or 'watch ads'). Interestingly enough, there are two examples where fundamentally atelic predications are made telic via subordinate modification ('jog a quarter hour' and 'wear a jersey for several days'). But there are also examples of atelic predications with no relevant type-shifting operators ('enjoy a high salary', 'sit in the car' and 'read'). But perhaps we impute too much structure in discussing the possibility of type shifting here. The most correct conclusion may be just that adverbials with iterative meaning apply felicitously to both telic and atelic predications.

Third, and finally, we examine twenty random sentences involving adverbials headed by *geleden* 'ago'. In order to save space, we do not list the predications and adverbials fully, but the report is quite simple: virtually all (19) of the twenty examples involve telic predications! This is interesting for two reasons. First, it is consistent with our hypothesis, advanced in the discussion of *tijdens*, that the border of telic vs. atelic may lie fairly far to the left in the scatterplot—in fact it ought to lie between these two adverbial heads.

But it is also interesting because it suggests that the affinities between adverbials and aspect are not exhaustively described by aspectual theory. As we noted above, there is no reason why a postposition such as *geleden*, which combines with an expression denoting a length of time to form a frame adverbial, should show a preference for one aspect over another. In particular, this sort of tendency seems to have nothing to do with the principles of aspectual interpretation based on type coercion that Moens and Steedman (1987) examined, nor with the sorts that Egg (2005) calls LANDING SITE COERCION. Since, however, predications involving *geleden* are always about the past, we perhaps see more telic predications because there is a tendency to view past actions as completed.[6]

Verbs: Despite some irregularities noted in the previous paragraphs, our data analysis of the adpositions shows a clear telicity continuum emerging from left to right. The next step is to plot the verbs against the same dimensions, to see whether the same continuum emerges, and if so, where the verbs appear in this continuum. In Figure 7, a sample of the 100 most frequent verbs is plotted in the first two dimensions.

Figure 7 shows the same tendency as Figure 6: a telicity continuum emerges from left to right, with typically telic verbs (*meld* 'report', *vertrek* 'leave' and *begin* 'begin') on the left, and typically atelic verbs (*werk* 'work', *blijf* 'stay' and *volg* 'follow') on the right.

To investigate the continuum for verbs, we again examined 20 randomly selected sentences for a number of verbs. Table 4 shows a number of sentences with the verbs *werk*, *blijf* and *volg*, appearing at the atelic end of the continuum. Practically all of the sentences indeed have an atelic reading; a few telic interpretations are also present, such as 'a training [session] followed around 6 o'clock'. It is revealing that these

---

[6]Comrie (1976) discusses interrelations between aspect and tense.

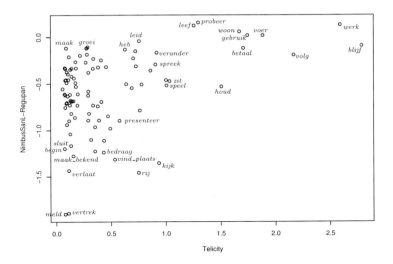

FIGURE 7 A graphical representation of verbs, showing the first two dimensions of the SVD

telic instances are only present with the verb *volg*, which appears already more to the left in the continuum.

	verb phrase	argument
	all immigrants [...] have worked	for three to five years
	Rotterdam works with health care information	since one year [ago]
	He wanted to work half time	after a year
	It stays dry	for five days in a row
	Bob Dylan stayed my hero	throughout the years
	The reporters followed the three women	during one year
	...followed by the FBI	since one year [ago]
	a training followed	around 6 o'clock

TABLE 4 Some verb-argument combinations for the verbs *werk*, *blijf* and *volg*, appearing at the atelic end of the continuum.

The other end of the spectrum shows the opposite picture: the majority of the sentences selected for the verbs *meld* 'report' and *vertrek* 'leave' are telic; atelic readings are possible with atypical cases, as in 'he reported ... for 20 minutes' (Table 5).

Next, we have evaluated two verbs that are located towards the

verb phrase	argument
Lindsay reported [herself]	a week and a half ago
124 voters reported	at 2 o'clock in the afternoon
The Greek media reported	on the day of her funeral
The man left	at 9 o'clock in the morning
Fricke left again	half an hour later
The hostage started	before 8 o'clock
He reported ...	for 20 minutes

TABLE 5 Some verb-argument combinations for the verbs *meld*, *vertrek* and *begin*, appearing at the telic end of the continuum.

middle of the continuum, namely the verbs *speel* 'play' and *kijk* 'look'. Some crucial sentences are shown in Tables 6 and 7. Both tables show a mix of telic and atelic verb phrases, in line with the telicity continuum. The first two sentences in Table 6 are telic instances; the five other sentences are atelic. In Table 7, the three first sentences are telic, the remaining four atelic.

verb phrase	argument
The band started playing	shortly after 8 o'clock
... the second game is played	within 14 days
He played in Greece	during those 3 years
No senior competitions are played anymore	since last year
... where the Yankees were playing	three days in a row
... who played with 9 players	for an hour
This station has played an important role	throughout history

TABLE 6 Some verb-argument combinations for the verb *speel*

7.4 Conclusion and Future work

This paper took the availability of increasingly large corpora as an impetus to investigate a statistical technique that seems suitable for investigating "latent" semantic phenomena quantitatively without requiring a manually annotated corpus. The aspectual phenomenon is latent in that it is not reflected simply in overt text; it is reflected indirectly in the sets of verbs and adpositions used. Our chosen technique relies on the availability of massive amounts of automatically annotated data, but it does not require that the annotations be flawless.

We have analyzed the co-occurrence data of verbs and aspectually

verb phrase	argument
Sluis himself went to look	two years ago
100.000 came to watch the movie	during the first 4 days
We looked at the same place	an hour later
... to watch the Dutch team	during the night
[We'll be] watching video's again	for one month
We looked what the possibilities are	during the last two years
... to watch tv commercials	4 hours in a row

TABLE 7 Some verb-argument combinations for the verb *kijk*

sensitive adverbials in an attempt to verify that the well-studied affinity
of atelic vs. telic predications for combination with only certain duratives could be detected, and, naturally, the degree to which it held.
The data analyzed consisted of parsed sentences from which the verb
heading the verb phrase was extracted, and also the preposition or
postposition heading the durative adverbial. We work from large tallies
showing which verbs were found in construction with which temporal
adpositions.

We applied singular value decomposition to extract simultaneously
the most significant principal components of the adpositions and also
of the verbs. The first two correspond with atelicity on the one hand,
and length of the time duration on the other. By examining random
samples of data in which different adverbials and different verbs occur,
we were able to confirm this interpretation, and also to note that the
characterizations are not categorical, but gradual—we found aspectual
mismatches in all of the sets of sentences we examined. From semantic
theory we know that mismatch is possible, but this study suggests
that it also occurs frequently. Interestingly, one of the cleanest sets of
examples did *not* involve aspectually selective adverbials, but rather the
aspectually aselective adverbials formed with the postposition *geleden*
'ago', which co-occur almost only with telic phrases. The SVD analysis
brought this out.

We conclude therefore that SVD allows us to to generalize over the
noisy data acquired from automatic parsing, and it successfully exposed
the aspectual tendencies in the telic and atelic verb phrases as well as
in the adverbials they construct with.

In future work, we plan to examine alternative methods of statistical analysis. Particularly, methods that bring about an entropy-based
dimension reduction (such as NON-NEGATIVE MATRIX FACTORIZATION
Lee and Seung 2000) look quite promising. In a similar vein, we want

to experiment with different weighting schemes (apart from PMI).

Further applications of this sort of analysis might also involve categories that are not simply marked in data, and for which the issue of semantic conditioning arises, e.g. negative or positive polarity items, or scope relations that are marked by these sorts of items. Further steps in these analyses might involve the examination of alternative hypotheses about the occurrence and co-occurrence of aspectual adverbials, and, indeed, the development of a more rigorous mode in which hypotheses might be tested using these techniques.

References

Berry, Michael. 1992. Large Scale Singular Value Computations. *International Journal of Supercomputer Applications* 6(3):13–49.

Brent, Michael. 1991. Automatic Semantic Classification of Verbs from their Syntactic Contexts: An Implented Classifier for Stativity. In *Proceedings of the 5th Meeting of the European ACL*, pages 222–226. Shroudsburg, PA: ACL.

Church, Kenneth Ward and Patrick Hanks. 1990. Word Association Norms, Mutual Information & Lexicography. *Computational Linguistics* 16(1):22–29.

Comrie, Bernard. 1976. *Aspect*. Cambridge: Cambridge University Press.

Deane, Paul. 2005. A Nonparametric Method for Extraction of Candidate Phrasal Terms. In *Proceedings of the 43rd Annual Meeting of Association for Computational Linguistics*, pages 605–613. Shroudsburg, PA: ACL.

Dowty, David. 1979. *Word Meaning and Montague Grammar*. Dordrecht: Reidel.

Egg, Markus. 2005. *Flexible Semantics for Reinterpretation Phenomena*. Stanford: CSLI.

Krifka, Manfred. 1987. Nominal Reference and Temporal Constitution: Toward a Semantics of Quantity. In *Proceedings of the 6th Amsterdam Colloquium*, pages 153–173. Amsterdam: Institute of Language, Logic and Information.

Landauer, Thomas and Se Dumais. 1997. A solution to Plato's problem: The Latent Semantic Analysis theory of the acquisition, induction, and representation of knowledge. *Psychology Review* 104:211–240.

Landauer, Thomas, Peter Foltz, and Darrell Laham. 1998. An Introduction to Latent Semantic Analysis. *Discourse Processes* 25:295–284.

Lee, Daniel D. and H. Sebastian Seung. 2000. Algorithms for Non-negative Matrix Factorization. In *NIPS*, pages 556–562.

Manning, Christopher and Hinrich Schütze. 2000. *Foundations of Statistical Natural Language Processing*. Cambridge, Massachussets: MIT Press.

Mehler, Alexander. 2007. Compositionality in Quantitative Semantics. In A. Mehler and R. Khler, eds., *Aspects of Automatic Text Analysis*, vol.

209 of *Studies in Fuzziness and Soft Computing*, pages 139–170. Berlin: Springer.

Moens, Marc and Mark Steedman. 1987. Temporal Ontology in Natural Language. In *25th Annual Meeting of the Association for Computational Linguistics. Proceedings of the Conference*, pages 1–7. Morristown, NJ: Association for Computational Linguistics.

Moens, Marc and Mark Steedman. 1988. Temporal Ontology and Temporal Reference. *Computational Linguistics* 14(1):3–14.

Nerbonne, John. 1996. Computational Semantics—Linguistics and Processing. In S. Lappin, ed., *Handbook of Contemporary Semantic Theory*, pages 459–82. London: Blackwell Publishers.

Schulte im Walde, Sabine. to appear. The Induction of Verb Frames and Verb Classes from Corpora. In A. Lüdeling and M. Kytö, eds., *Corpus Linguistics: An International Handbook*, chap. 61. Berlin: Mouton de Gruyter.

Siegel, Eric V. 1998. *Linguistic Indicators for Language Understanding: Using Machine Learning to Combine Corpus-Based Indicators for Aspectual Classification of Clauses*. Ph.D. thesis, Columbia.

Strang, Gilbert. 2003. *Introduction to Linear Algebra*. Wellesley: Wellesley-Cambridge Press.

van Noord, Gertjan. 2006. At Last Parsing Is Now Operational. In P. Mertens, C. Fairon, A. Dister, and P. Watrin, eds., *TALN06. Verbum Ex Machina. Actes de la 13e conference sur le traitement automatique des langues naturelles*, pages 20–42. Leuven.

Vendler, Zeno. 1967. *Linguistics in Philosophy*. Ithaca: Cornell University Press.

Villada Moirón, Begoña. 2005. *Data-Driven Identification of Fixed Expressions and their Modifiability*. Ph.D. thesis, University of Groningen.

Villavicencio, Aline, Francis Bond, Anna Korhonen, and Diana McCarthy. 2005. Introduction to the Special Issue on Multiword Expressions: Having a Crack at a Hard Nut. *Computer Speech and Language* 19(4):365–377.

8

know-how: **A compositional approach**[*]

CRAIGE ROBERTS

8.1   *de se* **know-how**

Consider John Perry's (1977) friend Rudolph Lingens, an amnesiac lost in the Stanford Library. Lingens is very intelligent and exceptionally well-read, and has access to all kinds of propositional information about a fellow named Rudolph Lingens. In the library, among other things, he has read that Rudolph Lingens is in aisle five, floor six, of the Main Library, Stanford. Moreover, (1) is true of the amnesiac Lingens:

(1)   The poor fellow knows that Rudolph Lingens can get out of the Stanford Library by going down to the first floor, turning right at the circulation desk, and exiting straight ahead.

But unfortunately, the poor fellow doesn't know that he* is Rudolph Lingens (in the sense of *he** due to Hector-Neri Castañeda, 1966). David

---

[*]This paper grew out of invited comments on a paper by Barbara Abbott that was presented at the Pacific Meetings of the American Philosophical Association in March, 2006. Thanks to the conference organizers and to Barbara Abbott for this stimulating opportunity. The analysis proposed here is based on unpublished work by David Dowty and Polly Jacobson, and I thank them for generously sharing it with me. I am also grateful to Polly Jacobson and an anonymous reviewer, who provided very valuable, detailed comments on a more recent draft. Rich Thomason gave excellent comments on the present version at the 2007 Michigan Workshop on Semantics and Philosophy, but unfortunately this too late to be reflected in the text; I hope to address those comments in future work on the subject. Thanks, as well, to Yusuke Kubota, for his assistance with the LaTeX preparation of the manuscript for publication.

Theory and Evidence in Semantics.
Erhard Hinrichs and John Nerbonne (eds.).
Copyright © 2009, CSLI Publications.

Lewis embroiders the story a bit. Suppose that Lingens has narrowed down his identity to one of two individuals, one of whom, Rudolph Lingens, is located on the sixth floor of the Stanford Library, and the other, Lester Reynolds, is located on the lowest level of the Widener Library, below street level. Lingens, standing among the stacks, just doesn't know which location he is in. Hence, though he wants to leave, he doesn't know whether to go down five floors or up three. It seems clear in this case that he doesn't know how to get out of the library. That is, there is a sense in which (2) is true in this scenario:

(2) Lingens doesn't know how to get out of the library.

Actually, just one additional piece of information would enable Lingens to get out, the self-ascription of the property of being Rudolph Lingens, which would permit him, on the basis of his propositional information, to locate himself in the Stanford Library. Hence, (3) is true, as well:

(3) If Lingens knew that he was Rudolph Lingens, he would know how to get out of the library.

But, as David Lewis (1979) has argued convincingly, the additional information Lingens needs is not propositional. On the view of a proposition as a set of possible worlds, the information Lingens needs does not distinguish between possible worlds, but between locations within one and the same world.

This, in a nutshell, is the central problem with a paper by Jason Stanley and Timothy Williamson (2001) on knowing-how. It argues cleverly for the thesis that knowledge-how, like knowledge-that, is propositional. But I will argue that knowledge-how is richer: It involves self-ascription, and hence is not reducible to propositional knowledge. This is clear in virtue of our intuitions about the meanings of examples like (1)–(3), intuitions that Barbara Abbott (2006) rightly defends in her response to Stanley and Williamson. But it also follows from systematic compositional semantic analysis of the constructions and lexical items involved, an analysis whose parts can all be independently motivated.

As Abbott demonstrates, in order to maintain their central thesis Stanley and Williamson have relied on some controversial assumptions about the infinitival *how to* construction, and, crucially, on the assumption of a "practical mode of presentation" which is not at all innocent from the perspective of the truth conditional distinction between knowing-how and knowing-that. I propose a linguistic analysis of the construction that is crucially different from that appealed to by

Stanley and Williamson. Given the *de se* character of knowledge-how statements observed above, I will argue that it isn't that we have a choice between two equally plausible linguistic analyses. Rather, the analysis sketched here is empirically superior in that it correctly predicts the attested interpretations more accurately than does Stanley and Williamson's analysis, which requires various *ad hoc* stipulations and leaves a number of loose ends, all of which have been pointed out by Abbott.

8.2   A compositional analysis of the *know how-to* construction

Here's what a fully adequate compositional semantic analysis of the *know how to* construction in English requires:

- a general account of the meaning of *to* infinitival phrases: Portner (1997)
- a general account of the meaning of interrogatives, and of interrogative complements in particular: Groenendijk and Stokhof (1984, 1997)
- an account of *wh*-infinitival complements that builds on the first two accounts: slight modification of Dowty and Jacobson (1991)
- an analysis of the meaning of *how*, as opposed to the other *wh*-words that occur in *wh*-infinitivals
- a general account of the meaning of *know* and of how that combines with the meaning of its *wh*-infinitival complement to yield the attested interpretation
- an account of the phenomenon of control, whereby the understood subject of the complement infinitival VP is conveyed

In the optimal theory, all these elements would be independently motivated, on the basis of the behavior of the components in other constructions. I think we can provide such an account, though convincing you of the independent motivation for each of the pieces would take a good deal more space than I have here. But I hope that in the following sketch of an analysis I can make the claim plausible, and suggest how the pieces of the puzzle fit together to yield the sorts of meanings we observe in the relevant examples. Moreover, I think the resulting account helps to explain why certain combinations are unattested, and why the combinations we do see fail to have certain readings. This is just what we want from a generative linguistic account supplemented by a semantic theory of the sort originally proposed by Richard Montague (e.g. 1973): a prediction of all and only the grammatically sanctioned strings and their interpretations.

Let's begin with infinitivals. Paul Portner (1997, p. 185) is concerned, among other things, with infinitival clauses like *for Joan to arrive in Richmond soon*. His account of these complements is summarized in the following truth conditions:[1]

(4) Given a set of situations S, a situation of evaluation $r \in S$, an infinitival formula ϕ, and an operator $\mathcal{F}$ that introduces the characteristic semantics of the infinitival construction:
$||\mathcal{F}(\phi)||^r = \{s \in S : s$ has as its initial segment a dispositional counterpart of r and for some $s' \leq s, s' \in ||\phi||^r\}$

For his (5), this means (p. 185):

(5) James wants for Joan to arrive in Richmond soon.
gloss: 'In all of James' buletic alternatives[2], Joan arrives in Richmond soon.'
embedded infinitive denotes: a set of situations which (speaking loosely) begin with James's wanting and extend into the future, eventually including a situation of Joan arriving in Richmond soon after the wanting.

Like imperatives (Portner, 2004, 2006), *to*-infinitivals are tenseless (Wurmbrand, 2005), but in both cases there is a futurity conventionally associated with the construction, as we see in (5), and this is crucial to their sense, distribution, and function. I'll assume that this is the correct general view of infinitivals.

Extending this analysis, we derive the following semantics for infinitival VPs:

(6) Given:
- an infinitival VP of the form *to δ*,
- a model with domain *Dom*, a set of situations S, and a situation of evaluation r, and
- Portner's operator $\mathcal{F}$ that introduces the characteristic semantics of the infinitival construction (as in (4) above),

$||$to $\delta||^r$ is that function $f \in (Dom \times Pow(S))$ such that for all $d \in Dom$, $f(d) = ||\mathcal{F}(\delta(d))||^r = \{s \in S : s$ has as its initial segment a d-dispositional counterpart of r and for some $s' \in s, s' \in ||\delta(d)||^r\}$.

---

[1]An anonymous reviewer claims that use of the operator $\mathcal{F}$ to introduce the characteristic semantics of the infinitival construction "sounds strangely uncompositional". This is Portner's terminology; one could simply take it as the meaning introduced by overt *to* in examples like (5) below.

[2]These are situations accessible to the situation of evaluation r under a buletic (conative) accessibility relation, one reflecting James' wishes or desires in r.

For any given agent d and situation r, a d-dispositional counterpart of r is a situation in which d has the same doxastic and buletic dispositions—the same beliefs and desires—as in r. The notion derives from the dispositional theory of action of Lewis (1986) and Stalnaker (1984); see Portner (1997), pp. 173 and 177, for discussion and implementation within his theory. If we add a temporal dimension to the model, d's dispositions must be the same in the two situations at the time of evaluation.

What about interrogative infinitival complements, of the sort we find in *know how to* constructions? These differ from the clausal infinitivals studied by Portner in two respects: They are interrogative, with an initial interrogative pronoun, and they cannot have an overt subject. To capture the interrogative component, Stanley and Williamson adopt the prominent theory of embedded questions of Karttunen (1977), on which (7) entails that Stuart knows all the true answers to the question of what Mark had for breakfast:

(7) Stuart knows what Mark had for breakfast.

If Mark had scrambled eggs, Stuart knows that Mark had scrambled eggs. If he had a bagel, Stuart knows this, etc. Groenendijk and Stokhof (1997) call Karttunen's theory *weakly exhaustive*, contrasting this with strongly exhaustive theories like their own. Strong exhaustivity adds a closure condition, so that on this account Stuart not only knows all the positive answers, he also knows all the negative answers to the question. The intuitive difference is that if the denotation of a question is the conjunction of all the true answers, this is just a proposition, which is what Stanley and Williamson assume; but if it is strongly exhaustive, then we know not only the exhaustive true answer, but *that it is the exhaustive true answer to that question*. More concretely, if Mark did not have pancakes for breakfast, Karttunen's theory cannot predict that (7) entails (8), whereas the strongly exhaustive theories can:

(8) Stuart knows whether Mark had pancakes for breakfast.

For this and a number of other reasons not directly relevant here, I'll adopt Groenendijk and Stokhof's theory. Formally the denotation of a question is a partition over the set of possible worlds, a set of (non-intersecting) propositions the union of which is identical to the set of all possible worlds. Any two worlds w and w' are in the same cell of the partition corresponding to *what did Mark have for breakfast?* in case Mark had exactly the same things for breakfast in w as in w'. The partition corresponding to the *whether*-clause in (8) divides the set of all possible worlds into two cells: those in which Mark had pancakes and those in which he did not. Because the question of whether Mark had pancakes is a subquestion of *what did Mark have for breakfast?*, the partition corresponding to the former is a sub-structure of that for the latter, so that knowing which cell corresponds to the correct answer for the super-question entails knowing it for the sub-question as well.

Stanley and Williamson assume that *wh*-infinitivals like *how to* are clausal, with a subject position in the syntax filled by a phonologically unrealized element, PRO. They appeal to the long literature in syntactic theory which attempts to explain how PRO gets its reference as a syntactic reflex of the control properties of the main-clause verb. In this literature, PRO may be obligatorily controlled by either one of the arguments of that main verb, as specified in the verb's lexical entry, or it can receive the so-called PRO_{arb} interpretation, where it denotes the arbitrary individual. I'll call the arbitrary interpretation *generic*.

I will argue for a different analysis of *wh*-infinitivals, one developed by David Dowty and Pauline Jacobson (1991). Their work builds both on the view of questions of Groenendijk and Stokhof and on a different kind of approach to infinitivals without overt subjects, one in which the infinitivals in question are VPs rather than sentential constituents. The agentive argument of the infinitival VP is not given as a syntactic subject—the implicit PRO of Stanley and Williamson's theory. Rather, other factors in the semantics and pragmatics of the utterance lead the hearer to understand who is entailed to have the property denoted by the VP.

In keeping with the VP status of these constituents, Dowty and Jacobson argue that infinitival questions denote not propositions, but properties of a certain sort: "Infinitival Questions denote hypothetical, unsaturated, appropriate actions". Note that the notion of action they have in mind is rather different from the colloquial sense, as we see in (9):

(9) Dowty and Jacobson's (1991) semantics of *wh*-infinitivals (informal):

"Infinitival Questions denote hypothetical, unsaturated, appropriate actions", i.e.

a) **actions**: properties which it is under an agent's control to possess or not to possess

b) **appropriate**: by some contextually implicit criterion, e.g. useful for attaining some goal, profitable, healthy, safe, legal, moral, pleasurable, etc.

c) **unsaturated**: the value of one or more arguments (represented by the *wh*-word) in the actions are unspecified; these correspond to the range of choices the agent will have in selecting the particular action to perform (now or later).

   d) **hypothetical**: it is presupposed that they are not yet carried out by an agent at the time referred to.

"That is, an Infinitival Question denotes a function from one or more arguments into a kind of property, what we call an action."

Dowty and Jacobson illustrate their proposal formally for the denotation of *what to eat* as in (10):

(10) *what to eat* denotes

$$\lambda x_{agent} \lambda w \lambda w' [\lambda y_{theme} [\text{ACT}(eat(w)(y))(x) = \text{ACT}(eat(w')(y))(x)]]$$

where $\text{ACT}(P)(x)$ means 'P is an action appropriately performed by x'   [with the sense of action in (9a), CR]

This is a function from individuals (agents) to partitions over the set of worlds. In (10) the partitioning is captured via a curried function, correlating to a relation over the set of worlds.[3] But any two worlds are in the same cell of the partition for a given agent just in case for any given edible object, either the agent acts so as to eat that object in both worlds or does not do so in either. Hence, a cell in the partition contains worlds where the agent aims to eat exactly the same things. This is the interrogative counterpart of an infinitival VP; instead of denoting a function from an individual to a proposition, it denotes a function from an individual to a question.

As noted, the sense in which these properties are actions is not that they are precisely actions to be undertaken. Dowty (1972, 1979) had discussed in detail the so-called "agentive statives" and their occurrence in imperatives such as *Don't worry!*, *Be polite!*, *Be a gentleman!*, and the like. These agentive statives also occur in *wh*-infinitival complements: *Marvin wondered how not to worry*. It is with a view to the occurrence of such statives in the construction of interest that Dowty and Jacobson use the notion of action in this constrained sense. Ginzburg and Sag (2000), noting the same issue, accordingly characterize the class of properties in the denotations of both infinitival questions and imperatives as *outcomes*. For reasons that will become clear, I prefer to choose a term that underlines the intentional character of the agent's relation

---

[3]Currying, sometimes called a *Schönfinkelization* (e.g., in Heim and Kratzer (1998), transforms a function taking a tuple of arguments into one which takes those arguments one at a time. E.g., from $f : (X \times Y) \mapsto Z$ into $X \mapsto (Y \mapsto Z)$. A partition takes any two worlds into a truth value (true just in case they're in the same cell of the partition); but the function in (10) instead takes any two worlds one at a time.

to these outcomes: As in Dowty and Jacobson's *actions* and Portner's analysis of imperatives, the denotations of these constructions represent the kind of eventualities the agent is (or might be) *committed to bringing about*. So for any given agent, I will call the set of such properties that agent's *goals*, keeping in mind the sense of that term in the philosophy of action and in Planning Theory in AI, wherein having a goal entails having a persistent commitment to achieving the goal (e.g. see Bratman, 1987, Pollack, 1986). Thus, I propose (11), with the associated conditions on goals in (12):[4]

(11) *what to eat* denotes

$\lambda x_{agent} \lambda w \lambda w' [\lambda y_{theme} [\text{GOAL}_x(eat(w)(y))(x) = \text{GOAL}_x(eat(w')(y))(x)]]$

where GOAL_x means 'is a rational goal given x's circumstances and commitments'

(12) **Goal Rationality**: It is only rational to adopt a goal if:

   a) **payoff**: there is a potential payoff if one achieves it. (This may be indirect; e.g., Mary hates codfish, but if she eats it, she stands a better chance of avoiding rickets.)

   b) **feasibility**: one has reason to think it's achievable, given the information one has.

   c) **compatibility**: one doesn't have pre-existing goals or commitments which preclude acting to achieve the goal in question.

   If any of these conditions fail, adopting the goal is at best a waste of one's time.

Though the change from (10) to (11) is to a large extent terminological,[5] the association of the type of actions in question with goals

---

[4]There is another benefit to characterizing Dowty and Jacobson's ACT as GOAL, though there isn't space to discuss that here: As Stanley and Williamson note, an infinitival *how-to* question typically has a mention-some interpretation, rather than mention-all. That is, for an answer to satisfactorily resolve (Ginzburg, 1995) a question about how to do y, it needn't entail all the ways that one might do y. One way would do. I would argue that this is due to the way that resolution of questions generally should be judged relative to the goals that the questions subserve. One way of doing x will typically serve the goal of getting x done as well as another, and so there is generally no need to specify more than one way, let alone all the possible ways one might accomplish it, unless there are questions about the feasibility of the various methods. Hence, the so-called "mention-some" interpretation (which I have argued elsewhere to be due to pragmatic domain restriction, instead of a distinct interpretation) arises out of the subsumption of the question-answering goal to the over-arching goal.

[5]I do not mean that Dowty or Jacobson would agree to the proposed modification, and in fact I know that Dowty (p.c.) prefers the original term. Rather, the

in the Planning sense brings out other features of this account which help to explain the properties of the *know how to* construction under discussion. When any of the conditions in (12) fail, adopting the goal in question would be irrational. So, one can only rationally adopt a goal so long as one believes it has not yet been accomplished; otherwise, there would be no pay-off and condition (a) would fail. In this respect, we can see how the futurity generally associated with infinitivals, as in Portner's analysis, makes them well-suited to the expression of goals; thus, the semantics of the *wh*-infinitivals is compatible with that for infinitivals more generally. We'll see some other virtues of this characterization shortly.

The futurity involved in both *wh*-infinitivals and infinitival VPs is not the only reason to assume that *wh*-infinitivals characterized as in (11) are derived from infinitival VPs with denotations like that in (6). To derive (11) compositionally, an interrogative pronoun would take an infinitival VP to make a function from individuals to a relation between worlds, i.e. a function from individuals to questions. According to Portner's analysis, infinitival VPs involve a disposition and what we might call an outcome; Portner doesn't make explicit the relationship between the disposition and the outcome, but I believe it would be in keeping with his conception, and with the Kratzer-style modal semantics on which it is based,[6] to characterize the latter as the ideal outcome given that disposition. The notion of a goal, as defined in Planning Theory and constrained by (12), is stronger than the usual colloquial notion of a disposition, since goals involve persistent commitments, while dispositions need not. But I believe we would say that anyone who has a given goal is disposed to attempt to achieve it, so that having a goal entails holding the corresponding disposition to act. Suppose we give the agent argument to the denotation of the *wh*-infinitival as characterized by Dowty and Jacobson and reframed in (11). The result is a question about what kind of goal it would be ideal for that agent to adopt, and hence a question about what kind of disposition that agent should cultivate. Suppose that in a situation s a given agent a has goal g. This entails that in s a has a disposition whose ideal outcome is g.

Working out the details of how we might derive (11) from (6) is nontrivial. Technically it involves the interrogative binding the situation-of-interpretation r in (6), so that the resulting question partitions the set of situations (or worlds—the maximal situations) into maximal sets

---

modification aims to preserve what is correct about their account, while drawing out some of the crucial features of what it is to adopt an ACT of the sort they describe.

[6]e.g., see Kratzer, 1981, 1989

in which the relevant agent shares the same dispositions. One challenge is to explain how, when an interrogative pronoun takes an infinitival VP as argument, this results in strengthening the disposition associated with the VP into a goal. Another is that since Portner's account is couched in situation semantics, we would have to transpose Dowty and Jacobson's possible worlds-based account into situation semantics in order to perform the derivation in a rigorous fashion. But this in turn would depend on a general account of questions in situation semantics, something which, to my knowledge, has not yet been satisfactorily worked out. Such an account in turn would require exploring the ramifications of interrogativity for a number of difficult issues that tend to arise in situation semantics, e.g. issues of persistence, genericity, and negation,[7] and tackling such issues would take us way beyond the current discussion. Another way of technically coordinating the two accounts would be to attempt to re-frame Portner's in terms of classical possible worlds; e.g. one might introduce temporal intervals, and characterize the agent's dispositions in a world-at-an-interval instead of in a situation. However, Portner's motivations for using situation semantics are quite subtle, and it isn't clear whether the transposition to the coarser-grained possible worlds framework would retain all the essential features of his account. I will not attempt to address these issues in the present paper, except to say that I suspect that all these challenges and more would face anyone attempting to give a compositional account of the denotation assumed by Stanley and Williamson. I only hope that I have made clear the intuitively plausible connection between Portner's infinitival VP denotations and Dowty and Jacobson's *wh*-infinitival denotations.

Now consider how (11) interacts with verbs that take *wh*-infinitival complements. For all such verbs, "some person knows, communicates, decides, etc. what values can be given to the unsaturated argument(s) to yield an action that is appropriate (for someone) in the implicitly relevant way" (Dowty and Jacobson). Different verbs entail different relations of the understood agent in question to the potential goal. Dowty and Jacobson point to the following classes of verbs that take infinitival question complements:[8]

---

[7]See Barwise and Perry, 1983, Veltman, 1984, Kratzer, 1989, and Portner's work for the flavor of these problems.

[8]I've added a few verbs to their lists and moved a couple to different categories. Some of these are slippery; for example, it isn't clear that *ask* or *suggest* or *recommend* entail an intention to act on the choice in question. But there do seem to be these general classes, exemplified by at least some of the verbs in the lists. In a fully detailed account, the point would not be to put these verbs in the appropri-

(13) Dowty and Jacobson's classes of verbs with infinitival question complements:
- I. Cognitive class: "pertain to a mental choice of one value for the unsaturated argument over another"
  - A. intransitive: *know, understand, discover, remember, wonder, notice, discern, forget, be unsure, be (un)certain, consider, contemplate, discuss*
  - B. subject infinitival complement: *elude, escape, be unclear, be obvious*
  - C. transitive: *demonstrate to, explain to, inform, advise, remind, convey to, mention (to)*
- II. Active class: "entail a choice of value for the unsaturated argument and an intention to act, given that choice"
  - A. intransitive: *ask, plan, decide, determine, resolve, practice*
  - B. transitive: *tell, ask, indicate to, advise, suggest to, recommend to*

I believe that the verbs in (13) form a natural class. Briefly, I note two features which they share semantically and which bear on the semantics of *knowing how*. First, note that none of the verbs in question are factive. Factives, like *surprise*, and other predicates that tend to implicate factivity, like *predict*, do not occur with infinitival complements (or subjects), as we see in these examples from Dowty and Jacobson:[9]

(14) *Where to go surprised me. (cf.: Where he went surprised me.)

(15) *John has predicted who to invite to the party. (cf.: John has predicted who he will invite to the party.) (Huntley, 1982)

But this follows if we assume that Portner's semantics for infinitivals is generally correct, since the unrealized, future entailment of the infinitival is incompatible with a presupposition or implication of factivity. I take this to capture the hypotheticality of Dowty and Jacobson's actions, as stipulated in their (9d).

Notice also that all but one of the verbs Dowty and Jacobson list are what I will call *epistemically reflective*, which is to say that they make the following schema true:

(16) A verb V is **epistemically reflective** if it truthfully instantiates the following schema: If for some relation R, you R something,

---

ate pre-existing category, but to determine for each its precise contributions to the truth conditions of the whole utterance in which it occurs. The categories would then exist only as generalizations over these verb-particular senses.

[9]See footnote 20 below for one possible exception.

194 / CRAIGE ROBERTS

then you know that you R it:

If you know something, you know that you know it.

If you wonder about something, you know that you wonder about it.

If you decide something, you know that you decide it.

If someone demonstrates to/explains to/informs/advises, etc. something to you, you know that they have done so (and they know they have done so, too).

Forget is not directly epistemically reflective, but it does involve a presupposition of epistemic reflectivity:

If you forget something, this presupposes that you once knew it, hence knew that you knew it.

Note that the epistemic reflectivity of the verbs in (13) doesn't necessarily entail knowledge of the correct answer to the question corresponding to its *wh*-infinitival complement; e.g., for *decide*, one must often decide what to do without knowing whether the course one has chosen is actually the best under the circumstances.

Not all predicates denoting mental attitudes are epistemically reflective in this sense. It is often argued that we can have merely implicit (or emergent) beliefs, and hence that if you believe something, you don't necessarily know that you believe it. It's interesting, then, that *believe* doesn't take infinitival questions:

(17) *Mary believed whether to eat/what to do/how to dance.

So far as I can determine, the predicates that take infinitival questions are all self-reflective, in this sense. They all either entail or presuppose self-reflective knowledge.

Of course, there is a long debate in epistemology over whether knowledge itself is self-reflective in this sense.[10] I do not mean to weigh in on that debate. Rather, I would only point out that the behavior of the verb *know* suggests that speakers of English treat it as self-reflective, since it classes with these other verbs in its behavior in the construction in question, which otherwise all seem to display self-reflectivity.

But of course the verbs in (13) differ semantically in some respects, among them whether the understood agent of the infinitival is entailed

---

[10]Polly Jacobson (p.c.) reports a high school saying: *He who knows not, and knows that he knows, he is a freshman; he who knows not and knows not that he knows not, he is a sophomore; he who knows and knows not that he knows, he is a junior; he who knows and knows that he knows, he is a senior.* The problem is the junior, and Socrates might argue that we're all juniors. This just underlines the reasons for the philosophical controversy. But to me, it seems to equivocate about what it means to know.

to have adopted the goal associated with the infinitival. For example, when *wonder* takes a *wh*-infinitival complement, the main subject is only entailed to entertain the infinitival question with a view to resolving the correct value for the understood agent. There is no entailment that the correct value has been determined, let alone the goal adopted. And one can understand what to do but decide not to do it. Knowing what to do seems to entail knowing what would be a rational goal under ideal circumstances of some relevant sort, but alas neither rationality nor ideal circumstances always obtain. But with *decide*, there is that commitment: The subject believes that she probably grasps the correct value for the *wh*-word, with herself as understood agent, and moreover she has adopted the goal entailed by the infinitival with that value for the gap. This pertains to another desirable feature of the proposed semantics for *wh*-infinitivals in (11): Combined with the feasibility condition on goal adoption, (12b), we know that any rational agent who has adopted the goal corresponding to an answer to the infinitival question must believe that she is capable of achieving the goal. So if, as with *decide*, there is entailed commitment to the corresponding goal, then this in turn by (12b) entails that that individual believes that she is probably capable of achieving the goal.

A verb like *demonstrate* directly entails that the subject *is* capable of achieving the goal in the manner demonstrated, so it entails ability. But since *know*, one of the verbs of "mental choice", does not entail that the goal has been adopted, the disputed implication of ability sometimes associated with the *know how to* construction only arises when there is a pragmatic implication that the goal has, in fact, been adopted. If we know that Georgia is looking for an ivory-billed woodpecker, and one of us says that she knows how to find one, this suggests that (assuming she is rational) she has adopted the goal of finding one in that fashion and therefore believes she is capable of pursuing it successfully. But capability is not entailed by the meaning of the *know-how* statement by itself. Hence, it is compatible to claim that *John knows what to eat but can't afford it*;[11] neither ability nor feasibility directly apply in this case. So in this way, the compositional semantic account of *know how to* can accommodate those whose intuitions correctly seize the implication of ability in many cases, while admitting the counterexamples to entailed ability offered by Ginet (1975) and others. Ginet argues that "ascriptions of knowledge-how do not even entail ascriptions of the corresponding abilities", and Stanley and Williamson illustrate this with the case of a ski instructor who knows how to perform a complex stunt

---

[11] This example was suggested by an anonymous reviewer.

without being able to perform it herself (due to Jeff King, p.c. to Stanley and Williamson), and that of a master pianist who has lost her arms in an accident and hence knows how to play a Beethoven sonata but no longer can.

In this way we can also explain why *know how to* statements often have the flavor of *could* statements, as Stanley and Williamson note: This is just the feasibility clause (12b) made hypothetical, in keeping with the infinitival's futurity. More generally, treating these properties in terms of goals also captures what Dowty and Jacobson seem to mean in calling them *hypothetical* in their informal characterization (9): One only rationally adopts goals conditional on the satisfaction of all the preconditions. The goal-orientation in the analysis also explains Stanley and Williamson's observation that there is sometimes a rather deontic flavor to *know how to* statements: Goals involve commitments, and commitments are things one should try to fulfill. But these different modal implications don't result from ambiguity: All the conditions on rational goals must obtain simultaneously, so that the feasibility and the deontic character co-exist. It's just that one of the modal flavors may seem to predominate in a given example, as a function of a variety of lexical and pragmatic factors.

The other feature Dowty and Jacobson claim for the properties denoted by infinitival questions is appropriateness. To see how this follows from the goal-based semantics, consider the following examples and paraphrases:

(18) Mary wondered whether to go to Shanghai.
  'Mary wondered about the value for $y \in$ {does/does not} such that $y(go\ to\ Shanghai)$ would be a rational goal to adopt, given what she knew and her other goals, commitments and intentions.'

To wonder about something suggests a puzzle, and in (18), given the rationality conditions on goal adoption in (12), the puzzle could be (a) whether there really is a potential payoff in going, or (b) whether circumstances might make it impossible or improbable to achieve the goal of going, or (c) whether one might have conflicting prior commitments. Here, going to Shanghai seems to allude to a particular potential trip, and so the question seems to be about Mary's going or not going on a particular occasion. The appropriateness condition follows from making her adoption of the infinitival goal conditional on whether it would be rational, in the sense outlined, including compatibility with her other goals, commitments and intentions.

Let's look at some more examples. (19) is more likely to have a generic reading, because of the bare present tense of *knows* and the non-specific indefinite *spicy food*:

(19) James knows what to drink with spicy food.
> 'James knows the value for *y* that would make *drink y with spicy food* a rational goal, given normal circumstances and lack of conflict with other, pre-established goals, commitments and intentions of the agent.'

In (20), we can get either the particular or the general readings:

(20) Jessica showed Mary how to fix her sink.
> 'Jessica demonstrated for Mary's benefit the procedure *y* such that *fix her sink via procedure y* would be a rational goal to adopt, given what is known and other pre-established goals, commitments and intentions.'

If there's any implication that the sink is actually broken, the example is likely to have the object-control reading; otherwise we get a generic reading. We can see the latter possibility more readily if we replace *her* with *a*: Maybe Jessica is teaching Mary how to be a plumber. The pay-off requirement on goals predicts one will only adopt the goal if the sink needs to be fixed and it would be useful to have it working. But just because Mary now knows how to fix the sink, even if it's broken (so that there would be a payoff), this doesn't mean that she adopts that goal: This might depend on whether she gets her APA paper finished in time! So, again, the hypothetical flavor captured in the paraphrase by *would* is really the presumption that the rational preconditions are satisfied, a sort of pragmatic presupposition arising from the requirement of rationality and what it is to fix a sink.

The proposed semantics for infinitival questions has another virtue: It works when they serve as subjects, as in (21), which has both a generic interpretation and one where the subject is taken to be some particular individual under discussion—perhaps poor Lingens:

(21) How to escape is obvious—it's what to do afterwards that's tough.
> 'The value for *y* such that *escape via procedure y* is a rational goal, given what's known and other pre-established goals, commitments and intentions of the agent, is obvious.'

The possibility of both kinds of readings here raises challenging questions for the type of linguistic theory that Stanley and Williamson appeal to in explaining the interpretation of PRO in their account, the linguistic theory of Control, which studies how such abstract, phonologically unrealized constituents get their interpretations. Control is generally assumed to involve governance of PRO in an infinitival complement by the main verb. But in (21) the infinitival is the subject, and verbs do not govern their subjects, at least in English. Still, here we see attested the same two types of readings we get for the earlier examples where the infinitival was a complement.

Control is a theory about verbs taking subjectless non-finite complements like the *wh*-infinitivals at issue here. The theory is intended to explain why with with some verbs, including *wonder* (18) and *know* (19), the implicit agent of the infinitival is taken to be the subject of the main verb, while with others, including *show* (20), *suggest* and *tell*, the subject of the infinitival is taken to be the object of the main verb. In syntactic theories of control, this is assumed to be a function of syntactic features of the governing verb, which assigns the proper referential index to the implicit PRO subject in its complement. But as with the purported sentential character of the infinitival, this type of theory of control is not universally accepted, and I think that a variety of problems argue for a non-syntactic account of Control, one in which the semantics of the matrix verb and various pragmatic factors combine to determine who is understood to be the agent of the infinitival. There is a significant body of literature which takes this general approach.[12]

Jackendoff and Culicover (2003) give a detailed, compelling critique of the syntactic approach to control involving PRO, arguing instead for three classes of control based on the lexical semantics of the matrix verb:[13]

(22) Jackendoff and Culicover's (2003) classes of control:

Unique control: e.g. in object complements of *persuade, promise, shout to, ask, request, be rude to*, etc.

Free control: e.g. in object complements of *beats, outranks, entails, is as good as*; and in subject complements of *help, important, ruin, intrigues*; etc.

---

[12] Jackendoff (1972, 1974), Rozicka (1983), Nishigauchi (1984), Williams (1985), Dowty (1985), Farkas (1988), Chierchia (1988), Sag and Pollard (1991), Pollard and Sag (1994), van Valin and LaPolla (1997), Culicover and Jackendoff (2001), and Jackendoff and Culicover (2003), the last of which provides a useful overview of the literature and issues.

[13] For those unfamiliar with the theory of Control, note that the classification of verbs into these three categories is orthogonal to the issue of which of the verb's arguments, if any, is the controller. That is, in an example where the subject of the main verb is understood to be the subject of the infinitival as well—so-called subject control—the verb may be in any of Jackendoff and Culicover's three classes. *Promise* typically exhibits unique subject-control, as in *Jane promised to come to the party*. In nearly-free *discuss*, we also often see subject-control, as in *Jane discussed coming to the party*.

Nearly free control: e.g. in object complements of verbs of communication and thought, including *talk about, mention, discuss*

In matrix verbs exhibiting unique control, Jackendoff and Culicover argue that the verb always selects for what they call an *Actional complement*, one felicitous in the context *what X did was...*, which may be an object or (less often) a subject. The matrix verb's lexical semantics entails that exactly one of its other arguments (that fulfilling a specified thematic role) should be understood as the controller; the thematic role of the controller differs from verb to verb (e.g. *promise* vs. *persuade*). However, they do note (p. 524) that even with verbs that normally exercise unique control, infinitival indirect question complements (in object or subject positions) may also have a generic control interpretation (the PRO_{arb} interpretation noted above). In their non-unique control, the verb does not select for an Actional infinitival. With free control, the controller is not semantically determined by the verb. The possibilities for controller in such cases include:

- the denotation of one of the explicit NP arguments of the verb,
- a split antecedent (the join of the denotations of two or more explicit arguments)
- a generic agent
- a long-distance controller—the denotation of an NP in a higher clause
- some entity under discussion in prior discourse
- the speaker or hearer, or the join of the speaker and another salient entity

In nearly free control, which involves verbs of communication or thought, the options are somewhat more restricted, but include the denotations of an argument of the matrix verb, a split antecedent, a discourse antecedent, or the generic interpretation.

   I agree with the general approach proposed by Jackendoff and Culicover. As argued in Dowty (1985), it is the lexical semantics of the verb, and not its syntactic properties *per se*, that are at the crux of obligatory control. But things are a bit more complex in certain cases than their account would suggest: Even with verbs that usually display unique control, pragmatics may also enter into the determination of the controller, as we can see when they take infinitival question complements. Consider:

(23) John promised Mary to mow the lawn.

(24) John asked Mary to mow the lawn.

(25) John asked Mary how to mow the lawn.

The verb *promise* takes three semantic arguments: an agent, a patient and a goal. Since a promise is a commitment on the part of the agent, and a commitment involves the intention to achieve a goal, the semantics of the verb here entails that the subject *John* is the controller of the goal-denoting infinitival; this is quite similar to the analysis of *promise* in Jackendoff and Culicover. It's a different matter to ask someone to do something, since that involves presenting them with a potential goal, which we propose that they adopt. Hence, in (24) the denotation of the *object* is the one to whom the goal is proposed: Mary is the one who would be making the commitment, it is she who would be the mower; hence, the object controls the infinitival, and again we needn't appeal to syntax. This is in keeping with the analysis of *ask* in Jackendoff and Culicover (2003), who argue that its semantics yields unique control.[14] In neither (23) nor (24) is there the possibility of a generic interpretation: The semantics of the verb plus the goal-denotation of the infinitival combine to entail that the argument who is entailed to make a commitment is the agent of the infinitival. Otherwise, the utterance would be incoherent.

But (25) demonstrates clearly that the control features of *ask* aren't due to its lexical semantics alone, let alone some arbitrary syntactic feature.[15] The same verb now permits either of two readings—generic or subject control—but not the object-control reading attested in (24). This is because what John proposes to Mary is not a goal in the world, as in (24), but the goal of answering the question corresponding to the *wh*-infinitival. Asking is posing a kind of request, proposing to the addressee that they adopt a given goal; but that goal may either be a particular type of action in the world (an Actional infinitival, as in (24)) or it may be informational—helping to resolve a question, as in (25). Without trying to pin down a full definition of *ask*, we can characterize this feature of its meaning via the following necessary conditions:

(26) Constraints on the meaning of *ask*:

   ask subcategorizes for a subject (agent of the request), an object

---

[14]See their section 4.2, discussion of their class 2, pp. 533–535. They acknowledge that such predicates have free control when they take *about* plus a gerund, but argue that they display unique control when they occur with infinitives. But the discussion of (25) just below argues that the semantics of the complement plays a role in the determination of control, so that it is not just an arbitrary fact about the *about* case that differentiates its control behavior from that of the canonical case with an infinitival VP complement.

[15]See Sag and Pollard (1991) for detailed discussion of these kinds of examples.

(addressee or patient), and a goal—an infinitival VP or
question

Take InfP to be either an infinitival VP or an infinitival question.
Then *ask*

presupposes: InfP has the right sort of denotation to serve as
a goal (e.g., if an infinitival VP, it is Actional in Jackendoff and Culicover's sense

has as a lexical entailment:

$$\lambda NP_{obj}\,\lambda InfP\,\lambda NP_{subj}\,[request(NP_{subj}, NP_{obj},$$
$$\text{Adopt-Goal}(NP_{obj}, InfP)]$$

If the goal is an action, then by virtue of what it is to adopt an action as one's goal, *ask* entails that what the agent requests is that the addressee be the agent of the proposed action, as argued by Jackendoff and Culicover. But if the goal is that the addressee resolve a question, the entailment by itself fails to say anything about the understood subject of the question. Hence, the nature of the denotation of the complement itself, and not the semantics of the verb alone, also plays a role in determining the understood controller. Moreover, in interpreting an utterance of (25), we must consider what possible motivation the agent (subject) might have for her request.

One frequent reason for asking how something is done is so that we can do it ourselves. If we take that to be John's motivation, which I think is the default case when we encounter (25) out of the blue, we will most likely take him to be the controller. But that isn't necessarily the case: John might be the instructor in a lawn maintenance course, quizzing Mary about what she has learned. In that case, he already knows the answer to the question, and the only reasonable interpretation seems to be the generic.[16] Hence, pragmatics plays a role in determining control, as well as the semantics of the verb and that of the complement.

Pragmatics also plays a role in control in examples with split antecedents, as in (27) and (28), due to Dowty and Jacobson, where in each case the antecedent of the underlined NP is taken to be the controller of the infinitival, which is in turn understood to be Mary and John:[17]

---

[16]E.g., if we change *the* to *her*, in the quiz-case we might take the question to be how Mary should mow her lawn—e.g., it might be seeded with a particular kind of grass seed that needs to be mowed at a certain height, etc.

[17]Moreover, control occurs not only with subjectless infinitivals, but with nominals as well, as discussed by Jackendoff and Culicover. Dowty and Jacobson note:

"[T]he same range of generic versus individual interpretations ... is found in sentences with the verb 'know' and all sorts of NPs denoting methods, not just

(27) John suggested to Mary how to amuse themselves during the afternoon.

(28) John reminded Mary what not to say to each other's parents.

Not all transitive predicates so readily permit split antecedent control, as we see in (29):

(29) #?John told Mary how to amuse themselves during the afternoon.

While *suggest* and *remind* are cooperative predicates, readily implicating that the suggested goal is to be cooperatively adopted, *tell* is directive, hence doesn't readily lend itself to the implication of cooperative goal-adoption that I believe is the necessary condition for split-antecedent control in general, including in cases like (27) and (28). The potential non-generic controller is the individual or set of individuals who are entailed or implicated to (potentially) adopt the goal associated with the infinitival. Jackendoff and Culicover (2003) characterize *remind* as a verb of unique control, and that seems correct when it takes a non-interrogative complement. But again, pragmatics plays a crucial role in determining control of an infinitival question.

But what about the generic reading of the infinitival questions? How does it arise? It is most likely when there are other indications in the infinitival that it describes not a particular situation or circumstance, but the general case. Another way of saying this is that generic control of the infinitival agent is a function of the genericity of the circumstance of evaluation. For example, in (19), the object of the infinitival is the mass indefinite *spicy food*, suggesting that the speaker is alluding to spicy food in general, not to the fare on some particular dining occasion; hence, the generic interpretation for the agent naturally arises. In (18) since travel to exotic places is not an ordinary issue and *wonder* entails an issue of concern to the subject, we take the infinitival question to have a particular interpretation; but cf. (30):

---

infinitival questions:

(46) John knows (a) a shortcut to Mary's house/(b) the formula for solving a quadratic equation/(c) Prolog/(d) a good recipe for carrots/(e) the right dress for the opera/(f) the best wine for this entrée.

"Some of these also have [a] more strongly generic than ... individual flavor, but not all need really be generic. If the shortcut John knows to Mary's house involves cutting through a back yard where there is a vicious dog that will attack anyone but him, (46a) is still appropriate, though it's not a "generic" shortcut. Notice that if [we] substitute "decided on" for "know" in the last sentence, then usually the individual "reading" is what comes to mind, e.g. "We decided on the best wine for this entrée, decided on a shortcut to Mary's house", etc."

(30) Whether to travel to exotic places is not a decision many of us have to make.

where the subject does have the generic interpretation.

Note that in Portner's semantics for the infinitival, interpretation is relativized to some situation r. That is, interpretation of infinitival questions is always deictically anchored to some understood situation, which is conveyed pragmatically. Let us call this the situation of interpretation for the infinitival. This may be either a particular situation relevant to the discussion—as in (18), one reading of (20) and (21), and the default interpretations of (23)–(25)—or the arbitrary, generic situation, as in (19) and the other readings of (20) and (21). Thus in (18), *to go to Shanghai* will be understood relative to a pragmatically implicated particular occasion, which may be either specific or non-specific, e.g. 'as part of the forthcoming business deal' or 'for a vacation'. We see a contextually-suggested specific definite situation of interpretation in (31):

(31) We were in a terrible mess during our vacation when we lost our passports in Turkey last summer. But we called John, and fortunately he knew what to do.

Besides a subject-control interpretation where John knows what he should do to save the day, on another prominent interpretation (31) means that John knew what the speaker and her companion(s) should do in their particular circumstance in Turkey. Again, the control here is largely pragmatically determined.

When the pragmatically conveyed situation of interpretation for the infinitival is particular, the resulting reading always involves non-generic control. There is another important property of these non-generic readings, given in (32):

(32) When an attitude verb takes an infinitival complement, the interpretation involving control of the infinitival by the experiencer of the attitude verb is always *de se*.

In such a control situation, no true *de dicto* readings arise, although the generic may in some cases entail a *de dicto* truth.

Stanley and Williamson come close to the generalization in (32) when they claim that "uses of 'PRO' where they are controlled by the subject in the main clause invariably give rise to "de se" readings, that is, readings involving a first-person mode of presentation."[18] The sole example they offer in support of this claim is (33) (from their footnote

---

[18]Stanley and Williamson give no references for this observation, so I assume it is theirs. I'd be interested to hear of any other claims in this vein from the literature.

26), which indeed can only be true if Hannah wants her*self to win the lottery:

(33) Hannah wants to win the lottery.

Parallel to this, *Lingens wants to win the lottery* can't mean only that Lingens wants that poor fellow Rudolph Lingens that he's been reading about to win the lottery, unaware that he* is that poor fellow. Although Stanley and Williamson's generalization seems correct for many control verbs, it over-generalizes in a way that is avoided by (32). For one thing, they ignore the possibility that the experiencer of an attitude predicate may not be the subject, a possibility illustrated by *excite* (or *dismay*, or *frighten*, etc.):

(34) It excited Lingens to find the map of the Stanford Library.

(34) can't merely mean that it excited Lingens that the fellow he'd been reading about, Rudolph Lingens, found the map of the Stanford Library. Instead, it entails that what excited Lingens was that he* had found the map. So here object-control is *de se*, since the object is the experiencer. But a non-experiencer object fails to yield a *de se* interpretation, as in (35):

(35) John believes Louis to be a vampire.

A *de se* interpretation, with its "first-person mode of presentation", presupposes a presentation of the relevant denotatum to the holder of an attitude. Since Louis is not entailed here to hold any attitude, nor is John entailed to hold any attitude pertaining to John, there can be no question of *de se* interpretation.

Stanley and Williamson's generalization is close to right because it seems to be the case that the majority of the verbs that take infinitival complements with interpretations involving subject control are in fact attitude verbs with subject experiencers, or at least entail attitudes on the part of the subject. Consider *connive*:

(36) Lingens connived to leave the library.

This entails a desire or wish on Lingens' part, hence a kind of attitude, and so we are not surprised to find that it conveys that Lingens was conniving for him*self to leave, and not necessarily for that fellow Rudolph Lingens to do so. Similarly with *contrive, desire, endeavor, expect* (with subject control), *fail* (which presupposes an attempt), *hope, long, manage* (again presupposing an attempt, hence a desire), *plan, plot, start, strain, strive, struggle, try, want, wish* and *yearn*.[19]

---

[19]This list of control verbs is drawn from the non-exhaustive list on Wiktionary: http://en.wiktionary.org/wiki/Category:English_control_verbs. The

Now note another generalization that I believe holds of all the predicates which fall under the generalization in (32):

(37) *de se* controllers are epistemically reflective with respect to the controller. That is, for any of the predicates denoted by these verbs, if the experiencer *Vs to δ*, then the experiencer knows that the experiencer *Vs to δ*, instantiating the schema in (16).

As (37) would lead us to expect, preliminary evidence suggests that non-epistemically reflective predicates do not license subject-control of infinitival complements:

(38) *John believes to be hungry.

An exhaustive consideration of English control verbs would be required to test these generalizations. But I think the preliminary evidence is strong. Then since all the predicates which take *wh*-interrogatives are (I have argued) epistemically reflective, this would lead us to expect that with experiencer control they would yield only the *de se* interpretation, as we observed earlier with *know how*. Note further that, as (32) and (37) predict, in the split antecedent examples in (27) and (28), both antecedents are epistemically reflective arguments of the verbs, and the only reading is *de se* with respect to that split antecedent.

But why should (32) hold in the more general case, and in particular for the predicates which take *wh*-infinitival complements? And why should there be this correlation between (32) and (37)? I strongly suspect that the answer lies beyond the present range of issues, and probably beyond my expertise. But I think we can say this much: The epistemic reflectivity of verbs like *know* suggests that in holding such an attitude the experiencer has a certain kind of privileged access to the relata, the intended denotations of the verb's arguments. By this, I don't mean to say that the experiencer knows who or what these relata are in some absolute sense, but that if the intended denotation entails certain relations (e.g., involving identity) among these relata, then the experiencer should have access to that information under the entailed epistemic reflectivity. Consider (39), the positive counterpart of (2):

(39) Lingens knows how to get out of the Stanford library.

---

only verb on that list that is a subject-control verb and doesn't seem to entail an attitude on the subject's part (at least in my dialect) is *proceed*: *Lingens proceeded to leave the library* doesn't entail an attitude or goal on Lingens' part, just reports a fact: Lingens then left the library (perhaps presupposing some preceding event just mentioned). I note that this factivity would appear at least *prima facia* to challenge Portner's analysis of infinitival VPs. Possibly the utterance doesn't literally mean that Lingens left, but only conversationally implicates it. But this warrants further consideration.

One of the relata in (39), the infinitival question, is about what would be the ideal goal for some individual. Suppose the intended interpretation involves non-generic control by the subject of *know*; this entails that the individual whose ideal goal is in question is the experiencer. Under epistemic reflectivity, the experiencer should have access to that information. Then the interpretation could be paraphrased 'Lingens knows that he* has the property of being an *x* such that *x* knows the value for *y* that would make *get out of the Stanford library via procedure y* a rational goal for *x*, given *x*'s own circumstances and other, pre-established goals, commitments and intentions'. The *he** in this paraphrase is justified by the epistemic reflectivity of the matrix verb, which I am treating thus as a kind of self-ascription. If something like this is the case, then the generalization in (32) follows from the semantics of the attitude verbs that take infinitival complements, including *wh*-infinitivals.

Whatever the reason for the correlation, the standard, syntactic theory of control adopted by Stanley and Williamson cannot account for these generalizations, because, as Castañeda pointed out, mere coreference, as guaranteed by coindexation of the controller with PRO, cannot guarantee the *de se* (or in his terms, the *he**) reading. The explanation must lie in the lexical semantics of the infinitival complement-taking verbs.

I have argued that the reading paraphrased is the one predicted for (39) on the basis of the independently motivated semantics for *wh*-infinitivals and an independently motivated theory of control.[20] I think this semantics does a far better job of explaining our intuitions about these examples than does Stanley and Williamson's, while shedding light on the difficulty of pinning those intuitions down. And it supports the contention of those from Ryle to Abbott, who have argued that knowing-how cannot be reduced to knowing-that.

8.3 Conjunction of unlike categories

Here is one objection that might be raised against the proposal just sketched: On this view, a *how-to* complement and a *that* complement are distinct both in syntactic character and in type of denotation (denoting a question vs. denoting a proposition). It is generally assumed that we can only conjoin like-categories, so on this account one might expect that *how-to* and *that* complements could not be conjoined. Yet

---

[20] I haven't attempted here a full semantics for *know*. However, deriving this interpretation for (39) relies mainly on the fact that it is a member of the epistemically-reflective class of verbs of interest.

Stanley and Williamson (2001) offer acceptable examples involving co-ordination of *wh*-infinitivals with *that*-complements:

(40) John knows that bicycle accidents can happen and also how to avoid them in most cases.

They assume that this is an argument for treating these two types of complements as identical in both syntactic category and semantic type.

But conjunction is not so simple as the like-category generalization might lead us to believe. Focusing on the case at hand, Groenendijk and Stokhof (1984) had pointed out that we can conjoin finite embedded questions with *that*-complements. The following are variants of non-finite examples in Stanley and Williamson (2001):

(41) a. John knows that Peter has left for Paris and how we can track him down.

b. Alex told Susan that someone was waiting for her, but not who it was.

But as discussed above, tensed *wh*-complements are generally argued to denote questions, not propositions. So in this respect, *how to* infinitivals are just acting like interrogative complements in general.

And the conjunction problem is even more complex than this. It has long been acknowledged in the linguistic literature, and discussed in detail in Sag et al. (1985), that both *that*-complements and infinitival questions can be conjoined with NPs. Here are (variants on) examples due to Dowty and Jacobson (1991):

(42) a. Mary explained to James both the question and how to find the answer.

b. Mary knows where to find the safe and the combination to the lock on it.

c. We asked her how to get home and several similar questions.

d. His answer and how he pronounced it both surprised me.

And the following examples, conjoining finite interrogative complements with infinitival questions or NPs, seem fine to me:

(43) a. Mary asked what articles she should read and where to get them.

b. Mary asked what articles she should read and the address of the nearest library.

c. Mary determined/learned the cost of the car and that she could buy it on credit.

d. Mary forgot both the address and how she was to get there.

There are other examples which don't seem as good, but these suffice to show, I think, that all the combinations are possible in principle, with no zeugma effect.

Dowty and Jacobson point out that this is not the only respect in which infinitival questions behave like nominal arguments:

- All verbs that subcategorize for infinitival question complements also subcategorize for (plain) NPs as well (with a few exceptions).
- All infinitival questions after transitive verbs (except for *wonder*, *resolve* and *decide*) passivize, as in:

(44) a. How to solve the problem is now understood by everyone.
      b. Where he found the mushrooms was discovered by his neighbor.

And we find that *that*-clauses behave as nominals in some respects as well. As Sag et al. (1985) discuss in detail (note that the title of the paper is a play on the issue), it seems that what constrains coordination isn't a matching requirement on the fully specified syntactic categories of the conjuncts, but whether they are of the same class of categories. Here, roughly speaking, the fact that the categories in question are all nominal in several respects is what seems to license coordination. Coordination is not an argument that they are all sentential (and hence proposition-denoting), or all property-denoting, or all NPs.[21]

In any case, any theory of coordination must wrestle with how to reconcile a fairly broad range of types of syntactico-semantic mismatch with the otherwise vigorous generalization that coordination involves like-constituents. Hence, the problem is far more general than the present issue and examples like (41)–(43) would suggest.

Moreover, from a purely semantic point of view we should keep in mind Lewis' point about the relationship between attitudes *de se* and *de dicto*:

---

[21] It is true, as Polly Jacobson (p.c.) points out, that in general NPs coordinated with interrogatives as in (42) and (43) can be construed as concealed questions, and this is probably a clue to why the coordination is acceptable. It seems that when one of these complements is a question, as in *how she was to get there* in (43d) and *how to pronounce it* in (42d), we understand that what the subject forgot or what surprised her was the answer to this question, an answer the speaker may or may not know. That is, in its interaction with the verb *forget* or *surprise*, the interrogative might be taken to be a non-specific stand-in for its answer. Then part of what would be at issue is whether any complement to such a verb—*that* clause, finite or non-finite interrogative, or NP—always denotes a question (with the verb entailing a relation to the answer to that question) or denotes something that could be understood to be an answer. Exploring this would take us beyond the current essay.

...if a map is made suitable for portable use by leaving off the "location of this map" ..., its incompleteness is not at all misleading. ...Knowledge *de dicto* is not the whole of knowledge *de se*. But there is no contradiction, or conflict, or unbridgeable gap, or even tension, between knowledge *de dicto* and the rest. They fit together as nicely as you please. (Lewis, 1979, p. 528)

Hence, the fact that *that*-complements denote propositions while *wh*-infinitivals do not does not preclude characterizing the information conveyed in comparable terms. So the argument from conjunction is not a strong one.

8.4 Comparatives and knowledge-how

Here is another argument for the proposed distinction in type between *that*-complements and *how to*-complements: We can felicitously compare knowledge of the *how-to* type, but not of the *that*-type:

(45) Marcus knows how to swim better than how to do pirouettes.

(46) #Marcus knows that he's learning to swim better than that he's learning to do pirouettes.

Now, it's not that we can never take a comparatively different stance with respect to one proposition than another:

(47) Mary admits to herself more readily that John loves her than that he's bad for her.

(48) Marcus confesses that he's learning to swim more comfortably than that he's learning to do pirouettes.

The difference between (46) and (47)/(48) is due to the difference in relation to their complement of the denotation of *know* vs. those of *admit/confess*. The point is that *know how* is not odd in comparatives.

I think we can explain this difference on the account due to Dowty and Jacobson. Knowing a proposition or a fact is an all or none matter: Either whatever conditions are necessary for knowledge obtain—the proposition is true and we believe it's true, etc.—or they do not. There's nothing in between. But knowing the answer to a question is not in general an all or none matter. For example, to the question *What does Moira take in her tea?*, there are several partial answers: *she takes sugar, she takes honey, she takes lemon, she takes milk*, etc. Knowing who someone is surely admits of degree in this respect; we can take a lifetime to get to know our own properties, let alone another's. Knowing how to do something is also a gradual matter—we might say that when Marcus is first learning to swim he has only a very partial answer to the question of how to swim, but that as he progresses, he knows more and more about how to swim, refining his methodology as he learns. Comparing where he stands on the scale from complete novice to master, we can see where he stands in this gradual process. The process involved in learning to do pirouettes is quite different, of course, but we can still talk about it in the abstract as involving a scale of mastery. And so we can compare where Marcus stands in the two processes of resolving the question of how to do something or other.

Interestingly, when we compare knowledge of the denotations of NP objects, they seem to be interpreted as concealed questions:

(49) Marcus knows chess better than poker.
> 'Marcus knows how to play chess better than how to play poker.'

Comparison isn't so felicitous with *knowing whether*:

(50) John knows whether to swim better than whether to do pirouettes.

But this is to be expected on the account just sketched. This is because a *whether-to* question has the same semantics as a yes-or-no question, with only two cells in the corresponding partition. Groenendijk and Stokhof define a partial answer as one that entails that one of the cells in the corresponding partition is not the correct answer. Hence, with only two cells, a partial answer is a complete answer. So there are no properly partial answers to *whether-to* questions, hence no proper scale of resolution for such questions: you either know the answer or you don't.

Again, the linguistic evidence converges on the conclusion that *how-to* infinitivals are of a different semantic type than *that*-complements: they are property-denoting VPs built on interrogative semantics. We cannot get this result if we regard the infinitival question as merely denoting (some or all) true answer(s) to a question, understood as mere propositions. It is true that we must understand the entailments deriving from these clauses in terms of the propositional content of the answer, but an *answer* is more than that—it also stands in relation to an underlying question and can be compared with other answers to the same question with respect to how well they resolve the question. This gradedness of answers in respect to resolution permits us to understand how we can compare degree of resolution of different questions. The semantics of *that*-complements does not provide us with such a notion.

References

Abbott, Barbara. 2006. Linguistic Solutions to Philosophical Problems. Paper given at the annual meeting of the Pacific APA, Portland, March, 2006.

Barwise, Jon and John Perry. 1983. *Situations and Attitudes*. Cambridge, MA: The MIT Press.

Bratman, Michael E. 1987. *Intentions, Plans and Practical Reason*. Cambridge, MA: Harvard University Press.

Castañeda, Hector-Neri. 1966. 'He': A study in the logic of self-consciousness. *Ratio* 8:130–157.

Chierchia, Gennaro. 1988. Structured Meanings, Thematic Roles and Control. In G. Chierchia, B. Partee, and R. Turner, eds., *Properties, Types and Meaning, Volume 2*, pages 131–166. Dordrecht: Kluwer Academic Publishers.

Culicover, Peter W. and Ray Jackendoff. 2001. Control is not movement. *Linguistic Inquiry* 32(3):493–512.

Dowty, David. 1972. *Studies in the Logic of Verb Aspect and Time Reference in English*. Ph.D. thesis, University of Texas, Austin.

Dowty, David. 1979. *Word Meaning in Montague Grammar*. Dordrecht, Holland: D. Reidel.

Dowty, David. 1985. On Recent Analyses of the Semantics of Control. *Linguistics and Philosophy* 8(3):291–331.

Dowty, David and Pauline Jacobson. 1991. Infinitival Questions. Unpublished manuscript for a talk delivered in colloquia at The University of California at Santa Cruz and Cornell University. The Ohio State University and Brown University.

Farkas, Donka F. 1988. On Obligatory Control. *Linguistics and Philosophy* 11(1):27–58.

Ginet, Carl. 1975. *Knowledge, Perception, and Memory*. Dordrecht, Holland: D. Reidel.

Ginzburg, Jonathan. 1995. Resolving Questions. *Linguistics and Philosophy* 18(5):459–527 (Part I) and 567–609 (Part II).

Ginzburg, Jonathan and Ivan A. Sag. 2000. *Interrogative Investigations: The Form, Meaning, and Use of English Interrogatives*. Stanford, California: CSLI Publications.

Groenendijk, Jeroen and Martin Stokhof. 1984. *Studies on the Semantics of Questions and the Pragmatics of Answers*. Ph.D. thesis, University of Amsterdam.

Groenendijk, Jeroen and Martin Stokhof. 1997. Questions. In J. van Benthem and A. ter Meulen, eds., *Handbook of Logic and Language*, chap. 19, pages 1055–1124. Amsterdam: Elsevier Science/MIT Press.

Heim, Irene and Angelika Kratzer. 1998. *Semantics in Generative Grammar*. Oxford: Blackwell Publishers.

Huntley, Martin. 1982. Imperatives and infinitival embedded questions. In *Papers from the Parasession on Non-declaratives*, pages 93–106. Chicago Linguistic Society.

Jackendoff, Ray. 1972. *Semantic Interpretation in Generative Grammar*. Cambridge, MA: MIT Press.

Jackendoff, Ray. 1974. A Deep Structure Projection Rule. *Linguistic Inquiry* 5(4):481–506.

Jackendoff, Ray and Peter W. Culicover. 2003. The Semantic Basis of Control in English. *Language* 79(3):517–556.

Karttunen, Lauri. 1977. Syntax and Semantics of Questions. *Linguistics and Philosophy* 1(1):3–44.

Kratzer, Angelika. 1981. The Notional Category of Modality. In H.-J. Eikmeyer and H. Rieser, eds., *Words, Worlds and Contexts*, pages 38–74. Berlin: Walter de Gruyter.

Kratzer, Angelika. 1989. An Investigation of the Lumps of Thought. *Linguistics and Philosophy* 12(5):607–653.

Lewis, David K. 1979. Attitudes *de Dicto* and *de Se*. *The Philosophical Review* 88:513–543.

Lewis, David K. 1986. *On the Plurality of Worlds*. Oxford: Basil Blackwell.

Montague, Richard. 1973. The Proper Treatment of Quantification in Ordinary English. In J. Hintikka, J. M. Moravcsik, and P. Suppes, eds., *Approaches to Natural Language: Proceedings of the 1970 Stanford Workshop on Grammar and Semantics*, pages 221–242. Dordrecht, Holland: D. Reidel. Reprinted in R.H. Thomason (ed.) (1974) *Formal Philosophy: Selected Papers of Richard Montague*. Yale University Press, 247–270.

Nishigauchi, Taisuke. 1984. Control and the Thematic Domain. *Language* 60(2):215–250.

Perry, John. 1977. Frege on Demonstratives. *The Philosophical Review* 86(4):474–497.

Pollack, Martha E. 1986. *Inferring Domain Plans in Question-Answering*. Ph.D. thesis, Dept. of Computer Science, University of Pennsylvania.

Pollard, Carl J. and Ivan A. Sag. 1994. *Head-Driven Phrase Structure Grammar*. Studies in Contemporary Linguistics. Chicago and London: University of Chicago Press.

Portner, Paul. 1997. The Semantics of Mood, Complementation, and Conversational Force. *Natural Language Semantics* 5(2):167–212.

Portner, Paul. 2004. The Semantics of Imperatives within a Theory of Clause Types. In K. Watanabe and R. B. Young, eds., *Proceedings of Semantics and Linguistic Theory 14*. Ithaca, NY: CLC Publications.

Portner, Paul. 2006. The Nature of Imperative Force in Imperative Subtypes. Fourth Workshop on Discourse Structure, UT Austin, March, 2006.

Rozicka, Rudolf. 1983. Remarks on Control. *Linguistic Inquiry* 14(2):309–324.

Sag, Ivan A., Gerald Gazdar, Thomas Wasow, and Steven Weisler. 1985. Coordination and How to Distinguish Categories. *Natural Language and Linguistic Theory* 3(2):117–171.

Sag, Ivan A. and Carl Pollard. 1991. An Integrated Theory of Complement Control. *Language* 67(1):63–113.

Stalnaker, Robert C. 1984. *Inquiry*. Cambridge, MA: The MIT Press.

Stanley, Jason and Timothy Williamson. 2001. Knowing How. *The Journal of Philosophy* 98(5):411–444.

van Valin, Robert D., Jr. and Randy J. LaPolla. 1997. *Syntax: Structure, Meaning and Function*. Cambridge: Cambridge University Press.

Veltman, Frank. 1984. Data Semantics. In J. Groenendijk, T. Janssen, and M. Stokhof, eds., *Truth, Interpretation, and Information: Selected Papers from the Third Amsterdam Colloquium*, pages 43–65. Dordrecht: Foris Publications.

Williams, Edwin. 1985. PRO and Subject of NP. *Natural Language and Linguistic Theory* 3(3):297–315.

Wurmbrand, Susi. 2005. Tense in Infinitives. Plenary talk at the Workshop New Horizons in the Grammar of Raising and Control, LSA.

9

Cells and paradigms in inflectional semantics

GREGORY STUMP

9.1   Introduction

In a realizational theory of inflection,[1] the morphology of a word w is deduced from (i) the lexeme L that w realizes together with (ii) the set σ of morphosyntactic properties associated with w; the pairing $\langle L, \sigma \rangle$ may be thought of as the unique characterization of a CELL in L's inflectional paradigm, and w may be thought of as the REALIZATION of this cell. On this view, various conceptions of the relation between a word's morphology and its semantics might be entertained. One possible hypothesis is (1).

(1) THE SEMANTIC FACTORIZATION HYPOTHESIS (SFH): For each contentive morphosyntactic property p there is a semantic operator O such that the interpretation of a word realizing p involves the operator O.

Corollary (a): all of the words in a paradigm that realize a particular contentive morphosyntactic property involve the corresponding semantic operator in their interpretation.

Corollary (b): words in different paradigms that realize the same morphosyntactic properties involve the same semantic operators in their interpretation.

---

[1] For discussion of the defining properties of a realizational theory of inflection and some instances of this sort of theory, see Stump (2001, pp. 1–30).

Theory and Evidence in Semantics.
Erhard Hinrichs and John Nerbonne (eds.).
Copyright © 2009, CSLI Publications.

Consider an example of a verb form whose semantics apparently conforms to this hypothesis. In Swahili, transitive verbs inflect for both tense and reflexiveness; for instance, one of the forms realizing the verbal lexeme ONA 'see' is *atajiona* 'he will see himself', whose morphological analysis is as in (2).

(2) Swahili: a-ta-ji-ona.

subj.infl	–	tense	–	obj.infl	–	stem
3.SG.GEND.1/2		FUTURE		REFLEXIVE		see

He will see himself/She will see herself.

The semantic interpretation of *atajiona* might be represented as in Figure 1, where (i) is the cell in the paradigm of ONA that *atajiona* realizes and (v) is its denotation. According to (v), *atajiona* is a predicate of events of seeing that are in the future and are reflexive. I here assume an event-based theory of thematic roles (cf. Dowty, 1989); thus, the lexeme ONA 'see' in cell (i) is interpreted as the set of events in (iv), and its Experiencer argument is represented as a variable indexed according to the grammatical function of the noun phrase by whose denotation it is to be bound.

The focal observation here is that the semantic effects of the three morphosyntactic properties in (i) are independent: the property 'future' in (i) denotes the future-tense operator in (ii); the property 'OBJ.INFL:reflexive' in (i) denotes the reflexive operator in (iii); and the subject-agreement property 'SUBJ.INFL:3rd sg gend.1/2' is semantically inert. The interpretation (v) thus arises through the composition of (ii)–(iv). This analysis is accordingly compatible with corollaries (a) and (b) of the SFH. The issue is whether an inflected word's morphosyntactic properties can, in general, be seen as possessing the sort of semantic independence in evidence here.

In the following sections, I argue that they cannot—that some languages require a more complex account of the relation between a word's morphosyntactic property set and its semantic interpretation. In section 9.2, I argue that Twi verb inflection presents instances in which (contrary to corollary (1a)) an inflected word's morphosyntactic properties contribute jointly (rather than independently) to its semantic interpretation; in section 9.3, I argue that Sanskrit verb inflection presents instances in which (contrary to corollary (1b)) an inflected word's semantic interpretation is sensitive not only to its own morphosyntactic properties, but to those of the other cells in its paradigm. Such evidence demonstrates that in some instances, the relation between a word's morphosyntactic properties and its semantic interpretation is more complex than the relation entailed by the SFH.

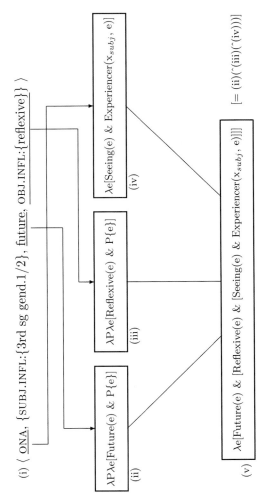

FIGURE 1 The semantic interpretation of the cell realized by Swahili *atajiona* 'he will see himself'

9.2 Counterevidence to the SFH from Twi

In Twi (Niger-Congo; Ghana), negation is expressed inflectionally by means of a low-toned homorganic nasal prefix, as the partial paradigm of the verb BISA 'ask' in Table 1 illustrates.

		Affirmative		Negative	
Habitual	1sg	mè-bìsá		mè-m̀-bìsá	
	2sg	wó-bìsá		wó-m̀-bìsá	
	3sg	ɔ̀-bìsá		ɔ̀-m̀-bìsá	
Progressive	1sg	mè-rè-bìsá		mé-ré-m̀-bìsá	
	2sg	wó-rè-bìsá		wó-ré-m̀-bìsá	
	3sg	ɔ̀-rè-bìsá		ɔ́-ré-m̀-bìsá	
		not before complement	*before complement*		
Remote past	1sg	mè-bìsá-è	mè-bìsá-à	m-à-m̀-bìsá	
	2sg	wó-bìsá-è	wó-bìsá-à	wó-á-m̀-bìsá	
	3sg	ɔ̀-bìsá-è	ɔ̀-bìsá-à	ɔ̀-à-m̀-bìsá	
				not before complement	*before complement*
Recent past	1sg	m-à-bísá		mè-m̀-bísá-è	mè-m̀-bísá-à
	2sg	wó-á-!bísá		wó-ḿ-!bísá-è	wó-ḿ-!bísá-à
	3sg	ɔ̀-à-bísá		ɔ̀-m̀-bísá-è	ɔ̀-m̀-bísá-à

TABLE 1 Some affirmative and negative forms of the Asante Twi verb BISA 'ask' (Dolphyne, 1988, p. 182f)

The remote-past and recent-past tenses, however, present a complication. Although the negative prefix appears, as expected, in negative remote-past and negative recent-past forms, negative forms in these tenses exhibit an apparent reversal in tense morphology: the tense morphology of negative remote-past forms is that of affirmative recent-past forms and that of negative recent-past forms is that of affirmative remote-past forms;[2] for instance, *m-à-m̀-bìsá* 'I didn't ask' shares the tense prefix *à-* of *m-à-bísá* 'I have asked' and *mè-m̀-bísá-è* 'I haven't asked' shares the tense suffix *-è* of *mè-bìsá-è* 'I asked'. Notice, moreover, that affirmative remote-past forms exhibit alternate shapes according to whether or not they precede their complement; if they do, the tense suffix is supplanted by a lengthening of the stem-final vowel (*mèbìsáá nò* 'I asked him'). Thus, an additional reflection of the tense reversal

[2]This apparent reversal in tense morphology is widely noted; see Balmer and Grant (1929, p. 71), Berry and Aidoo (1975, p. 179), Dolphyne (1988, p. 93), Dolphyne (1996, p. 93), Redden (1963, p. 81), Stewart (1963), Welmers (1946, p. 55).

is the fact that this same alternation appears in the negative recent-past tense (and not in the negative remote-past tense, which follows the affirmative recent-past tense in failing to exhibit it).

On first consideration, this reversal in tense morphology might be attributed to two rules of referral, as in (3).

(3) a. Any exponent of a property set {affirmative remote-past X} likewise acts as an exponent of the property set {negative recent-past}.

b. Any exponent of a property set {affirmative recent-past X} likewise acts as an exponent of the property set {negative remote-past}.

In accordance with rule (3a), the cells in (4a) and (5a) would have the parallel realizations in (4b) and (5b); in accordance with (3b), the cells in (6a) and (7a) would have the parallel realizations in (6b) and (7b).

(4) a. ⟨ BISA, {1st sg affirmative remote-past} ⟩
   b. mè-bìsá-è 'I asked'

(5) a. ⟨ BISA, {1st sg negative recent-past} ⟩
   b. mè-m̀-bísá-è 'I haven't asked'

(6) a. ⟨ BISA, {1st sg affirmative recent-past} ⟩
   b. m-à-bísá 'I have asked'

(7) a. ⟨ BISA, {1st sg negative remote-past} ⟩
   b. m-à-m̀-bìsá 'I didn't ask'

This solution is problematic, however, because it presumes a morphosyntactic contrast between remote-past and recent-past tenses, as in Table 2; yet, this presumed contrast is supported by neither syntactic nor morphological evidence, but only by semantic evidence. Semantic evidence alone, however, is insufficient to justify the postulation of morphosyntactic distinctions, which, as their name implies, require some kind of grammatical grounding.

In the clearest cases, two word forms are assumed to possess contrasting morphosyntactic properties because they participate in a regular difference in behavior with respect to rules of both syntax and morphology: for instance, the fact that *dog* and *dogs* impose different requirements on agreeing constituents (*this/*these dog, these/*this dogs*) and differ concomitantly in their inflectional form (*dogs* = the morphologically unanalyzable stem *dog* suffixed with -*s*) supports the assumption that they possess contrasting morphosyntactic properties. In some

	Remote past	Recent past
Affirmative	mèbìsáè 'I asked'	màbísá 'I have asked'
Negative	màm̀bìsá 'I didn't ask'	mèm̀bísáè 'I haven't asked'

TABLE 2 'Remote past' and 'recent past' as morphosyntactic properties in Twi

instances, however, the postulation of a morphosyntactic contrast depends essentially on a difference in syntactic behavior. In French, for example, the gender contrast between *livre* and *table* is supported by syntactic but not morphological evidence; in particular, these nouns' contrasting behavior with respect to gender agreement isn't accompanied by any concomitant contrast in inflectional form. Similarly, the postulation of a morphosyntactic contrast may depend essentially on a difference in morphology. In English, for instance, the assumed tense contrast between *sings* and *sang* is supported by their difference in inflectional form, but not by any concomitant contrast in syntactic behavior. (Syntactic principles are, of course, sensitive to a verb form's finiteness, but not to differences in tense among finite forms.) Thus, the postulation of a morphosyntactic distinction requires either syntactic or morphological justification, or both.

In Twi, as in English, there is no syntactic motivation for the postulation of tense distinctions. Moreover, the morphological evidence would, on its own, actually lead one to assume that the morphosyntactic classification of Twi verb forms is based on the properties 'tense$_1$' and 'tense$_2$' in Table 3 rather than on the properties 'remote past' and 'recent past' in Table 2.[3] The postulation of the properties 'remote

---

[3]One might attempt to argue that there is morphological evidence in favor of the property 'recent past' in Table 1, namely the high tonality of the root's initial syllable in all of the recent-past forms, affirmative or negative. But independent evidence suggests that the tonality of a verb root's initial syllable is instead determined by principles of tone sandhi. Note first that the prefix à- generally causes an adjacent root-initial syllable to have high tone, e.g. mè-dà-è 'I slept' but m-à-dá 'I have slept'; note, in addition, that the tonality of the root-initial vowel in a negative form is (in certain tenses in certain conjugations) the opposite of its tonality in the corresponding affirmative form, e.g. 1sg habitual mè-tɔ́ń 'I sell' but mè-ǹ-tɔ̀ǹ 'I don't sell', 1sg progressive mè-rè-tɔ̀ǹ 'I am selling' but mé-ré-ǹ-tɔ́ń 'I am not selling', and so on. Given these two factors, the high tonality of the root-initial syllable in the recent-past forms in Table 1 need not be seen as an exponent of the recent-past tense. Instead, this high tonality can be seen as a sandhi effect of the prefix à- in recent-past forms such as m-à-bísá 'I have asked' and an effect of negation in recent-past forms such as mè-m̀-bísá-è 'I haven't asked'; the low tonality of the root-initial syllable in remote-past forms such as m-à-m̀-bìsá 'I didn't ask' can

past' and 'recent past' wrongly implies that the mismatch embodied by the verb forms in Table 2 is at the interface of morphology and syntax when, in fact, it is at the interface of morphosyntax with semantics.

	Tense$_1$	Tense$_2$
Affirmative	*mèbìsáè* 'I asked'	*màbísá* 'I have asked'
Negative	*mèm̀bísáè* 'I haven't asked'	*màm̀bìsá* 'I didn't ask'

TABLE 3 'Tense$_1$' and 'tense$_2$' as morphosyntactic properties in Twi

If one assumes the classification in Table 3, then the rules of referral in (3) are unnecessary. What is needed in their place are rules of semantic interpretation whose construal of the properties 'tense$_1$' and 'tense$_2$' in the interpretation of a given verb form is sensitive to whether this form is associated with the property 'negative': by these rules, affirmative tense$_1$ verbs and negative tense$_2$ verbs receive a remote-past interpretation while affirmative tense$_2$ and negative tense$_1$ verbs receive a recent-past interpretation. These rules might be formulated as in (8).

(8) Rules for the interpretation of the morphosyntactic properties 'tense$_1$' and 'tense$_2$' in Twi:

    a. In any cell $\langle$ L, {negative tense$_1$ X} $\rangle$, the morphosyntactic property 'tense$_1$' denotes the recent-past operator $\lambda P \lambda e[\text{Recent-past}(e) \;\&\; P\{e\}]$; otherwise, 'tense$_1$' denotes the remote-past operator $\lambda P \lambda e[\text{Remote-past}(e) \;\&\; P\{e\}]$.

    b. In any cell $\langle$ L, {negative tense$_2$ X} $\rangle$, the morphosyntactic property 'tense$_2$' denotes the remote-past operator $\lambda P \lambda e[\text{Remote-past}(e) \;\&\; P\{e\}]$; otherwise, 'tense$_2$' denotes the recent-past operator $\lambda P \lambda e[\text{Recent-past}(e) \;\&\; P\{e\}]$.

If the four verb forms in Table 3 realize the cells in (9a–d), then in accordance with the rules in (8), the tense properties in (9a) and (9d) have the denotation in (10a), while the tense properties in (9b) and (9c) have the denotation in (10b).

(9)   a.   i. Cell: $\langle$ BISA, {1st sg affirmative tense$_1$} $\rangle$
           ii. Realization: *mè-bìsá-è* 'I asked'
      b.   i. Cell: $\langle$ BISA, {1st sg negative tense$_1$} $\rangle$
           ii. Realization: *mè-m̀-bísá-è* 'I haven't asked'

---

likewise be attributed to negation.

c. i. Cell: ⟨ BISA, {1st sg affirmative tense₂} ⟩
    ii. Realization: *m-à-bísá* 'I have asked'
d. i. Cell: ⟨ BISA, {1st sg negative tense₂} ⟩
    ii. Realization: *m-à-ṁ-bìsá* 'I didn't ask'

(10) a. λPλe[Remote-past(e) & P{e}]
      b. λPλe[Recent-past(e) & P{e}]

The morphosyntactic properties 'tense₁' and 'tense₂' assumed by
this analysis are morphologically and syntactically unremarkable. They
do, however, possess a special semantic characteristic, in that their interpretation depends on the accompanying property of polarity. In this
sense, they are similar to the property 'past participle' in English, whose
semantic interpretation is likewise sensitive to some part of its context:
in construction with the auxiliary BE, a past participle receives a passive interpretation, while in construction with the auxiliary HAVE, it
instead receives a perfect interpretation. Thus, just as past participles
are a morphologically coherent but semantically heterogeneous class of
forms in English, so, too, in Twi, are the class of tense₁ verb forms
and that of tense₂ verb forms. The properties 'tense₁' and 'tense₂' in
Twi and the property 'past participle' in English are all instances of
what Aronoff (1994) has called MORPHOMES—units of linguistic analysis whose only coherent construal is in the morphological component;
more particularly, these properties might be characterized as CONTEXT-
DEPENDENT morphomes, since their semantics depends systematically
on some aspect of their context. The properties 'tense₁' and 'tense₂' in
Twi might be characterized even more narrowly as CELL-DEPENDENT
morphomes, since the domain of their dependency is the morphosyntactic property set associated with a particular cell.

The Twi evidence disconfirms corollary (a) of the SFH, demonstrating that the relation between an inflected word's morphosyntactic properties and its semantic operators is potentially an oblique one. The Twi
facts exclude the possibility that the tense₁ suffix *-è* and the tense₂
prefix *à-* are simply listed in the lexicon as morphemes (i.e. minimal
form/meaning pairings), since the meanings they are used to express
vary according to the morphosyntactic properties of the cells they are
used to realize.[4]

---

[4]Ofori (2006) proposes a nonlinear phonological account of these facts. According
to this analysis, the segmental content of the recent-past and remote-past affixes
is unspecified, arising purely as an effect of general phonological principles of Twi
(Akan) phonology. The distributional properties of these affixes is then accounted
for by means of four assumptions: (i) the negative affix must be adjacent to the verb
root and must precede it; the recent-past affix is a floating mora that (ii) must be

I now turn to a counterexample to corollary (b) of the SFH, namely Sanskrit middle verbs.

9.3 A counterexample to corollary (b) of the SFH: Ātmanepadin verbs in Sanskrit

In Sanskrit, some verbal lexemes (e.g. PAC 'cook') exhibit distinct active and middle morphology: middle forms designate events that directly affect their subject's referent (*pacate* 'cooks for self'); active forms designate events that lack this sort of effect (*pacati* 'cooks for someone else'). The complete present indicative paradigm of PAC is given in Table 4.

		Singular	Dual	Plural
Active	1st	pacāmi	pacāvaḥ	pacāmaḥ
	2nd	pacasi	pacathaḥ	pacatha
	3rd	pacati	pacataḥ	pacanti
Middle	1st	pace	pacāvahe	pacāmahe
	2nd	pacase	pacethe	pacadhve
	3rd	pacate	pacete	pacante

TABLE 4 Present indicative paradigm of the Sanskrit U-verb PAC 'cook'

---

adjacent to the verb root and (iii) is ordinarily prefixal; and (iv) the remote-past affix is a floating mora that is ordinarily suffixal. Thus, the prefixal position of the tense affix in *m-à-bísá* 'I have asked' follows from (iii); the suffixal position of the tense affix in *mè-bìsá-è* 'I asked' follows from (iv); the suffixal position of the tense affix in *mè-m̀-bísá-è* 'I haven't asked' follows from (ii) together with the assumption that the satisfaction of (i) and (ii) overrides that of (iii); and the prefixal position of the tense affix in *m-à-m̀-bìsá* 'I didn't ask' follows if one assumes that (iv) is overridden by the need to avoid homophony between the negative remote past and the negative recent past.

There are obvious grounds for skepticism about this analysis. First, there is no independent motivation for the postulation of floating moras in this language; second, the analysis portrays as coincidental the fact that it is exactly the two floating affixes that are segmentally unspecified moras; and third, the analysis depends on the assumption that an affix's distributional properties may be overridden by the need to avoid homophony. While homophony avoidance may well be a force in language change, it is far from clear that it ever functions as a synchronic grammatical constraint, particularly in view of the widespread incidence of syncretism in morphology (as well as that of lexical homonymy and syntactic ambiguity). Moreover, the negative remote-past and negative recent-past forms of many verbs (e.g. BISA 'ask') would be at no risk of homophony even if (iv) were strictly adhered to, since they differ tonally in any event.

Other lexemes, however, have only active forms or only middle forms; examples are the active verb SPṚŚ 'touch' (Table 5) and the middle verb LABH 'obtain' (Table 6). In his grammar of Sanskrit, Pāṇini distinguishes these three classes of verbs by means of the rules in (11).

		Singular	Dual	Plural
Active	1st	spṛśāmi	spṛśāvaḥ	spṛśāmaḥ
	2nd	spṛśasi	spṛśathaḥ	spṛśatha
	3rd	spṛśati	spṛśataḥ	spṛśanti

TABLE 5 Present indicative paradigm of the Sanskrit P-verb SPṚŚ 'touch'

		Singular	Dual	Plural
Middle	1st	labhe	labhāvahe	labhāmahe
	2nd	labhase	labhethe	labhadhve
	3rd	labhate	labhete	labhante

TABLE 6 Present indicative paradigm of the Sanskrit Ā-verb LABH 'obtain'

(11) Three rules from Pāṇini's *Aṣṭādhyāyī*

Rule 1.3.12: prescribes the exclusive use of middle or *ātmanepada*[5] inflections with a particular class of verbs, the so-called ĀTMANEPADIN verbs (e.g. LABH 'obtain').

Rule 1.3.72: prescribes the conditional use of middle inflections with a distinct class of verbs, the so-called UBHAYAPADIN[6] verbs (e.g. PAC 'cook'): here, middle inflections are used only if the action denoted by the verb affects the agent; otherwise, active inflections are used.

Rule 1.3.78: prescribes the use of active or *parasmaipada*[7] inflections as the default for any verb whose subject denotes the agent of the action it describes; verbs adhering exclusively to this default are PARASMAIPADIN verbs (e.g. SPṚŚ 'touch').

Drawing on the traditional terminology in (11), I refer to these three classes of verbs as Ā-verbs, U-verbs, and P-verbs, respectively.

---

[5] *Ātmane pada* 'word for oneself'.

[6] *Ubhayapadin* 'having words for both [oneself and another]' (< *ubhaya-* 'both' + *pada-* 'word').

[7] *Parasmai pada* 'word for another'.

9.3.1   A morphosemantic paradox

One might expect to be able to distinguish the membership of these three verb classes purely by virtue of their meaning; that is, one might suppose that the voice marking of P-verbs is exclusively active simply because their meaning would be incompatible with middle marking, and that active marking would be similarly incompatible with the semantics of Ā-verbs. But P-verbs, Ā-verbs, and U-verbs cannot, in fact, be distinguished on purely semantic grounds. First, there are sets of synonymous verbs that cut across the classes of U-verbs, P-verbs, and Ā-verbs; for instance, the verb STU 'praise' is a U-verb, but the synonymous verb ŚAMS is a P-verb, and the synonymous verb ŚLĀGH is an Ā-verb.[8] Secondly, there are verbs in Sanskrit that inflect as members of one class in one tense but as a member of another class in another tense; so, for instance, the verb VṚT 'turn' inflects as an Ā-verb in the present, exhibiting only middle forms (*vartate* 'it turns'), but instead inflects as a P-verb in the perfect, exhibiting only active forms (*vavarta* 'it turned'). Thus, we have an apparent paradox: active morphology doesn't always coincide with active semantics, nor does middle morphology always coincide with middle semantics.

There are two apparent ways out of this paradox. The first of these is to assume that P-verbs and Ā-verbs actually have full paradigms of active and middle forms, i.e. that they involve heavy syncretism. On this assumption, a P-verb such as SPṚŚ 'touch', whose forms all appear to be active, would be said to have middle forms as well, but middle forms which are always syncretic with their active counterparts. The paradigm of the Ā-verb LABH 'obtain' would likewise be assumed to contain identical active and middle subparadigms. But this approach is implausible given the evidence of the periphrastic perfect.

---

[8]This is not to say, of course, that the kinds of meanings expressed by P-verbs, Ā-verbs and U-verbs tend not to be of different sorts. Indeed, it would be astonishing if that were the case. It is natural to assume that in pre-Sanskrit, the middle/active distinction expressed a comparatively straightforward distinction between affected and unaffected agents. On that assumption, one would expect that historically, verbs denoting actions that inherently affect their agent would tend to become Ā-verbs and verbs denoting actions that inherently fail to affect their agent would tend to become P-verbs. But the effects of these tendencies are at best statistical, since other, analogical factors have also presumably influenced the historical differentiation of P-verbs, Ā-verbs and U-verbs. Consequently, we cannot attribute the synchronic distinction between P-verbs, Ā-verbs and U-verbs in attested Sanskrit to the semantics of voice (nor to any other purely semantic determinant); we must instead view this distinction as the lexical residue of cross-cutting historical processes. (See Xu, Aronoff, and Anshen (2007) for discussion of the semantic differences between deponent and nondeponent verbs in Latin, which clearly constitute a similar sort of lexical residue.)

The periphrastic perfect is a construction in which the main verb appears in a nominalized form bearing the suffix -ām and is accompanied by the appropriate finite perfect form of an auxiliary verb. Voice in the periphrastic perfect is expressed by the auxiliary verb, and the relevant auxiliary verb is ordinarily a U-verb. Given this fact, one might expect that at least in the periphrastic perfect, P-verbs and Ā-verbs should actually exhibit distinct active and middle subparadigms. And yet, this isn't the case: in the periphrastic perfect, P-verbs always take the active forms of the auxiliary verb, and Ā-verbs invariably take the middle forms. For instance, the P-verb VID 'understand' always takes active forms of the auxiliary KṚ 'do' in the periphrastic perfect (e.g. *vidām cakāra* 's/he understood'), while the Ā-verb ĪKṢ 'see' always takes middle forms of KṚ (e.g. *īkṣām cakre* 's/he saw'). Thus, the periphrastic perfect shows that P-verbs and Ā-verbs truly do have defective paradigms: they can't be thought of as simply having syncretic paradigms in which active and middle receive the same realization, since even when they appear in construction with an auxiliary verb that is capable of exhibiting overt active/middle contrasts, no such contrast appears.

Another way of getting around the apparent paradox presented by P-verbs and Ā-verbs would be to say that active and middle are really just inflection classes in Sanskrit. The analogy here would be to the distinction between causative and noncausative verbs in Sanskrit. In the present-tense system, Sanskrit verbs fall into ten different conjugations; for instance, the verbs CUR 'steal' and BHṚ 'carry' belong to the first and tenth conjugations, respectively. But causativization in Sanskrit is expressed as a shift in membership from a given conjugation class to the tenth conjugation; for instance, if the first-conjugation verb BHṚ 'carry' is transferred into the tenth conjugation, the effect is to produce a causative verb meaning 'cause to carry', as in Table 7. One might therefore envision an approach to Sanskrit verbal morphology according to which there are two conjugations, one active and one middle: LABH 'obtain', an Ā-verb, would belong to the middle conjugation, while SPṚŚ 'touch', a P-verb, would belong to the active conjugation. The U-verb PAC 'cook', which is able to take either active or middle inflections, would then be seen as a verb which is basically active but which gets shifted into the middle conjugation; as a concomitant of this shift, it takes on middle semantics. On this view, there would be a complete parallelism between the shift in conjugation associated with causative semantics in Table 7 and the shift in conjugation associated with middle semantics in Table 8. Note that because basic members of the class of middle verbs wouldn't involve any shift in conjugation, this account correctly predicts that such forms shouldn't invariably possess middle semantics.

	1st conjugation	10th conjugation
CUR 'steal'		*corayati* 's/he steals'
BHṚ 'carry' ↓ 'cause to carry'	*bharati* 's/he carries'	*bhārayati* 's/he causes to carry'

TABLE 7 Causativization realized as a shift to the 10th conjugation in Sanskrit

	Active conjugation	Middle conjugation
LABH 'obtain'		*labhate* 's/he obtains'
SPṚŚ 'touch'	*spṛśati* 's/he touches'	
PAC 'cook' ↓ 'cook for oneself'	*pacati* 's/he cooks'	*pacate* 's/he cooks for self'

TABLE 8 The active/middle contrast portrayed as the effect of a shift to a hypothetical "middle conjugation" in Sanskrit

Ultimately, however, this is not a viable approach to understanding the active/middle distinction in Sanskrit. We've already seen that in the periphrastic perfect, an auxiliary verb joining with an Ā-verb itself has to be middle in inflection (and one joining with a P-verb itself has to be active in inflection). In the context of an approach in which active and middle were portrayed as conjugation classes, this would mean that the auxiliary verb would have to be seen as agreeing with respect to a P-verb or Ā-verb's conjugation-class membership. But conjugation class membership is not a locus of agreement relations in language.

This evidence shows that active and middle must well and truly be regarded as morphosyntactic properties and not as inflection-class labels. As a consequence, we really do seem to be left with a kind of paradox: the fact that the voice morphology of P-verbs and Ā-verbs doesn't inevitably coincide with the expected voice semantics.

9.3.2 The pragmatics of the active voice in U-verbs

One might assume that the property 'active' ordinarily denotes the active-voice operator in (12), which entails that the event described by an active verb doesn't affect the referent of that verb's subject. If we assume that 'active' has this denotation, then P-verbs clearly involve a morphosemantic mismatch.

(12) $\lambda P \lambda e[\neg \text{Affects}(e, x_{subj}) \mathrel{\&} P\{e\}]$

   (where x_{subj} is bound by the denotation of the verb's subject)

There is, however, reason for doubting whether 'active' actually has the denotation in (12), hence whether P-verbs actually involve any sort of morphosemantic mismatch. There are certain circumstances in which U-verbs exhibit active morphology even though the event being described clearly does affect the referent of the verb's subject. In the examples in (13), there is an explicit reflexive pronoun appearing in the complement of the U-verb. It is therefore clear that the event being described is one that affects the referent of the verb's subject. And yet, active voice is a possibility here, as the acceptability of (13b) shows. By Pāṇini's rule 1.3.77, the use of the middle voice rather than the active is merely optional in the presence of an overtly reflexive complement; it's as though the job of identifying this as an event affecting the referent of the verb's subject is done by the reflexive pronoun, which therefore obviates the need for middle voice morphology on the verb itself.

(13) a. svaṃ   kaṭam   kurute
          own.ACC.SG   mat.ACC.SG   make.3SG.PRES.INDIC.MIDDLE
          's/he makes her/his own mat'

      b. svaṃ   kaṭam   karoti
                                      make.3SG.PRES.INDIC.ACTIVE
          's/he makes her/his own mat'   [Katre (1987, p. 72)]

In (14b), there is an explicit reciprocal pronoun appearing in the complement of the U-verb; here again, it is clear that the event being described is one that affects the referents of the verb's subject. And yet, here again, active voice is used. Indeed, according to Pāṇini, it must be used: by Pāṇini's rule 1.3.14, middle verb forms are ordinarily used to denote reciprocal action, as in (14a); but this rule is overridden by rule 1.3.16, according to which the active is instead used with an overtly reciprocal complement, as in (14b).

(14) a. vyatilunate
          reap.3PL.PRES.INDIC.MIDDLE

'they reap for one another'
b. anyonyasya   vyatilunanti
   one.another.GEN.SG   reap.3PL.PRES.INDIC.ACTIVE
   'they reap each other's (grain)'   [Katre (1987, p. 56)]

It is clear from these examples that even if one restricts one's attention to U-verbs, active voice can't simply be seen as denoting the active operator in (12); I therefore instead assume that the morphosyntactic property 'active' denotes an identity function—that it is semantically empty. At the same time, I do assume that the use of an active voice form rather than the corresponding middle voice form conversationally implicates that the event described by the verb doesn't affect the subject's referent. This sort of conversational implicature takes place in the interpretation of U-verbs but not in the interpretation of P-verbs, since the middle voice only exists as a more informative alternative to the active voice in the paradigms of U-verbs. Moreover, the implicature is cancellable in the interpretation of U-verbs, as in examples (13b) and (14b).

9.3.3 A paradigmatic conception of middle voice semantics in Sanskrit

But even if we can say that P-verbs don't involve any real morphosemantic mismatch (i.e. that active morphology doesn't entail active semantics), we can't make an analogous claim about Ā-verbs. The semantics of a U-verb's middle-voice forms genuinely involves a middle operator, while that of an Ā-verb's middle-voice forms does not. Thus, I propose that there is a rule of semantic interpretation for the morphosyntactic property 'middle' in Sanskrit and that this rule is sensitive to the type of paradigm in which it appears. According to (15a), in any paradigm in which the properties 'active' and 'middle' directly contrast with one another, the property 'middle' denotes a middle-voice operator; this operator entails that the event described by the middle verb directly affects the referent of the verb's subject. By contrast, the default rule in (15b) entails that in those cases not covered by rule (15a), the morphosyntactic property 'middle' denotes an identity function (i.e. is semantically empty). Together, the rules in (15) entail that the interpretation of the property 'middle' depends on the sort of paradigm in which it appears.

(15) Rules for the interpretation of the morphosyntactic property 'middle' in Sanskrit:

    a. In any pair of cells $\langle$ L, {active X} $\rangle$, $\langle$ L, {middle X} $\rangle$ appearing in the paradigm of a lexeme L, 'middle' denotes the operator λ Pλ e[Affects(e, x$_{subj}$) & P{e}]

    b. By default, 'middle' denotes an identity function.

The proposed analysis is schematized in Table 9. Section A of Table 9 pertains to U-verbs (such as PAC 'cook'), which have both active and middle cells in their paradigms. In the interpretation of such verbs, the active voice is semantically empty (i.e. it denotes an identity function), but because there are contrasting active and middle forms in a U-verb's paradigm, there is a conversational implicature attendant on the use of the active voice; this is the implicature that the subject's referent is unaffected by the event described by the verb. The interpretation of the middle verbs in a U-verb's paradigm involves a middle-voice operator, by virtue of rule (15a). Section B of Table 9 pertains to P-verbs (such as SPṚŚ 'touch'), which have only active cells in their paradigm. The active voice is, again, semantically empty, but here there is no conversational implicature attendant upon its use, because there is no direct contrast between active and middle forms in a P-verb's paradigm. Finally, section C of Table 9 pertains to Ā-verbs (such as LABH 'obtain'), which have only middle cells in their paradigms. Here, there is no contrast between 'active' and 'middle' forms; accordingly, the property 'middle' is semantically empty by virtue of rule (15b).

The analysis proposed here can be seen as embodying Pāṇini's analysis in (11), according to which middle semantics is found only with verbs whose paradigms exhibit a direct contrast between active and middle.

What we've seen here is that the Sanskrit middle voice is another instance of a morphome. Semantically, it doesn't have a single coherent interpretation; its only really coherent characterization is at the morphological level, where it is associated with certain types of markings on verbs. Like tense$_1$ and tense$_2$ in Twi, it is a context-dependent morphome, since its semantic interpretation depends on the context in which it appears. But unlike tense$_1$ and tense$_2$ in Twi, the middle voice in Sanskrit is a PARADIGM-DEPENDENT morphome—that is, how 'middle' gets interpreted in one cell of a paradigm depends upon whether it directly contrasts with the property 'active' in an otherwise identical cell of that paradigm.[9]

---

[9]Stump (2007) presents Sanskrit voice inflections as one instance of a noncanonical pattern of deponency, citing other instances of this pattern from Sora (Austro-

	active	middle
A. Paradigm of PAC 'cook' (U-verb)	⟨ PAC, {active 1sg pres indic} ⟩ ... ⟨ PAC, {active 3pl pres indic} ⟩	⟨ PAC, {middle 1sg pres indic} ⟩ ... ⟨ PAC, {middle 3pl pres indic} ⟩
Denotation of voice property	identity function	$\lambda P \lambda e[\text{Affects}(e, x_{subj})$ & $P\{e\}]$
Conversational implicature	$\neg\,[\text{Affects}(e, x_{subj})]$	
B. Paradigm of SPṚŚ 'touch' (P-verb)	⟨ SPṚŚ, {active 1sg pres indic} ⟩ ... ⟨ SPṚŚ, {active 3pl pres indic} ⟩	
Denotation of voice property	identity function	
Conversational implicature	none	
C. Paradigm of LABH 'obtain' (A-verb)		⟨ LABH , {middle 1sg pres indic} ⟩ ... ⟨ LABH, {middle 3pl pres indic} ⟩
Denotation of voice property		identity function

TABLE 9 Denotations of voice properties in three Sanskrit paradigms

9.4 Conclusions and discussion

Here, I have presented evidence for two types of context-dependent morphomes in natural language. A cell-dependent morphome is a morphosyntactic property whose semantic content in a given cell depends on the presence (in that cell) of some morphosyntactic property belonging to a different inflectional category; Twi tense$_1$ and tense$_2$ are examples. A paradigm-dependent morphome, by contrast, is a morphosyntactic property whose semantic content in a given paradigm depends on whether it directly contrasts (in that paradigm) with some other property belonging to the same inflectional category; the Sanskrit middle is the exemplar in this case. The existence of these types of morphomes basically excludes the SFH, and by extension, it excludes morpheme-based approaches to inflectional semantics. In particular, it would be impossible to take the Twi affixes in (16) and to list them in the lexicon with their meanings, simply because their meanings depend upon which cell in a paradigm they are used to realize. By the same token, it would be impossible to take the Sanskrit suffix -te in (17), which expresses the third-person singular indicative middle, and associate it with any kind of meaning, because again, whether it has a meaning depends upon what sorts of cells exist in the paradigm whose cells it is used to realize.

(16) Twi:
　　a. -è (realizes the property set {tense$_1$})
　　b. à- (realizes the property set {tense$_2$})

(17) Sanskrit: -te (realizes the property set {3rd singular indicative middle})

References

Aronoff, Mark. 1994. *Morphology by itself: Stems and inflectional classes*. Cambridge: MIT Press.

Balmer, William T. and F. C. F. Grant. 1929. *A Grammar of the Fante-Akan language*. London: Atlantis Press.

Berry, Jack and Agnes Akosua Aidoo. 1975. *An Introduction to Akan*. Evanston: Northwestern University.

Dolphyne, Florence Abena. 1988. *The Akan (Twi-Fante) language: Its sound system and tonal structure*. Accra: Ghana Universities Press.

Dolphyne, Florence Abena. 1996. *A comprehensive course in Twi (Asante)*. Accra: Ghana Universities Press.

Asiatic; India) and Muna (Austronesian; Indonesia).

Dowty, David R. 1989. On the semantic content of the notion 'thematic role'. In G. Chierchia, B. Partee, and R. Turner, eds., *Properties, types, and meaning*, pages 69–129. Dordrecht: D. Reidel.

Katre, Sumitra Mangesh. 1987. *Aṣṭādhyāyī of Pāṇini*. Austin: University of Texas Press.

Ofori, Seth Antwi. 2006. *Topics in Akan grammar*. Ph.D. thesis, Indiana University.

Redden, James E. 1963. *Twi basic course*. Madison: Audio-Forum.

Stewart, J. M. 1963. Twi tenses in the negative. In *Actes du 2ème colloque internationale de linguistique négro-africaine*, pages 182–190. Dakar: Université de Dakar.

Stump, Gregory T. 2001. *Inflectional morphology*. Cambridge University Press.

Stump, Gregory T. 2007. A non-canonical pattern of deponency and its implications. In M. Baerman, G. G. Corbett, D. Brown, and A. Hippisley, eds., *Deponency and morphological mismatches*, pages 71–95. Oxford: Oxford University Press.

Welmers, William Everett. 1946. A descriptive grammar of fanti. *(Language dissertation no. 39), supplement to Language* 22. Baltimore: Linguistic Society of America.

Xu, Zheng, Mark Aronoff, and Frank Anshen. 2007. Deponency in Latin. In M. Baerman, G. G. Corbett, D. Brown, and A. Hippisley, eds., *Deponency and morphological mismatches*, pages 127–143. Oxford: Oxford University Press.

10

Right-Node Wrapping: Multimodal Categorial Grammar and the 'Friends in Low Places' Coordination

NEAL WHITMAN

10.1   Introduction

In October 1990, singer Garth Brooks's recording of 'Friends in Low Places' topped the *Billboard* country charts, and could be heard on United States radio stations and in bars and dance halls across the country. In addition to being a good song for two-stepping, as of the time of this writing, it occupies the top spot on Country Music Television's list of the '40 Greatest Drinking Songs'. The refrain goes like this:

(1) I've got friends in low places,
     where the whiskey drowns and the beer chases
     my blues away.
     ('Friends in Low Places', Earl Bud Lee and DeWayne Blackwell)

Whenever I heard this line during the early 1990s, I had to stop and try to parse it. There are two ways of taking the coordination in this refrain to be strictly parallel. One is to take *the whiskey drowns* and *the beer chases my blues away* to be two coordinated clauses. That is, in these low places of which Garth sings, two things happen:

Theory and Evidence in Semantics.
Erhard Hinrichs and John Nerbonne (eds.).
Copyright © 2009, CSLI Publications.

(2) a. The whiskey drowns.
   b. The beer chases Garth's blues away.

The other way is to take *the whiskey drowns* and just *the beer chases* as coordinated clauses lacking direct objects (DOs). Each of these partial clauses is completed by the DO *my blues away*. So under this parsing, the two things that happen are:

(3) a. The whiskey drowns Garth's blues away.
   b. The beer chases Garth's blues away.

Under both parsings, the part about the beer is fine. Under both parsings, the part about the whiskey is decidedly unidiomatic. Whiskey does not drown, as in reading (2a). And even if you drown something which then goes away, saying that you drowned it away, as in (3a), just does not sound right.[1]

Of course, the intended meaning is that *these* two things happen (presumably in reverse order):

(4) a. The whiskey drowns Garth's blues.
   b. The beer chases Garth's blues away.

In other words, the intended reading is the one that could be phrased as either of the following parallel coordinations:

(5) a. The whiskey drowns, and the beer chases away, my blues.
   b. The whiskey drowns my blues, and the beer chases them away.

However, if the writers had opted for (5a), they would have had to get rid of the next line in the refrain, *and I'll be okay*, and replace it with something that rhymed with *blues*. (5b) would have ruined the meter entirely. So for more than a decade, I accepted the lyrics as a case of poetic license. In recent years, however, I have had to question my assumption, as I have found more and more attestations of 'Friends in Low Places' coordinations.

10.2 Definition and Attestations

'Friends in Low Places' coordinations are very similar to one kind of nonconstituent coordination (NCC), two examples of which are given

---

[1]Lance Nathan (p.c.) informs me that the phrasal verb *drown [something] away* is attested in several other songs, found in a Google search. The line 'Started raining—drown my blues away' appears in the song 'Preachin' Blues' by Robert Johnson; 'I keep drinking malted milk / Tryin' to drown my blues away' in 'Malted Milk' by Jonny Lang; and 'Drowning my sorrows away' in 'Quicksand' by the band Travis. Even so, I will keep the name 'Friends in Low Places' coordination, since many other examples have come to light that do parallel the parsing of *the whiskey drowns and the beer chases my blues away* in which *drowns* is a simple transitive verb.

in (6). (6a) illustrates right-sided NCC, in which the coordinated non-constituent sequences *rice on Monday* and *beans on Tuesday* appear to the right of the factor[2] *ate*. (6b) is an example of left-sided NCC (commonly referred to for historical reasons as right-node raising, or RNR[3]), in which the coordinated nonconstituent sequences *John caught* and *Mary ate* appear to the left of the factor *the fish*. In fact, (5a) is another example of RNR, complicated by the fact that the second verb is the phrasal verb *chases away* instead of the simple transitive verb *ate*.

(6) a. John ate [rice on Monday] and [beans on Tuesday].
        (Dowty, 1996, (22b))
     b. [John caught] and [Mary ate] the fish.
        (Dowty, 1996, (24a))

The 'Friends in Low Places' coordination bears a strong resemblance to RNR. In both constructions, two sequences are coordinated: *the whiskey drowns* and *the beer chases* in (1); *John caught* and *Mary ate* in (6b). In both constructions, the factor (viz. the DO) appears to the right of the coordinates: *my blues* in (1), and *the fish* in (6b). The difference is that the *chases* in (1) is part of the phrasal verb *chases away*, which wraps around its DO. Taking *chases away* as a discontinuous constituent, the resultative phrase *away* is semantically part of one (and only one) of the coordinates, and yet is located syntactically outside the coordination, inasmuch as it appears to the right of the factor. For this reason, I adopt the name *right-node wrapping* (RNW) for what I have casually referred to as the 'Friends in Low Places' coordination, defined below:

---

[2] In discussing the anatomy of coordinate structures, I follow Pullum and Zwicky (1986, p. 754) in using *factor* to refer to the 'material which acts as a sister to a coordinate constituent C—material bearing syntactic and semantic relations to ... all the conjuncts in' the coordinate structure, analogous to the factor *x* in mathematical expressions such as $x(y + z)$. In addition, I follow the usage of Huddleston and Pullum (2002) in referring to coordinated elements as *coordinates*.

[3] Dowty (1996) notes that there are differences between fairly ordinary-sounding coordinations such as (6b), and more prosodically marked ones such as *John committed, and Mary was an accessory to, the crime*. In his words: 'A Right-Node-Raising construction may exist independently of left-sided NCC—a right-sided across-the-board extraction construction....' (p. 15). For present purposes, however, I will defer to common usage and use RNR as a synonym for left-sided NCC.

> A 'Friends in Low Places' (right-node wrapping) coordination has:
>
> 1. the form [**A conjunction B**] **C D**,
> 2. with meaning composed as if the form were
>   [**A C**] **conjunction** [**B C D**],
> 3. *not* as if it were [**A C D**] **conjunction** [**B C D**].

Most of the examples of RNW coordination have a DO for part C of the construction, with a resultative or other adverbial phrase for part D, as does the original example. One difference between the following examples and (1) is that in the following examples, parts A and B coordinate just partial VPs, with a single subject appearing to the left. In these and subsequent examples, the A and B portions will be enclosed in square brackets, and the D portion underlined. Additionally, B will be underlined inside its brackets, to indicate its affinity with D. In some examples, it is possible to construe D with both A and B, but in each case, the context of the attestation made it clear that this was not the intended reading. For example, (7f) is not asking the shopper to tap their card through the cardreader, but to tap it on the screen or slide it through the reader.

(7) a. The blast [upended] and [nearly sliced] an armored Chevrolet Suburban in half. . . .
         (Henry Chu and Megan K. Stack, '3 Americans die in bomb attack in Gaza', *The Los Angeles Times*, October 16, 2003, p. A1)

     b. There is little or no incentive for the contractor to [reduce] or [keep] cost down.
         (Bunnatine Greenhouse, quoted in Larry Margasak, 'Top Officer Objected to Halliburton Deal', The Associated Press, October 30, 2004)

     c. It [rejuvenates] and [pushes] abstraction to a fresh level. [4]
         (Michael Kimmelman, 'Abstract art's new world, forged for all', *The New York Times*, June 7, 2005)

     d. Senators [sign] and [trade] Hossa for Heatley. [5]
         (headline on www.tsn.ca website on August 23, 2005)

---

[4]Thanks to Mark Liberman for this attestation, which he discusses in the Language Log posting 'Cubist Syntax', at http://itre.cis.upenn.edu/~myl/languagelog/archives/002235.html.

[5]Thanks to Bob Kennedy for this attestation, which he discusses in the Piloklok posting, 'Sign and trade X for Y', at http://biloklok.blogspot.com/2005/08/sign-and-trade-x-for-y.html.

e. During the War of 1812, American troops [occupied] and [burned] the town to the ground.
(Mike Michaelson, 'Through the Mist', *Home & Away,* September/October 2005, p. 18)

f. [Tap] or [slide] your card through the cardreader.
(sign at a self-checkout machine at a grocery store, observed July 2006)

g. Several years ago, in a Washington, D.C. suburb, an undercover police officer [followed] and [then shot] a young motorist eight times.
(Michele Norris, interviewing author Marita Golden on *All Things Considered,* National Public Radio, July 5, 2006)

h. What was her story, like why was she collecting so many cats and then either [killing] or [allowing] them to die?
(Terry Gross, interviewing Dr. Melinda Merck on *Fresh Air,* National Public Radio, May 14, 2007)

i. Heavily armed deputies were sent at night to the home of an 18-year-old student suspected of [assaulting] and [robbing] another student of a video game. [6]
('No-fault Sheriffing', *Star News Online.com,* February 21, 2007, `http://www.wilmingtonstar.com/apps/pbcs.dll/article?AID=` `/20070221/EDITORIAL/702210369`)

j. I'm gonna [take] and [put] this in the checkbook.
(author's wife, March 2007)

k. Hey, Dad, can you [bring over] and [squirt] some ketchup onto my plate?
(author's son, October 2007)

Some of these examples coordinate more than two partial VPs (in which case the schema [A **conj** B] should be understood as [A$_1$, ..., A$_n$ **conj** B]):

---

[6] Thanks to Glen Whitman for this attestation.

(8) a. A Monroe County man, convicted yesterday of [raping], [beat-
ing] and [stuffing] a 7-year-old girl into an abandoned well,
could be executed by lethal injection.
(article from *The Columbus (Ohio) Dispatch*, December 2004)

b. Picasso [designed], [built], and [gave] a giant sculpture to
Chicago.
(tour guide, March 2005)

c. Members of the platoon testified that they [punched], [kicked]
and [struck] the detainee with their rifles.[7]
(noted by *Washington Post* copyeditor Bill Walsh, on the June 17,
2005 posting on Blogslot, `http://theslot.blogspot.com/2005/`
`06/potpourri.html`)

d. The FBI will bring to bear all of its national resources ... to
make sure that we [track], [apprehend], and [put] this person
or persons behind bars where they belong.
(FBI Special Agent Herb Brown regarding an arsonist responsible
for a wildfire in California, October 28, 2007)

e. After using dishes, please [wash], [dry], and [put] them away
in the proper place.
(sign in a church kitchen, observed November 2004)

f. ... without somebody wanting me to [cook for], [clean up af-
ter], or [drive] them somewhere. [8] (*Zits* comic strip, by Jerry
Scott and Jim Borgman, November 25, 2007)

The last two examples are particularly interesting, since unlike earlier
examples, here the wrapping of B and D around C is obligatory, since
part C is a pronoun. Other examples can be made parallel by way
of Heavy NP shift; e.g., *upended and nearly sliced in half a Chevrolet
Suburban,* or *designed, built, and gave to Chicago a giant sculpture.* In
contrast, *Wash, dry, and put away them* is unquestionably ungrammatical. This fact points in the direction of RNW being not an error,

---

[7]Thanks to Chris Waigl for this attestation.
[8]Thanks to Mark Liberman for this attestation, which he notes in the Language
Log posting, 'FLoP in the Funny Papers', at `http://itre.cis.upenn.edu/~myl/`
`languagelog/archives/005155.html`.

but a productive construction that is a natural development of the grammar in places where RNR and wrapping interact.

10.3   A Multimodal Categorial Grammar Analysis

In this section I present an analysis of RNW in the framework of multimodal categorial grammar. RNW is a natural candidate for such an analysis, in light of work done in Dowty (1988, 1996). Dowty (1988) shows how an associative Lambek categorial grammar can provide a simple analysis of NCC, such as the examples in (6). However, sentences such as (9) pose a problem. The categorial grammar analysis of NCC presented in Dowty (1988) derives this sentence by assigning *gave* a category such that it combines first with its DO and then with its oblique object.[9] But for independent and crosslinguistic reasons noted in Bach (1980, 1984), it is desirable to analyze *give* (and indeed any three-argument verb) as combining with its oblique object before its DO—in other words, 'wrapping' around the DO. Dowty (1996), building on an analysis of Dutch word order by Moortgat and Oehrle (1994), shows how such a wrapping mode in categorial grammar can resolve the contradiction.

(9)   Mary gave [a book to John] and [a record to Bill].
      (Dowty, 1996, (3))

Sentence (9) is an example of right-sided NCC interacting with wrapping. Another such example that Dowty derives is (10), where the DO is part of the factor:

(10)   Mary gave a book [to John yesterday] and [to Bill today].
       (Dowty, 1996, (59)–(61))

Taken together, the analyses in Dowty (1988, 1996) elegantly handle right-sided NCC without wrapping, as in (6a); left-sided NCC without wrapping (aka RNR), as in (6b); and right-sided NCC with wrapping, as in (9)–(10). The remaining, unexplored possibility is left-sided NCC with wrapping, i.e. RNW.

Given space considerations, I will assume basic knowledge of associative Lambek categorial grammar, and begin the theoretical background with the extension to a multimodal system. As in a Lambek categorial grammar, the set of syntactic categories is the transitive closure of

---

[9]When I say that a sequence can be derived, it should be taken as shorthand for 'the sequence is licensed because it can be proven with the logical and structural rules of the grammar'; it is not intended to imply an actual process of derivation that takes place in a speaker's mind.

a small number of atomic categories under all category constructors, typically / and \. In a multimodal system, however, there is more than one mode of syntactically combining expressions. The typical means of associative concatenation would be one, but there could be others; for example, nonassociative concatenation, or for our purposes, wrapping.

In a multimodal system with i modes of combination, each category constructor comes in i varieties, and there are i sets of rules of logical inference, where each set of rules is the same basic set of slash elimination and introduction. These rules are presented in (11), in natural-deduction style sequent presentation:

(11) Rules of inference

    a. Axiom

$$\frac{}{a:\alpha:A \vdash a:\alpha:A}\text{Axiom}$$

    b. Slash elimination rules

$$\frac{\Gamma \vdash a:\alpha:A/_iB \quad \Delta \vdash b:\beta:B}{(\Gamma,\Delta)^i \vdash a\circ_i b:\alpha(\beta):A}/_i\text{E}$$

$$\frac{\Delta \vdash b:\beta:B \quad \Gamma \vdash a:\alpha:B\backslash_iA}{(\Delta,\Gamma)^i \vdash b\circ_i a:\alpha(\beta):A}\backslash_i\text{E}$$

    c. Slash introduction rules

$$\frac{(\Gamma,b:x:B)^i \vdash a\circ_i b:\alpha:A}{\Gamma \vdash a:\lambda x.\,\alpha:A/_iB}/_i\text{I}$$

$$\frac{(b:x:B,\Gamma)^i \vdash b\circ_i a:\alpha:A}{\Gamma \vdash a:\lambda x.\,\alpha:B\backslash_iA}\backslash_i\text{I}$$

In these rules, the uppercase Greek letters on the left of the turnstiles stand for structured lists of linguistic expressions. $(\Gamma,\Delta)^i$ and $(\Delta,\Gamma)^i$ refer to two such lists combined via mode i. To the right of the turnstiles are single linguistic expressions. For these, the prosodic form is represented by lowercase Roman letters, with $\circ_i$ representing the prosodic combination operation in mode i. The semantic term for each expression is represented with lowercase Greek letters, or the variable x. The categorial information for each expression is represented with capital Roman letters, and the constructors for mode i, $/_i$ and $\backslash_i$.

These rules, however, are often used in abbreviated form. To illustrate, consider the derivation of *likes John*:[10]

---

[10]In these derivations, *vp* is used as an abbreviation for $np\backslash s$. In addition, the $\circ$, $/$, and $\backslash$ are not labeled with mode subscripts, as associative concatenation will be taken as the default mode.

(12) Deriving *likes John* as *vp*

$$\dfrac{\dfrac{}{likes:\textbf{like}':vp/np \vdash likes:\textbf{like}':vp/np}\text{Ax} \quad \dfrac{}{John:\textbf{j}':np \vdash John:\textbf{j}':np}\text{Ax}}{(likes:\textbf{like}':vp/np, John:\textbf{j}':np) \vdash (likes \circ John):\textbf{like}'(\textbf{j}'):vp}\text{/E}$$

It quickly becomes cumbersome to write the entire structure represented by Γ and Δ in the rules; even to add just a subject to the VP to derive *Mary likes John* makes the derivation difficult to fit on the page. So in practice, the material to the left of the turnstile is often omitted, and replaced by the prosodic portion of the expression to the right of the turnstile. On the right side of the turnstile, then, only the semantic term and syntactic category are shown. Thus, the abbreviated form of the derivation of *Mary likes John* would be as shown in (13):

(13) Deriving *Mary likes John* as *s*

$$\dfrac{\dfrac{}{Mary \vdash \textbf{m}':np}\text{Ax} \quad \dfrac{\dfrac{}{likes \vdash \textbf{like}':vp/np}\text{Ax} \quad \dfrac{}{John \vdash \textbf{j}':np}\text{Ax}}{likes \circ John \vdash \textbf{like}'(\textbf{j}'):vp}\text{/E}}{Mary \circ (likes \circ John) \vdash \textbf{like}'(\textbf{j}')(\textbf{m}'):s}\text{\textbackslash E}$$

In addition to the inference rules, each mode may have its own set of structural rules stating how expressions combined in that mode can be manipulated. In associative Lambek categorial grammar, the only structural rules are those of Associativity, shown in (14).

(14) Structural rules of Associativity

$$\dfrac{((\Delta_1, \Delta_2), \Delta_3) \vdash (a \circ b) \circ c:\alpha:A}{(\Delta_1, (\Delta_2, \Delta_3)) \vdash a \circ (b \circ c):\alpha:A}\text{Assoc1}$$

$$\dfrac{(\Delta_1, (\Delta_2, \Delta_3)) \vdash a \circ (b \circ c):\alpha:A}{((\Delta_1, \Delta_2), \Delta_3) \vdash (a \circ b) \circ c:\alpha:A}\text{Assoc2}$$

To see how a structural rule works, as well as the /I rule, consider the derivation of *Mary likes* as an *s/np*, in the abbreviated notation described above. In this derivation, the *e* in $e:x:np$ represents the null string:

(15) Deriving *Mary likes* as s/np

$$
\cfrac{
  Mary \vdash \mathbf{m'}:np \qquad
  \cfrac{
    \cfrac{
      \cfrac{likes \vdash \mathbf{like'}:vp/np}{}\ \text{Ax} \qquad
      \cfrac{e \vdash x:np}{}\ \text{Ax}
    }{likes \circ e \vdash \mathbf{like'}(x):vp}\ \text{/E}
  }{}
}{}
$$

$$
\cfrac{
  \cfrac{
    \cfrac{
      \cfrac{Mary \vdash \mathbf{m'}:np \qquad likes \circ e \vdash \mathbf{like'}(x):vp}{Mary \circ (likes \circ e) \vdash \mathbf{like'}(x)(\mathbf{m'}):s}\ \text{\\E}
    }{(Mary \circ likes) \circ e \vdash \mathbf{like'}(x)(\mathbf{m'}):s}\ \text{Assoc2}
  }{Mary \circ likes \vdash \lambda x.\mathbf{like'}(x)(\mathbf{m'}):s/np}\ \text{/I}
}{}
$$

In addition to declaring how expressions combined in a single mode can be manipulated, structural rules can also specify how expressions combined in one mode can interact with those combined in other modes. At this point we transition from a presentation of multimodal categorial grammars in general to the one presented in Dowty (1996), which makes use of the following structural rules:

(16) Structural rules for mode interaction employed in Dowty (1996)

$$
\cfrac{((\Delta_1, \Delta_2), \Delta_3)^w \vdash (a \circ b) \circ_w c:\alpha:A}{((\Delta_1, \Delta_3)^w, \Delta_2) \vdash (a \circ_w c) \circ b:\alpha:A}\ \text{M-Comm2}
$$

$$
\cfrac{(\Delta_1, (\Delta_2, \Delta_3))^w \vdash a \circ_w (b \circ c):\alpha:A}{((\Delta_1, \Delta_2)^w, \Delta_3) \vdash (a \circ_w b) \circ c:\alpha:A}\ \text{M-Assoc1}
$$

$$
\cfrac{((\Delta_1, \Delta_2), \Delta_3)^w \vdash (a \circ b) \circ_w c:\alpha:A}{(\Delta_1, (\Delta_2, \Delta_3)^w) \vdash a \circ (b \circ_w c):\alpha:A}\ \text{M-Assoc2}
$$

Mixed Commutativity (M-Comm2) states that a sequence $(a \circ_w c) \circ b$ can be derived from sequence $(a \circ b) \circ_w c$. It is this rule that allows the NP *a book* to combine with *gave to John yesterday and to Bill today* and end up adjacent to *gave* in Dowty's analysis. Mixed Associativity (M-Assoc) 1 and 2 allow reassociation such that when an element is combined via wrapping with a pair of elements that have been combined in the associative mode, it can become more closely associated with the closer of those two elements. M-Assoc1 is used in Dowty's derivation of *gave a book to John and a record to Bill.* Dowty later uses M-Assoc2 to allow the phrase *easy to please* to wrap around *person* to yield *easy person to please.* Of these mode interaction rules, M-Comm2 and M-Assoc2 are relevant in the analysis of RNW.

In addition to the above rules, Dowty's analysis entails the use of a third Mixed Associativity rule, one which was not directly relevant to his proposal. To see the need for it, consider again the string *Mary likes.* Under Dowty's analysis, all DOs combine with their verbs in the wrapping mode, whether or not actual wrapping takes place. Thus, *likes* would have the category $vp/_w np$. Therefore, after the \E step in (15), instead of $Mary \circ (likes \circ e)$, we would have $Mary \circ (likes \circ_w e)$. To allow the reassociation $(Mary \circ likes) \circ_w e$, we need the following rule:

(17) Additional Mixed Associativity rule for English

$$\frac{(\Delta_1, (\Delta_2, \Delta_3)^w) \vdash a \circ (b \circ_w c) : \alpha : A}{((\Delta_1, \Delta_2), \Delta_3)^w \vdash (a \circ b) \circ_w c : \alpha : A} \text{ M-Assoc3}$$

The last components of Dowty's analysis are inclusion rules and type sorting for prosodic classes of expressions. These components are necessary because the rules as presented thus far overgenerate. Though it is already possible to derive sentences such as (9) and (10), it is also possible to derive sentences such as **Mary gave to John yesterday (and Bill today) a book* because there is no requirement that the structural rules be used in a derivation. Dowty's solution is to assume that in English, a phrase is complete only when all elements have been combined in the associative mode, and that the wrapping mode becomes inactive (radioactively decays to associative mode, as it were) only when two elements combined in the wrapping mode meet a certain condition. What is that condition? The condition is that whatever lexical item originally had a syntactic category constructed with $/_w$ or $\backslash_w$ must come to be in a wrapping configuration with another element.

Dowty, following Moortgat and Oehrle (1994), accomplishes this with type-sorting of prosodic classes of expressions. First, there is a sorting into *words*, which are a subset of *clusters* (e.g. clitic-host combinations), which are a subset of *phrases*. Second, an inclusion rule stipulates that all words with a category of form $A/_w B$ or $B\backslash_w A$ are members of the prosodic class of "infixing triggers":

(18) Inclusion rule adapted from Dowty (1996, (56))

$$\frac{\Gamma \vdash (a_i \circ_w b)_{ph} : \alpha : A}{\Gamma \vdash (a_i \circ b)_c : \alpha : A} \text{ Incl}$$

The subscript *ph, c,* and *i* in this rule stand for *phrase, cluster,* and *infix*. This rule declares that a phrase consisting of an infixing trigger a_i combined with an element via the wrapping mode, indicated by $\circ_w$, counts prosodically as a cluster created via the ordinary mode. In other words, in Dowty's analysis, the deactivation of the wrapping mode simultaneously creates a cluster out of the wrapping word and the element that comes to be adjacent to it; thus *gave the book* or *easy person* would count as clusters. The motivation for such a move comes from evidence that pronominal DOs in verb+DO clusters behave phonologically similarly to clitics, and even when the DO is nonpronominal, 'the one exceptional position in which an adverb *cannot* appear is between verb and object' (Dowty, 1996, pp. 24–25).

At this point, derivation of *the whiskey drowns and the beer chases my blues away* can proceed. The basic strategy will be to derive both *the whiskey drowns* and *the beer chases away* as $s/_wnp$, coordinate the two, and then wrap *chases away* around *my blues*. We will start with the derivation of *the beer chases away* as $s/_wnp$.

For reasons of space, this derivation is divided into two parts. In part 1 in (19), *chases away* plus the null string e is derived as vp. For easier readability, prosodic class subscripts are suppressed, and the infixing trigger *chases* is indicated by boldface type. The resultative *away* is assigned the category $(vp/_wnp)\backslash(vp/_wnp)$ instead of the ordinary adverbial category $vp\backslash vp$, in light of its status as an object-modifying adjunct: What ends up away is the blues, not the beer. (For further reasoning behind the categorization of object-modifying adjuncts, see Dowty (2007, sec. 6).) Derivation of *drowns* plus e as a vp (not shown) is done in the same way, except that no $\backslash E$ step is needed, since there is no resultative phrase that *drowns* needs to combine with.

(19) Deriving *the beer chases away* as $s/_wnp$, part 1

$$
\cfrac{
  \cfrac{
    \cfrac{
      \overline{\textit{chases} \vdash \mathbf{chase}' : vp/_wnp}^{\text{Ax}} \quad
      \overline{\textit{away} \vdash \mathbf{away}' : (vp/_wnp)\backslash(vp/_wnp)}^{\text{Ax}}
    }{
      \textit{chases} \circ \textit{away} \vdash \mathbf{chase}'(\mathbf{away}') : vp/_wnp
    }\scriptstyle \backslash E \quad
    \overline{e \vdash x : np}^{\text{Ax}}
  }{
    (\textit{chases} \circ \textit{away}) \circ_w e \vdash \mathbf{chase}'(\mathbf{away}')(x) : vp
  }\scriptstyle /_wE
}{}
$$

For part 2 of this subderivation in (20), *the beer chases away* combines with *the beer* via the ordinary $\backslash E$ rule. At this point the M-Assoc3 rule applies, paving the way for application of the $/_wI$ rule to finish the derivation. Derivation of *the whiskey drowns* proceeds in the same way.

(20) *the beer chases away* as $s/_wnp$, part 2

$$
\cfrac{
  \cfrac{
    \cfrac{
      \overline{\textit{the-beer} \vdash \iota(\mathbf{beer}') : np}^{\text{Ax}} \quad
      (\textit{chases} \circ \textit{away}) \circ_w e \vdash \mathbf{chase}'(\mathbf{away}')(x) : vp
    }{
      \textit{the-beer} \circ ((\textit{chases} \circ \textit{away}) \circ_w e) \vdash \mathbf{chase}'(\mathbf{away}')(x)(\iota(\mathbf{beer}')) : s
    }\scriptstyle \backslash E
  }{
    (\textit{the-beer} \circ (\textit{chases} \circ \textit{away})) \circ_w e \vdash \mathbf{chase}'(\mathbf{away}')(x)(\iota(\mathbf{beer}')) : s
  }\scriptstyle \text{M-Assoc3}
}{
  \textit{the-beer} \circ (\textit{chases} \circ \textit{away}) \vdash \lambda x.\mathbf{chase}'(\mathbf{away}')(x)(\iota(\mathbf{beer}')) : s/_wnp
}\scriptstyle /_wI
$$

Coordinating *the whiskey drowns* and *the beer chases away*, shown in (21), is simple. The polymorphic category $(X\backslash X)/X$ is used for *and*; in this derivation, X stands for $s/_wnp$. Spacing considerations again force a simplification; in this case, semantic terms are omitted, but will be discussed following the derivation.

(21) Deriving *the whiskey drowns and the beer chases away* as $s/_w np$

$$
\cfrac{
\textit{the-whiskey} \circ \textbf{\textit{drowns}} \vdash s/_w np \quad
\cfrac{
\textit{and} \vdash (X\backslash X)/X \quad \textit{the-beer} \circ (\textbf{\textit{chases}} \circ \textit{away}) \vdash s/_w np
}{
\textit{and} \circ (\textit{the-beer} \circ (\textbf{\textit{chases}} \circ \textit{away})) : X\backslash X
} \text{/E}
}{
(\textit{the-whiskey} \circ \textbf{\textit{drowns}}) \circ (\textit{and} \circ (\textit{the-beer} \circ (\textbf{\textit{chases}} \circ \textit{away}))) \vdash s/_w np
} \text{\textbackslash E}
$$

The semantic term for *and* will be **Coor(and)**, a function defined on Boolean semantic types as in (22), adapted from Carpenter (1997, p. 180):

(22)   a. $\textbf{Coor}_t(\textbf{and})(\beta_1)(\beta_2) = \beta_1 \wedge \beta_2$

        b. $\textbf{Coor}_{\langle \sigma, \tau \rangle}(\textbf{and})(\beta_1)(\beta_2) = \lambda x^\sigma . \textbf{Coor}_\tau(\textbf{and})(\beta_1(x))(\beta_2(x))$

Thus, if *the whiskey drowns* is associated with the semantic term $\lambda y.\textbf{drown}'(y)(\iota(\textbf{whiskey}'))$, and *the beer chases away* with the term $\lambda x.\textbf{chase}'(\textbf{away}')(x)(\iota(\textbf{beer}'))$, then the conjunction of the two works out to be $\lambda z.(\textbf{drown}'(z)(\iota(\textbf{w}')) \wedge \textbf{chase}'(\textbf{away}')(z)(\iota(\textbf{b}')))$.

Finally, *chases away* can be wrapped around *my blues*, as shown in (23).

(23) Deriving *the whiskey drowns and the beer chases my blues away* as s

$$
\cfrac{
\cfrac{
\cfrac{
\cfrac{
\cfrac{
\cfrac{
\cfrac{
(\textit{the-whiskey} \circ \textbf{\textit{drowns}}) \circ (\textit{and} \circ (\textit{the-beer} \circ (\textbf{\textit{chases}} \circ \textit{away}))) \vdash s/_w np \quad \textit{my-blues} \vdash np
}{
((\textit{the-whiskey} \circ \textbf{\textit{drowns}}) \circ (\textit{and} \circ (\textit{the-beer} \circ (\textbf{\textit{chases}} \circ \textit{away})))) \circ_w \textit{my-blues} \vdash s
} \text{/}_w\text{E}
}{
(((\textit{the-whiskey} \circ \textbf{\textit{drowns}}) \circ \textit{and}) \circ (\textit{the-beer} \circ (\textbf{\textit{chases}} \circ \textit{away}))) \circ_w \textit{my-blues} \vdash s
} \text{Assoc2}
}{
((((\textit{the-whiskey} \circ \textbf{\textit{drowns}}) \circ \textit{and}) \circ \textit{the-beer}) \circ (\textbf{\textit{chases}} \circ \textit{away})) \circ_w \textit{my-blues} \vdash s
} \text{Assoc2}
}{
(((((\textit{the-whiskey} \circ \textbf{\textit{drowns}}) \circ \textit{and}) \circ \textit{the-beer}) \circ \textbf{\textit{chases}}) \circ \textit{away}) \circ_w \textit{my-blues} \vdash s
} \text{Assoc2}
}{
(((((\textit{the-whiskey} \circ \textbf{\textit{drowns}}) \circ \textit{and}) \circ \textit{the-beer}) \circ \textbf{\textit{chases}}) \circ_w \textit{my-blues}) \circ \textit{away} \vdash s
} \text{M-C2}
}{
((((\textit{the-whiskey} \circ \textbf{\textit{drowns}}) \circ \textit{and}) \circ \textit{the-beer}) \circ (\textbf{\textit{chases}} \circ_w \textit{my-blues})) \circ \textit{away} \vdash s
} \text{M-A2}
}{
((((\textit{the-whiskey} \circ \textbf{\textit{drowns}}) \circ \textit{and}) \circ \textit{the-beer}) \circ (\textbf{\textit{chases}} \circ \textit{my-blues})_c) \circ \textit{away} \vdash s
} \text{Incl}
$$

In this derivation, semantic terms are omitted, but after the first line, the semantic term will remain $\textbf{drown}'(\textbf{my-blues}'))(\iota(\textbf{w}')) \wedge \textbf{chase}'(\textbf{away}')(\textbf{my-blues}'))(\iota(\textbf{b}'))$ throughout. The first step is for the $s/_w np$ *the whiskey drowns and the beer chases* to combine with *my blues* by way of the $/_w$E rule. Next, Assoc2 applies repeatedly in order to reassociate the component chunks until we have a structure of form $(a \circ b) \circ_w c$, where $b = away$, and $c = my\ blues$. At this point, M-Comm2 applies to permute these two elements, so that *chases away* wraps around *my blues*. We now focus in on the string *the whiskey drowns and the beer chases my blues* without the *away*. This structure is of form $(a \circ b) \circ_w c$, where $b = chases$ and $c = my\ blues$. This structure is eligible for M-Assoc2, which reassociates *chases* with *my blues.* Now, *chases* is in a wrapping structure with a phrase to its right, and is eligible for the Incl rule to finalize the sequence. Incl deactivates the wrapping mode and converts *chases my blues* into a phonological cluster, thus concluding the derivation.

The other RNW coordinations in (7) and (8) can be derived similarly, but with one fewer applications of Assoc2, since the subject is not part of the coordination in these examples.

10.4 Complications

The good news is that the RNWs seen so far can be derived using nothing more than was already proposed in Dowty (1996). The bad news is that this analysis both overgenerates and undergenerates. One overgeneration problem can be identified by inspecting the derivation in (23). If M-Comm2 is applied before the application of Assoc2, the ungrammatical *the whiskey drowns my blues and the beer chases away* is derived.

Another overgeneration occurs if both coordinated verbs are phrasal verbs. For example, a sentence such as (24) could be easily derived with the rules as currently proposed:

(24) *John [put away] and then [got] the dishes <u>back out</u>.

Even though RNW coordinations are not entirely grammatical for me, I find that (24) sounds worse; furthermore, in the years in which I have been hyperaware of RNW coordinations, I have yet to hear one with this pattern.

Regarding undergeneration, I have found attestations in which A_1 is a phrasal verb; A_2 is an ordinary transitive; B is a phrasal verb; and D completes both A_1 and B. These 'RNW sandwiches' are listed in (25), where both A_1 and B are underlined along with D:

(25) a. Led by France and Canada, a majority of countries are as-
         serting the right of governments to [safeguard], [promote] and
         even [protect] their cultures <u>from outside competition</u>.[11]
         (Alan Riding, 'A global culture war pits protectionists against free
         trade', *The New York Times*, February 7, 2005)

      b. What I do mourn is what we lose when by official policy or
         official neglect we [allow], [confuse], or [encourage] our soldiers
         <u>to forget</u> ... that <u>which</u> is our greatest <u>strength</u>. ...
         (John R. McCain, 'Torture's terrible toll', *Newsweek*, November 21,
         2005, p. 36)

---

[11]Thanks to Glen Whitman for this attestation.

These RNW sandwiches are not derivable with the current structural rules. The trouble is that part D, for example, *to forget ... in* (25b), would need to be placed right next to A_1, in this case *allow*, in order for the derivation to proceed. It cannot be placed there, however, because it also needs to be placed next to B, *encourage*. It is possible to introduce modes which allow an expression to be used more than once; this has in fact been done for parasitic gaps (Morrill et al., 1990). However, an investigation of how such a mode would interact with the wrapping mode goes beyond the scope of this paper.

In other RNW attestations, parts B and D do not form a syntactic/semantic unit that wraps around part C, as they have in the earlier examples. In the following examples, part D is neither a complement of B nor a modifier of it. As a result, derivations like the one shown in section 10.3 are impossible. The first such example involves infinitive-taking adjectives:

(26) Please move from the exit rows if you are [unwilling] or [unable] to perform the necessary actions <u>without injury</u>.
(spoken during a pre-flight safety presentation, December 2004)

If we assumed that part B *unable* was a wrapping-type word, with category $adj/_w vp_{inf}$, and took part D *without injury* to be a modifier of *unable*, with category $(adj/_w vp_{inf})\backslash(adj/_w vp_{inf})$, we could derive (26) in the same way as we derived the RNW coordination in section 10.3. However, *without injury* does not modify *unable* (nor is it a complement to it). Rather, it modifies the complement to *unable*, i.e. part C *to perform the necessary actions*. The discontinuous string *unable ... without injury* is not a constituent that wraps around *to perform the necessary actions*.

An anonymous reviewer points out that having *without injury* be of category $vp_{inf}\backslash_w vp_{inf}$ would allow the derivation to succeed. Unfortunately, such an analysis would also require *without injury* to be a member of the prosodic class of infix triggers, which are defined as a subset of the *word* class. Since *without injury* is a (non-word) phrase, assigning it to this class would require an additional, ill-motivated, inclusion rule.

A similar though more complicated problem occurs in (27):

(27) In the players' box was Tony Nadal, the [uncle] and [coach] of Rafael Nadal <u>since he started playing as a youngster</u>.[12]
(noted by *Washington Post* copyeditor Bill Walsh, on the June 17,

---

[12]Thanks to Chris Waigl for this attestation.

2006 posting on Blogslot, http://theslot.blogspot.com/2005/06/
potpourri.html))

Once again, B and D (in this case *coach* and *since he started playing
as a youngster*) do not form a semantic unit. *Since he started playing
. . .* is neither complement to nor modifier of *coach*; instead, it modifies
the entire proposition that Tony Nadal is Rafael's coach. As far as I can
see, the only way to make an RNW-style derivation succeed here is to
ignore this fact, and moreover stipulate that relational nouns such as
coach have category $n/_wpp_{of}$ and that *since* clauses can have category
$(n/_wpp_{of})\backslash(n/_wpp_{of})$.

More troublesome still are attestations such as the following:

(28) a. [Mothers now cheerfully push strollers] and [kids dash] through
his sculptures <u>as if they were playgrounds</u>. [13]
(Michael Kimmelman, 'Abstract art's new world, forged for all',
The New York Times, June 7, 2005)

   b. We've got information on [where else] and [what else] he's
wanted <u>for</u>.
(teaser <u>for</u> an evening newscast regarding a suspected criminal,
heard September 2005)

(28a) could be derived in the same way as the verbal RNWs by
type raising *kids dash* from s to $s/_w(s\backslash_w s)$, and declaring the *as* clause
to have category $s\backslash_w s$, but again, motivation for this categorization is
questionable. Furthermore, even with *kids dash* having the wrapping
category $s/_w(s\backslash_w s)$, there is no lexical item that starts out with this
category, and therefore no lexical item to trigger the Incl rule at the
appropriate time.

Like the other troublesome examples, (28b) could be derived with a
suitable choice of category for *what else* and *for* such that they could
be parsed as a discontinuous constituent wrapping around *he's wanted*.
Again, though, the choice would be unmotivated.

There is one additional drawback to forcing the examples in (26)–
(28) to be derived as RNW coordinations by means of unmotivated
category choices. Doing so would imply that part B and part D of
these various examples could appear adjacent to each other, forming an
ordinary continuous constituent instead of a discontinuous one. Thus,
in the same way as we could derive *the whiskey drowns and the beer
chases away my blues*, we could also derive the following:

(29) ?? . . . if you are [unwilling] or [unable without injury] to perform
the necessary actions.

---

[13] Thanks to Mark Liberman for this attestation, as noted also for (7c).

?? Tony Nadal, the [uncle] and [coach since he started playing as a youngster] of Spanish tennis champion Rafael Nadal

* [Mothers now cheerfully push strollers] and [kids dash as if they were playgrounds] through his sculptures.

?? We've got information on [where else] and [what else for] he's wanted.

To be fair, some of the badness of (29) can be attributed to the lack of a clear referent for *they* after moving it to before *his sculptures*, but even without this problem, it would probably be at least as awkward as the others.

So either the proposed analysis of RNW is wrong, or the examples in (26)–(29) are not the same kind of phenomenon as the verbal RNWs seen in (1), (7), and (8). Even if we take the latter position, however, there are still the verbal RNW sandwiches of (25) that remain to be derived, and unattested coordinations such as the one in (24) to rule out, so the analysis presented in section 10.3 must be considered incomplete. Moreover, the question remains of how the examples in (26)–(29) should be analyzed, if they are not true cases of RNW.

10.5 A Unary-Constructor Analysis?

Some, but not all, of the problems noted in section 10.4 can be solved by replacing the multimodal analysis with one that makes use of a unary category constructor. In the earlier analysis, the only category constructors were $/_i$ and $\backslash_i$ (with i standing for any of various modes of combination). These constructors are binary: A new category $A/_iB$ or $A\backslash_iB$ is constructed from two existing categories, A and B. The unary analog of the $/_i$ and $\backslash_i$ constructors is $\Box$, with rules of elimination and introduction as follows (adapted from Morrill (1994), Moortgat (1999), among others):

(30) Rules of inference for $\Box$

$$\frac{\Gamma \vdash a : \alpha : \Box A}{\langle \Gamma \rangle \vdash \langle a \rangle : \alpha : A} \Box E \qquad \frac{\langle \Gamma \rangle \vdash \langle a \rangle : \alpha : A}{\Gamma \vdash a : \alpha : \Box A} \Box I$$

The angle brackets around around the Γ are analogous to the parentheses around Γ and Δ in the E and I rules for the binary constructors $/$ and $\backslash$. Just as (Γ, Δ) denotes *two* structures put together in the way associated with $/$ or $\backslash$, so $\langle \Gamma \rangle$ denotes *one* structure, put together with nothing else, in the way associated with $\Box$.

These angle brackets are an overloaded notation, as they are also used to enclose the prosodic portion of the expression to the right of the turnstile. Here, they are analogous to the $a \circ_w b$ notation for the / and $\backslash$ rules. Just as $a \circ_w b$ denotes two prosodic strings put together in the way associated with / and $\backslash$, so $\langle a \rangle$ denotes just one prosodic string, put together with nothing else, in the way associated with $\square$.[14]

To get the wrapping effect, the M-Assoc rules are replaced with the following rule of Permutation:

(31) Structural rule of Permutation (adapted from Moortgat 1999)

$$\frac{((\Delta_1, \langle \Delta_3 \rangle), \Delta_2) \vdash (a \circ \langle c \rangle) \circ b : \alpha : A}{((\Delta_1, \Delta_2), \langle \Delta_3 \rangle) \vdash (a \circ b) \circ \langle c \rangle : \alpha : A} \; \text{P1}$$

Our canonical RNW is derived in much the same way as it was before, except that the binary wrapping modality is gone, and *away* has the category $\square((vp/np)\backslash(vp/np))$. The string *the whiskey drowns* is derived as before, but now has non-wrapping category s/np. *The beer chases away* is derived as s/np shown in (32) and (33). Part 1 in (32) is like the derivation in (19), but with a $\square$E step preceding the $\backslash$E step:

(32) Deriving *the beer chases away* as s/np, part 1

$$\frac{\cfrac{}{chases \vdash \textbf{chase}' : vp/np} \text{Ax} \quad \cfrac{\cfrac{}{away \vdash \textbf{away}' : \square((vp/np)\backslash(vp/np))} \text{Ax}}{\langle away \rangle \vdash \textbf{away}' : (vp/np)\backslash(vp/np)} \square \text{E}}{\cfrac{chases \circ \langle away \rangle \vdash \textbf{chase}'(\textbf{away}') : vp/np}{(chases \circ \langle away \rangle) \circ e \vdash \textbf{chase}'(\textbf{away}')(x) : vp}} \backslash \text{E} \quad \cfrac{}{e \vdash x : np} \text{Ax}}{/\text{E}}$$

Part 2 in (33) is like the derivation of *the beer chases away* in (20), except that instead of the M-Assoc3 step, we now have an Assoc2 step—in other words, this part of the derivation is precisely parallel to the derivation of *Mary likes* in (15).

(33) Deriving *the beer chases away* as s/np, part 2

$$\frac{\cfrac{\cfrac{}{the\text{-}beer \vdash \iota(\textbf{b}') : np} \quad (chases \circ \langle away \rangle) \circ e \vdash \textbf{chase}'(\textbf{away}')(x) : vp}{the\text{-}beer \circ ((chases \circ \langle away \rangle) \circ e) \vdash \textbf{chase}'(\textbf{away}')(x)(\iota(\textbf{b}')) : s} \backslash \text{E}}{\cfrac{(the\text{-}beer \circ (chases \circ \langle away \rangle)) \circ e \vdash \textbf{chase}'(\textbf{away}')(x)(\iota(\textbf{b}')) : s}{the\text{-}beer \circ (chases \circ \langle away \rangle) \vdash \lambda x.\textbf{chase}'(\textbf{away}')(x)(\iota(\textbf{b}')) : s/np} /\text{I}} \text{Assoc2}}$$

Coordination of *the whiskey drowns* and *the beer chases away* is achieved in the same way as in (21), with the same resulting semantic term: $\lambda z.(\textbf{drown}'(z)(\iota(\textbf{w}')) \wedge \textbf{chase}'(\textbf{away}')(z)(\iota(\textbf{b}')))$.

---

[14]There are also unary analogs for the semantic term, but for our purposes, the semantic portion remains unchanged.

The last portion of the derivation is shown in (34), with semantic terms omitted. As before, after the first line, the semantic term will be **drown′(my-blues′))(ι(w′))** $\land$ **chase′(away′)(my-blues′))(ι(b′))**.

(34) Deriving *the whiskey drowns and the beer chases my blues away* as *s*

$$
\frac{\frac{\frac{\frac{\frac{\frac{(\textit{the-whiskey} \circ \textbf{\textit{drowns}}) \circ (\textit{and} \circ (\textit{the-beer} \circ (\textbf{\textit{chases}} \circ \langle \textit{away} \rangle))) \vdash s/np \quad \textit{my-blues} \vdash np}{((\textit{the-whiskey} \circ \textbf{\textit{drowns}}) \circ (\textit{and} \circ (\textit{the-beer} \circ (\textbf{\textit{chases}} \circ \langle \textit{away} \rangle)))) \circ \textit{my-blues} \vdash s} \text{/E}}{(((\textit{the-whiskey} \circ \textbf{\textit{drowns}}) \circ \textit{and}) \circ (\textit{the-beer} \circ (\textbf{\textit{chases}} \circ \langle \textit{away} \rangle))) \circ \textit{my-blues} \vdash s} \text{Assoc2}}{((((\textit{the-whiskey} \circ \textbf{\textit{drowns}}) \circ \textit{and}) \circ \textit{the-beer}) \circ (\textbf{\textit{chases}} \circ \langle \textit{away} \rangle)) \circ \textit{my-blues} \vdash s} \text{Assoc2}}{(((((\textit{the-whiskey} \circ \textbf{\textit{drowns}}) \circ \textit{and}) \circ \textit{the-beer}) \circ \textbf{\textit{chases}}) \circ \langle \textit{away} \rangle) \circ \textit{my-blues} \vdash s} \text{Assoc2}}{(((((\textit{the-whiskey} \circ \textbf{\textit{drowns}}) \circ \textit{and}) \circ \textit{the-beer}) \circ \textbf{\textit{chases}}) \circ \textit{my-blues}) \circ \langle \textit{away} \rangle \vdash s} \text{P1}
$$

In this derivation, the only point at which P1 can apply is after the three Assoc2 steps, since only then is $\langle \textit{away} \rangle$ in the proper configuration.

This analysis improves on the multimodal one in ruling out *The whiskey drowns my blues and the beer chases away*. However, it brings with it a disadvantage, in that it will generate coordinations such as (35), where the first verb is a phrasal verb:

(35) *John put the dishes away and took back out.

Furthermore, the present analysis still overgenerates sentences such as (24), *John put away and got the dishes back out*, and still fails to generate the other kinds of RNWs noted in (25)–(28a). For these reasons, neither the multimodal analysis of section 10.3 nor the unary-constructor analysis presented here has a clear advantage over the other as far as RNWs are concerned.

10.6 Conclusion

Cases of RNW, i.e. 'Friends in Low Places' coordinations, were successfully derived in two ways: by using the multimodal categorial grammar analysis of wrapping and NCC of Dowty (1996) with no alterations necessary, and by using the unary constructor □ and P1 rule of Moortgat (1999). Cases of RNW that did not involve object-wrapping verbs were not covered under this analysis, and it is an open question whether RNW is a unified phenomenon that requires a different analysis than the one proposed here, or there are different processes at work for the RNWs not involving verbs.

In introducing his analysis of wrapping and NCC, Dowty states that one goal of the paper is 'to lay the groundwork for a thorough linguistic description of English non-constituent coordination and related phenomena (Gapping, etc.) in a framework that assumes an object-wrapping analysis' Dowty (1996, p. 1). The analysis of RNW presented here is intended to be a step toward such a description. Another step that has been taken is the treatment of gapping in Morrill and Solias (1993), though wrapping does not play a part in their analysis.

Beyond gapping, there are other kinds of NCC or asymmetric coordination that should be considered. For example, there are the subject-gap in finite/fronting (SGF) constructions and similar coordinations such as the one in (36), first noted by Höhle (see for example Höhle (1990)), and later given HPSG and LFG analyses (Kathol 1999, Frank 2002). In this example, the VPs 'went into the forest' and 'caught a hare' are coordinated, but the PP 'into the forest' (*in den Wald*) is topicalized. Given German's V2 syntax, 'went' (*ging*) comes next, with the subject 'the hunter' (*der Jäger*) appearing afterward. VPs are coordinated, but the subject for both VPs appears inside the coordination, much like the object does in the RNW constructions. As a result, *der Jäger* is embedded inside one coordinate, though it is semantically linked to both.

(36) [In den Wald ging] der Jäger und [fing einen Hasen].
　　 in the forest went the hunter and caught a hare
　　 'Into the forest went the hunter and caught a hare.'

In fact, there is a categorial analysis of SGF, in Steedman (1990). However, Frank (2002) notes that it overgenerates somewhat, and the version of categorial grammar used (combinatory categorial grammar) differs significantly from the type-logical multimodal system used here. Even so, it would be good to take Steedman's insights and see how they could be integrated into a multimodal categorial grammar analysis.

Though SGF is considered mainly a German construction, it also exists in English, as illustrated in (37). Because of the locative inversion in the first VP, not only does *Santa* appear inside the coordination, but *will* appears inside one of the coordinates despite semantically scoping over both *come* and *fill*. (The parentheses indicate that semantically it belongs outside the coordinate.) A similar case occurs with quotative inversion, shown in (38):

(37) [Down (will) come (Santa)] and [fill the stockings].

(38) a. ['No', said (John)], and [left the room].
　　 b. ['No', (John) said], and [left the room].

Other asymmetric coordinations involve markers of negation, modality, or interrogation/relativization that scope over coordinated clauses, but are infixed inside only the first coordinate. For example, in (39a), the modal *can* scopes over both clauses, but surfaces inside just the first one. In (39b), the negative *didn't* behaves similarly. In (39c) *can't* carries both modality and negation for both bracketed clauses, but appears inside only the first one. In (39d), the question marking by subject-auxiliary inversion scopes over both clauses, but is realized only on the first.

(39) a. [I (can) be on the computer] and [she's talking on the phone].
   b. I was amazed [the car (didn't) crash] and [Jim go flying through the windshield].
   c. You can push this and these'll move, but [you (can't) push these] and [this will move].
   d. [Did you reboot] but [the problem still wasn't fixed]?

Will the normal and wrapping modes of combination discussed in this paper prove sufficient to allow for analyses of RNW and other varieties of unusual coordination? If not, the questions are how many and what kinds of modes would be sufficient for the task (and could be sufficiently motivated independently), and whether the unexplored interaction of these modes would prove to be a source of overgeneration. And finally, there is the question of what light such analyses could shed on the analysis of coordination phenomena in other languages, or vice versa.

References

Bach, Emmon. 1980. In Defense of Passive. *Linguistics and Philosophy* 3(3):297–341.

Bach, Emmon. 1984. Some Generalizations of Categorial Grammars. In F. Landman and F. Veltman, eds., *Varieties of Formal Semantics*, pages 1–23. Dordrecht: Foris Publications.

Carpenter, Bob. 1997. *Type-Logical Semantics*. Cambridge, Massachusetts: MIT Press.

Dowty, David. 1988. Type Raising, Functional Composition, and Non-Constituent Coordination. In R. T. Oehrle, E. Bach, and D. Wheeler, eds., *Categorial Grammars and Natural Language Structures*, vol. 32 of *Studies in Linguistics and Philosophy*, pages 153–198. Dordrecht: Kluwer.

Dowty, David. 1996. Non-Constituent Coordination, Wrapping, and Multimodal Categorial Grammars. Expanded draft of Aug 96 paper from International Congress of Logic, Methodology and Philosophy of Science, In M. L. D. Chiara, K. Doets, D. Mundici, and J. van Benthem, eds., *Structures and Norms in Science*, pages 347–368, 1997. [Retrieved from ftp://ftp.ling.ohio-state.edu/pub/dowty/nccwmmcg.ps.gz on November 15, 2006].

Dowty, David. 2007. Compositionality as an empirical problem. In C. Barker and P. Jacobson, eds., *Direct Compositionality*, pages 23–101. Oxford: Oxford University Press.

Frank, Anette. 2002. A (Discourse) Functional Analysis of Asymmetric Co-ordination. In M. Butt and T. H. King, eds., *Proceedings of the LFG02 Conference*, pages 174–196. Athens: CSLI.

Höhle, Tilman N. 1990. Assumptions about asymmetric coordination in German. In J. Mascaró and M. Nespor, eds., *Grammar in Progress*, pages 221–235. Dordrecht: Foris.

Huddleston, Rodney and Geoffrey K. Pullum. 2002. *The Cambridge Grammar of the English Language*. Cambridge: Cambridge University Press.

Kathol, Andreas. 1999. Linearization vs. phrase structure in German coordination constructions. *Cognitive Linguistics* 10:303–342.

Moortgat, Michael. 1999. Constants of grammatical reasoning. In E. Hinrichs and G. Bouma, eds., *Constraints and Resources in Natural Language Syntax and Semantics*, pages 195–219. Stanford, California: CSLI.

Moortgat, Michael and Richard T. Oehrle. 1994. Adjacency, dependence, and order. In P. Dekker and M. Stokhof, eds., *Proceedings of the Ninth Amsterdam Colloquium*, pages 447–466. Universiteit van Amsterdam: Instituut voor Taal, Logica, en Informatica.

Morrill, Glyn. 1994. *Type Logical Grammar: Categorial Logic of Signs*. Dordrecht: Kluwer.

Morrill, Glyn, Neil Leslie, Mark Hepple, and Guy Barry. 1990. Categorial deductions and structural operations. In G. Barry and G. Morrill, eds., *Studies in Categorial Grammar*, vol. 5 of *Edinburgh Working Papers in Cognitive Science*, pages 1–21. Edinburgh: Center for Cognitive Science.

Morrill, Glyn and Teresa Solias. 1993. Tuples, Discontinuity, and Gapping in Categorial Grammar. In *Proceedings of the Sixth Conference of the European Chapter of the Association for Computational Linguistics*, pages 287–297. Morristown, NJ: Association for Computational Linguistics.

Pullum, Geoffrey K. and Arnold M. Zwicky. 1986. Phonological Resolution of Syntactic Feature Conflict. *Language* 62(4):751–773.

Steedman, Mark J. 1990. Gapping as Constituent Coordination. *Linguistics and Philosophy* 13(2):207–263.

Index